Human Rights and the Body

Hidden in Plain Sight

ANNABELLE MOONEY
University of Roehampton, UK

Routledge
Taylor & Francis Group
LONDON AND NEW YORK

First published 2014 by Ashgate Publishing

2 Park Square, Milton Park, Abingdon, Oxfordshire OX14 4RN
52 Vanderbilt Avenue, New York, NY 10017

Routledge is an imprint of the Taylor & Francis Group, an informa business

First issued in paperback 2020

British Library Cataloguing in Publication Data
A catalogue record for this book is available from the British Library

The Library of Congress Cataloging-in-Publication Data has been applied for

ISBN 978-1-4724-2259-0 (hbk)
ISBN 978-0-367-60038-9 (pbk)

HUMAN RIGHTS AND THE BODY

Bare, embodied life, traditionally conceived of as pre-political and pre-legal, emerges in Annabelle Mooney's sensitive account as the very origin and index of being human, and hence as the only proper foundation for a truly universal set of basic human rights. The thinking enacted in this brilliant book will be a welcome contribution to the debate about universalism versus cultural relativism in the theory of human rights.

Louis E. Wolcher, University of Washington, Seattle, USA

Annabelle Mooney's book is a landmark in the literature on human rights and our common humanity. Importantly, the main stress here is not so much on "rights" as on "human". The two main reference points are the vulnerable human body and universal human concepts. This is novel and revealing. Highly recommended.

Anna Wierzbicka, Australian National University, Australia

By moving away from strictly defined aspects to what Dr Mooney refers to as Bare Human Rights, she helps us to look deeper into the human condition from a perspective of disenfranchisement and de-humanizing the other. Human Rights and the Body *is at once thought-provoking and holistic in its approach to human rights. As corporate and political globalization marginalizes more and more of our world's population, this is a timely text which should be read by those in the fields of world politics, law and business.*

Jack B. Hamlin, National University, USA

What a bold and inspiring book, refreshingly disrespectful of the traditional boundaries between disciplines. Straddling philosophy, law and linguistics, the book invites us to reflect not only on human rights and the body, but effectively on the human condition itself.

Gerlinde Mautner, Vienna University of Economics and Business, Austria

Law, Language and Communication

Series Editors
Anne Wagner, Lille University – Nord de France, Centre for Legal Research and Perspectives of Law, René Demogue Group, France and Vijay Kumar Bhatia, City University of Hong Kong

This series encourages innovative and integrated perspectives within and across the boundaries of law, language and communication, with particular emphasis on issues of communication in specialized socio-legal and professional contexts. It seeks to bring together a range of diverse yet cumulative research traditions related to these fields in order to identify and encourage interdisciplinary research.

The series welcomes proposals – both edited collections as well as single-authored monographs – emphasizing critical approaches to law, language and communication, identifying and discussing issues, proposing solutions to problems, offering analyses in areas such as legal construction, interpretation, translation and de-codification.

For Christopher

Contents

List of Tables

Acknowledgements

I have been thinking about the foundations of human rights for a while now. During these many years, a number of people have been influential, supportive and generous in all manner of ways. From conversations overheard about gravity to discussions about blood, many encounters have helped this project along. The impetus for the project is directly connected to classes I took as a linguistics student at the Australian National University with Professor Anna Wierzbicka. While I can only aspire to the clarity and precision of her thought, she made clear to me that for all the differences between languages and people there is something we share. Her approach to language and to variation has had a profound effect on me and on this work.

The majority of this work has taken place while I have been at the University of Roehampton. The first phase of research was supported through sabbatical as was the completion of this text. I was extremely fortunate to have been welcomed by the Faculty of Law at University of Washington for a period of some months in 2010 as a Visiting Scholar. During this time, I was fortunate to meet with Professor Talbott in the Department of Philosophy; talking with him clarified a great deal for me. I also had the pleasure of spending time at the The Helen Riaboff Whiteley Center for which I am very grateful. The thinking behind Chapter 2 was developed there. During my time at the University of Washington, Professor Louis Wolcher was, and has continued to be, generous as a scholar and as a human. His work has been an inspiration and conversations with him will stay with me for many years. As well as introducing me to a great many fascinating and kind people in his circle, he also introduced me to the Critical Legal Conference which seeded many ideas in this work and provided a venue for presenting papers connected to the project. Feedback on work presented and the general tenor of this conference have been invaluable. Thanks are due to Dr Tom Frost for introducing me to Agamben's concept of 'whatever being' at this conference. I've had a great deal of feedback from conference delegates and various anonymous reviewers and it has been appreciated; it has led me in new directions and shaped this project in important ways. Special thanks to Dr Jack Hamlin for his enthusiasm about the work in Chapter 5. I'd also like to thank Professor Anne Wagner; my work on law started and continues with her support. My colleagues at Roehampton, especially Dr Judith Broadbent, Dr Evi Sifaki and Professor Jennifer Coates, have been extremely supportive throughout this work; always ready to help with expertise on sleep, syntax, theoretical linguistics and Latin. Being exposed to Dr Lynn Thomas's work on human rights was also extremely valuable. Dr Betsy Evans, as ever, has been a critical and constructive reader and my faithful and patient friend. Thanks to her, Jonathan Goodman, Ellen Kaisse and Gary Roberts for welcoming me to Seattle and providing safe refuge, even when stranded by the eruption of Eyjafjallajökull. Thanks also to the series editors, Professor Wagner and Professor Bhatia for supporting this project. Ashgate have also been extremely helpful, especially Celia Barlow and Alison Kirk.

Material in Chapter 2 was previously published as 'Human Rights: Law, language and the bare human being', *Language and Communication* (2012) 32: 169–81 and reproduced with the kind permission of Elsevier. The poem, 'The Dark' on page 66 is reproduced with the kind permission of Dr Simon West; Simon West, 'The Dark' in *First Names* (Puncher and Wattmann 2006). Material in Chapter 5 was previously published as 'Restoring Trust: Plachimada, the Human Trust and Anticipatory Negligence as Restorative Justice', *International Journal for the Semiotic of Law* (2012) online first. This is reproduced with the kind permission of Springer. The table of NSM on page 167 is reproduced with the kind permission of Professor Anna Wierzbicka and Professor Cliff Goddard. The script lines on page 177–8 are reproduced from Karen Stollznow, 'Dehumanisation in language and thought' (2008) 7(2), *Journal of Language and Politics* 177–200 with the kind permission of John Benjamins Publishing Company, Amsterdam/Philadelphia.

This book is dedicated to Christopher Marlow, who always believes in me.

Introduction:
We Were Promised Jet Packs

At Poliochni, on the island of Lemnos in Greece, one finds what some scholars think is the first ever parliament. A room has been unearthed that appears to have been used for discussion and debate.

> Two impressively large buildings, one at either side of the city gates, have been interpreted by their excavators as a granary and as a 'theatre' or 'assembly hall' (bouleuterion) respectively. The latter of these buildings was provided with rows of seats arranged in theatrical manner along its long sides.[1]

There is debate about exactly what kind of activity took place here, about who met and how they were chosen[2] but it is the adjacent building I want to consider. The size of the granary room suggests that the community at Poliochni had about thirteen square kilometres of land under cultivation. This was a community that did not intend to go hungry. It was also a fortified community; protected by walls on one side, cliffs and the ocean on the other. The lines of sight were good.

The proximity of these two rooms may not be accidental. Once the body is fed, discussion about other matters can take place. Once hunger has been chased away, there is time to talk of law. But before one's hunger has been sated, it is difficult to think of anything else. In the words of Ulysses:

> Nevertheless, let me sup in spite of sorrow, for an empty stomach is a very importunate thing, and thrusts itself on a man's notice no matter how dire is his distress. I am in great trouble, yet it insists that I shall eat and drink, bids

1 Christos Doumas, 'The emergence of central authority in the Aegean', in Paul Sinclair (ed.), *The Development of Urbanism from a Global Perspective* (Uppsala University 1996) 4. http://www.arkeologi.uu.se/digitalAssets/9/9397_doumas.pdf [accessed 5 October 2010] citing L. Bernabo Brea, *Poliochni: città prehistorica nell'isola di Lemnos*, 2 Vols. (L'Erma di Bredschneider 1964) 177.

2 M. Jones, 'Landscape, Law and Justice: Concepts and Issues – a preliminary overview', in Z. Roca, T. Spek, T. Terkenli, T. Plieninger and F. Höchtl (eds), *European Landscapes and Lifestyles: The Mediterranean and Beyond* (Edições Universitárias Lusófonas 2007) 438–59.

> me lay aside all memory of my sorrows and dwell only on the due replenishing of itself.[3]

The argument in this book is in a sense a statement of the obvious. Humans have bodies. All people are embodied. People, as a concept and as beings, presuppose a body. Our body is our mode of being in the world, our mode of being human in the world. What seems to be less obvious is that being embodied has consequences and preconditions. For the body to exist, to live, certain substances need to be available; the environment – physical and social – needs to be hospitable to human habitation. This has consequences for human rights. If human rights are *human* rights, they should first and foremost, attend to the body.

The argument in this book is underpinned by an apocalyptic view of the world. It considers the possibility that humans may cease to exist altogether; this is the horizon to which I orient. However, given the state of the planet and the human activity that continues on it, this horizon may not be quite so distant. There are many people living at this horizon already in the sense that their lives are utterly precarious. Their worlds, their lands, their bodies, are already ending. Whether this is because of drought and famine or chronic unemployment, the suffering is real. I want to suggest that looking at the body, through the body, teaches us something about what it means to be human and therefore what human rights we need.

This is not a book about the law of human rights. While I draw on legal concepts and consider aspects of the law of human rights, my aim is to provide a universally defensible set of human rights and a foundation for them. It should be said at the outset that the foundation is not a foundation but a frame. The frame with which we should look at human rights is the human body. It is the human condition, human embodiment and suffering, that is universal. The body is that which we cannot escape. But in some ways we have forgotten this, we have forgotten how to look. In the haste of the going forward we have neglected to look back, to look up or down, to look properly. This book is a response to the crisis in human rights, to the very real concern that without a secure foundation for the concept of human rights, their very existence is threatened. The answer is to look.

The argument that follows is divided into sections that have distinct focal points and deal with issues related to the corporeal frame for human rights. I begin in Chapter 1 by considering some of the central debates around the universality of human rights, focusing on cultural variation and whether or not foundations are needed for human rights at all. I argue that even accounts that eschew foundations nevertheless rely on something. Close attention to work about foundations in human rights shows that the nation state and a particular understanding of the individual are generally taken for granted. While these may not seem to be 'cultural' constructs at first glance, they are certainly ideological and have consequences for how human rights are imagined. More importantly, they are not defensibly universal and they do not give proper attention to real people. There

3 Homer, *The Odyssey*, Samuel Butler (trans) (Plain Label Books 2009) 56.

are, however, models of human rights that do focus on real people, providing space for consideration of human well-being and human suffering. I conclude the chapter by thinking about what a human is and acknowledging the inevitability, and universality, of pain.

The theories of human rights examined in the first chapter come from perspectives that may not be familiar to all people. Because of this, the second chapter considers the meanings of 'human rights' of which people should be aware as it examines media representations of human rights in the UK and the USA. Looking at this data makes clear that the most dominant presence in human rights is the law. I thus argue for a distinction between 'legal human rights' and 'bare human rights', while noting that the former is not the law in fact, but rather, a specific imagining of how the law deals with human rights. The data also make clear that human rights do not belong to 'us', instead, they are apparently claimed by and given to the Other. It seems that we are not yet at home with human rights. This may be a consequence of the way that legal human rights have been represented; more often than not, the human rights we see in the mass media are those claimed by 'criminals' and 'monsters'. To realise that we all have human rights, and to understand what they might be, requires looking to the margins of the data. Here, the bare human rights that attach to each and every person are found. These rights are predicated upon and protect the human body. Bare human rights include rights to food, water, shelter and sleep.

The human body is hidden in the margins and needs to be closely examined. In Chapter 3, I document the way the body is currently treated in human rights, legal theory and philosophy. The body has received a great deal of attention, especially from feminist scholars, and it is important to understand the associations the body has traditionally had as this helps understand how it has been banished from the state, law and human rights. However, most approaches to the body treat it either as a surface or a text. The body serves as a page on which cultural and legal discourses can be written, either to construct or dismember it. As a great deal of work has shown, these discourses are arbitrary and oppressive and can be resisted. However, once the body is understood as caught up in chains of signification, it is impossible to see the body itself. I want to argue that the body itself does exist, that it exists outside of arbitrary cultural discourses.

Chapter 4 sets out my reading of the body. I argue that as our body is fundamental to our existence, it should be considered our zero institution. A zero institution is that without which nothing else makes sense; as such, it describes our embodiment. While the zero institution is usually a signifier, if the body is our zero institution it cannot be. The body is not a signifier; it shows itself. Rather than reading bodies as texts or Saussurean signs I argue that we should understand the body as an index. The body as index points to itself and it shows us something. It shows us that the body needs food, water, sleep and shelter to exist. This chapter also makes an argument for connecting the 'is' of human embodiment to the 'ought' of human rights. As already mentioned, it seems to me that without protection of the human body, 'human' itself may cease to have meaning; its referent may cease to exist. This becomes clear when considering the effects that human activity has had on the natural world; humans now wield a geological force. Fortunately, exactly because of other human activity, we now know this. In short, because humans rely on the planet, environmental rights are now clearly human rights. Bodies cannot be fed or given water if the environment cannot provide these things.

Focusing on the importance of the natural world also questions the dominance of the nation state. Environmental systems do not respect the lines that humans have drawn on the globe. This suggests that the figure that should be at the heart of human rights is not the nation state but that which the state has banished: bare life. Indeed, the body as index is bare life. But bare life does not exist in isolation. Treating the body as an index shows us this; people depend on other people. Thus it is important to consider the presence of the Other and how she might be approached. Although each individual depends for their original existence on other people, each individual is individual. It is impossible to know the Other; she can only be greeted.

Chapter 5 considers how the needs of bare life might be protected as this has consequences for the way people live together. This chapter takes as an example the human right to water and considers a legal case in Plachimada, India, in order to show how the environment might be protected. The facts of this case show that one of the central problems is the way the environment is treated as property. Because bare life relies on the natural world, putting a price on the environment is tantamount to commodifying human life. Tracing a strand of the judgments in the Plachimada case, I argue that environmental goods should be taken out of property relations altogether and instead conceived as a 'human trust'. In addition to this, I propose a private law action, anticipatory negligence, a development of *quia timet* injunctions, to protect bare life and the environment on which it depends. Finally, the human trust serves as a model for human community. Rather than the social contract of the nation state, bare life demands a human community of trust.

Having dealt with the bare corporeal needs of humans, in the final two chapters I consider what else humans are and share. To do this, I pay attention to the connection between language and the body in Chapter 6 and to linguistic universals in Chapter 7. In Chapter 6, I document the connections between language and the body through work from cognitive linguistics. This involves explanation of a particular theory of metaphor, one that structures cognition and is ultimately linked to the body. Attention to metaphor and language demonstrates that while these do vary across cultures, there are some commonalities. This mirrors the arguments traced in Chapter 1 in relation to cultural variation. Significantly, however, cognitive linguistics confirms our basic commonality: the body. Language is embodied.

The first frame of human rights is the human body, seen as an index, reliant on the natural world. However, as consideration of the environment shows, other frames are needed. To fully protect the environment, a global frame is needed. As this seems to be far outside the corporeal existence of people, it needs to be constructed in relation to and grounded in a way that aligns with the human body.

I suggest that it is possible to imagine the global frame in a corporeal way if the connection between the body and language is traced. Some of the metaphors documented by cognitive linguists suggest that an image may be appropriate, an image that captures the global frame: the earth as seen from outside. I argue that this global frame is necessary if bare life is to be protected.

Finally, Chapter 7 argues for the third and final frame: language. Here, I draw on the work of Anna Wierzbicka and colleagues who have documented a set of linguistic universals. Natural Semantic Metalanguage (NSM) is a mini-language, complete with words and syntax. The word, the primes, are both universal and undecomposable into simpler parts. Consideration of NSM provides a universal, linguistic frame to supplement the frame of the human body and the globe. NSM tells us what people are over and above their embodiment. As such, it suggests a human right to supplement the rights to food, water, shelter and sleep and those that protect the natural world. This is a right against dehumanisation. This right relies on an understanding of what it means to be a person, not only in terms of bare life but also in terms of how people apprehend and interact with the world. To understand the consequences of this, I consider the root causes of dehumanisation. I argue that the personification of non-human entities and the treatment of people as commodities are both caused by the deification of the market. In short, the religion of capitalism is the root cause of a great many human rights abuses, either directly or indirectly, by way of a more general dehumanisation of people.

For all the differences between each and every person, we nevertheless share some things. All humans are embodied and have language; this can inform the development of a new model of human rights that takes the human condition seriously. In this book, I suggest that the proper frames for human rights are, first, the human body, second, the globe and finally, language. These three frames generate rights to food, water, sleep and shelter, environmental protection and a right against dehumanisation. These frames, these rights, only make sense if we see that we are all embodied and all absolutely unique. They only make sense if we see that people rely on each other and on the natural environment. They only make sense if we see people as people.

To come finally to the title of this chapter; we were promised jetpacks. We were promised a great deal, or at least we imagined that a great technological promise would be fulfilled. We imagined new modes of travel, freedom from the 'natural' limitations of our bodies, freedom borne of technological innovation. We imagined uploading our consciousness to neural nets, terraforming and the immediate synthesis of food and drink (in the words of Jean Luc Picard, 'Tea, Earl Grey; hot'). We are not there, yet. We may never arrive at the promised land of technological utopia. It is not enough to place all our trust in technology; we cannot assume that it will be able to provide an utterly new environment. But there are other possibilities. Language, philosophy, and indeed law, are also technologies of a kind. If we can remember that these are also human inventions, it may be possible to apply their potential in the interests of people. It should be possible to use them in order to see people as people.

Currently the body is everywhere and nowhere in human rights.[4] It is suspended, as though in a teleportation loop, passing in and out of visibility. I argue that it is time to bring the body home, to be at home in the body and to recognise – as though for the first time – the connection between the body, the world and being human. In 'The Third Mountain' Wolcher meditates on a form of knowing that lies beyond dualities, grounds and foundations. While acknowledging that the request may sound 'flaky and mystical', nevertheless, he writes

> I want to stay within the realm of the obvious and the simple, and thereby try to avoid what Kierkegaard calls the 'martyrdom of being uncomprehended'. I want to invite you to experience what requires no supernatural beliefs to be seen – what anyone can see, in fact, lying right before their eyes, if only they would just look.[5]

We cannot see what we are not disposed to see; we cannot see something that we think we don't need to consider. And yet, humans are embodied. This simple assertion could provide the foundation and substance of human rights. We only need to look.

4 William MacNeil, 'Law's Corpus Delicti: The Fantasmic Body of Rights Discourse' (1998) 9(1) *Law and Critique* 37.

5 Louis E. Wolcher, 'The Third Mountain: A Meditation on Chaos and Order' (2002) 15, *International Journal for the Semiotics of Law* 25, 50.

Chapter 1
Universals and Foundations

Human rights matter. The concept is important legally, politically and culturally. But exactly what human rights are and precisely where they come from is not settled. The lack of a clear, convincing foundation threatens the continuing acceptance of human rights and hence undermines the very real protections they offer.

Brown observes, 'Virtually everything encompassed by the notion of "human rights" is the subject of controversy.'[1] Controversy, contest and categorisation[2] would be a reasonable way to describe work in the field of human rights. But there is one sense in which 'human rights' is generally uncontroversial. The idea that humans are equal and that everyone is a subject of human rights simply because of their humanity has gained acceptance, rhetorically, if not in practice.[3] The move from this abstract idea to any realisation of rights, however, involves contact with politics, law and culture. Who should have particular rights, what these rights should be and where they come from are all subjects of a great deal of debate and discussion. Because of the exponential growth of work in human rights in the last few decades and because of the range of disciplines it comes from and issues it engages with, it is not possible to offer a complete survey of the field here.[4] Rather, in this chapter, I argue that the existing human rights system rests on foundations that are largely hidden. The human rights system depends on the

1 Chris Brown, 'Universal Human Rights: A Critique' (1997) 1(2), *Intl J Hum Rts* 41.

2 Because of the range of work, it has also been necessary to try and categorise approaches; not in order to reduce the complexity but in order to manage it, focus debate and provide some points of orientation. Thus Serena Parekh describes contemporary human rights work as being either essentialist or anti-essentialist, while Dembour argues that there are four schools of thought in relation to the existence of human rights; 'natural scholars' conceive of human rights as given; 'deliberative scholars' as agreed upon; 'protest scholars' as fought for; and 'discourse scholars' as talked about. Thus, natural scholars argue that human rights exist because they are given, and so on. Serena Parekh, (2007), 'Resisting "Dull and Torpid" Assent: Returning to the Debate over the Foundations of Human Rights' (2007) 29 *Hum. Rts. Q.* 754; Marie-Bénédicte Dembour, 'What are Human Rights? Four Schools of Thought' (2010) 32(1), *Hum. Rts. Q.* 1.

3 This parallels attitudes to feminism in the West in so far as it is generally accepted that women are equal; this does not mean that women are in fact treated equally.

4 For broad and inclusive accounts of human rights see Costas Douzinas, *The End of Human Rights* (Hart 2000); Michael Freeman, *Human Rights: Key Concepts* (Polity 2002); Jack Donnelly, *Universal Human Rights: In theory and practice* 2nd ed (Cornell University Press 2003); Micheline R. Ishay, *The History of Human Rights: From Ancient Times to*

acceptance of the nation state, a particular construction of the individual and a contractual conception of rights. These are cultural, and ultimately, ideological constructs. Because they are so dominant, however, it is not routine to see them as constructed.

For all the diversity and disagreement around human rights, there are some facts. Cultural variation is clear however it is described and critiqued. The difference human rights as a discourse and practice have made to the lives of at least some individuals is also not in doubt.[5] It is also clear that there is a lack of agreement on the substance of, reasons for and history of human rights. Finally, violation of and resistance to even the most basic human rights norms is widely documented. The net result of these facts is that human rights are under threat, both at the level of individual rights and more generally at a conceptual level. Human rights are in crisis, indeed, 'the battle for human rights meanings has arguably never been more urgent'.[6] What human rights means, why they are important, and why they should be protected are questions that need a response. Conor Gearty frames the issue clearly when he argues that 'the subject of human rights needs a better answer to the question of the basis of its authority than it seems currently able to provide, and if it fails to deliver such a response then its medium to long term future cannot be assured'.[7] This answer cannot be given by passing new laws or ratifying new conventions; as Sen observes, 'The difficult questions regarding the status and standing of human rights arise in the domain of ideas, before [any] legalization occurs.'[8] The answer can only be found by paying close attention to the ideas that underpin the current human rights system. While there are problems with the current human rights system, this does not mean that human rights should be abandoned altogether. To be clear, I take the position that the concept 'human rights' exists, and should continue to exist. I believe in the potential of the concept to make positive changes in the world. It seems to me, however, that the concept could be re-invented in such a way as to allow for more positive changes for more people in the world.

---

the Globalization Era (University of California Press 2004); Charles R. Beitz, *The Idea of Human Rights* (Oxford University Press 2009).

5 For a nice example, see James Griffin, *On Human Rights* (Oxford University Press 2008) 19.

6 Anna Grear, *Redirecting Human Rights: Facing the Challenge of Corporate Legal Humanity* (Palgrave 2010) 155.

7 Connor Gearty, *Can Human Rights Survive? The Hamlyn Lectures* (Cambridge University Press 2006) 11.

8 Amartya Sen, 'Elements of a Theory of Human Rights' (2004) 32(4), *Philosophy and Public Affairs* 315, 318. Of course, the way in which legalisation occurs, what is encoded in law and how these laws are upheld, matters a great deal. See Saladin Meckled-García and Başak Çali (eds), *The Legalization of Human Rights: Multidisciplinary Perspectives on Human Rights and Human Rights Law* (Routledge 2006); Luke McNamara, *Human Rights Controversies: The Impact of Legal Form* (Routledge Cavendish 2007).

In this book, I propose a new foundation, new frames, for human rights. Both the body and language are universal and can provide a response to urgent questions in the field of human rights. Before outlining these answers, however, it is important to understand the current system of human rights and how 'human rights' is understood more generally. In the next chapter, I consider mass media use of 'human rights' to establish how it is generally understood. In this chapter, however, I consider the international human rights system that is taken to include the United Nations bodies and texts as well as regional bodies such as the European Court of Human Rights. My interest is not in the particular bodies, procedures, texts and laws of this system, but rather, its general contours and the conceptual foundations on which it relies. It then becomes possible to see what is lacking in the system: a real person.

The sacred heart of human rights is their conceptual universality. I begin with this in order to distinguish it from the rather more complicated issue of substantive universality. While it is widely accepted that human rights belong to all people, exactly what belongs to all people is less clear. I then consider the most obvious barrier to a universal set of rights, the variation that exists among human cultures. Cultural variation is a fact, but whether it is fatal to universal human rights is not settled. To be sure, existing models of human rights have suggested ways of dealing with this difference, for example, by focusing on functional consensus rather than absolute agreement. But the challenge that cultural variation presents may suggest that it would be desirable to avoid foundations altogether. Approaches of this kind do exist, and tend to be pragmatic and results driven, eschewing and even attacking the idea that a universal foundation for human rights is required. But even these considered calls to action depend, at the very least, on attaching a value to human life and in asserting the equality of human beings. This deserves attention as the real suffering that humans experience should be a central concern of any thinking about human rights. Less positive is the way these models accept the position of the nation state and the general contours of international politics and law. International institutions and frameworks have been essential in establishing the idea of human rights, promoting them and securing a level of acceptance. But these institutions bring with them their own ideological underpinnings that are not always in line with what is good for humans.

The hidden foundations of human rights are clear in Beitz's descriptive account of the current system. This work demonstrates the centrality of the nation state, a particular conception of the individual, and the nature of rights generally to international human rights. While hegemonic, the nation, the individual subject of rights and rights themselves are nevertheless cultural constructs. They need to be closely considered if foundations for human rights are to be truly universal and even remotely humane. I then examine two recent arguments (Talbott and Griffin) that produce fresh models and lists of human rights. These models are, at least in part, predicated on a specific construction of the individual and implicitly rely on the nation state. However, these models also make important contributions to a humane human rights in that they provide a space of recognition for real people. These arguments show that it is possible to re-invent human rights by paying attention to people. In the last part of this chapter I consider the human. The individual in existing human rights system is rational and bloodless; the human who should be the subject of human rights is a person who lives, breathes, eats and suffers. The human we need to consider is ultimately the person, every person, in pain.

Universality of Human Rights

Even though 'universality' suggests singularity, in relation to human rights it has two meanings. The 'universality' of human rights may relate to either the conceptual or substantive universality of rights.[9] The first, conceptual universality, means that human rights attach to all people, universally, simply on the basis of being human. The second, substantive universality, relates to universal agreement about the content of human rights and is often discussed in terms of 'agreement theories' rather than 'universality'.[10] Substantive agreement takes many forms; it may be established empirically, through reference to laws, authoritative texts, state practice or national policy, ratification of treaties and similar documents or based on some kind of logical necessity.

The first meaning, conceptual universality, is not so much a topic of debate as a point of departure. That is, if one agrees that human rights exist (at any level of theory or practice) by definition they apply to all people. The idea that human rights attach to all individuals is inherent in the very concept. There are issues that emerge around universality, but they do not really challenge the idea that, by definition, human rights belong to all. Schaefer, for example, wonders whether 'women's human rights' can be universal given that they only apply to women. This is answered in two ways. First, he argues that they are universal in that they apply to all women.[11] Alternatively, he argues that these 'derived' rights are not, strictly speaking, human rights, as they are not universally held.[12] This is a nice solution to the apparent difficulty. Even so, Schaefer's distinction between derived 'honorary' rights and true human rights indicates the strength of the connection between 'human rights' and universality. That is, reserving 'true' human rights for those rights that belong to all people can be understood as a strategy to protect the

9 Jack Donnelly, 'The Relative Universality of Human Rights' (2007) 29(2) *Hum. Rts. Q.* 281.

10 Beitz (n 4).

11 Brian Schaefer, 'Human Rights: Problems with the Foundationless Approach' (2005) 31(1) *Social Theory and Practice* 27, 29.

12 Ibid.

idea of *universal* human rights. Insisting that the subject of human rights is only ever the individual is also evidence of the importance of conceptual universality.[13]

The second meaning of universality, the substantive universality of human rights, is problematic. As mentioned, universal agreement on human rights can be established in a number of ways. While some approaches focus on generating rights from a foundation, others pay attention to actual agreement on rights and are less concerned with where rights come from. The latter approach is routine and can be linked to the history and status of the Universal Declaration of Human Rights (UDHR). Indeed, the UDHR is often given as evidence for the modicum of universal agreement that does exist. Moreover, narratives about its construction add force to the argument that reasons for agreement are not necessary. Recounting the oft cited story,[14] Schapiro writes

> The comments of Jacques Maritain, a leading French philosopher and one of the participants in the negotiations that resulted in the Universal Declaration of Human Rights, illustrate this nonfoundational approach. In response to expressions of surprise at mustering widespread agreement to the Universal Declaration, Maritain stated that '[y]es, we agree about the rights but on condition no one asks us why'.[15]

Reliance on and endorsement of the particular set of rights in the UDHR is widespread, the document is described as 'a textual golden thread running through the international legal order'.[16] It should be noted that this reliance is not always

---

13 This presents a challenge for any claim to group rights. One solution is to derive these from individual rights. As Donnelly points out, in the terms of the Covenants (ICESCR and ICCPR) 'Individuals belonging to minorities, not minorities (collective entities), have these rights.' Donnelly, *Universal Human Rights* (n 4) 25; There are, of course, other ways of conceiving of groups in relation to human rights; see Ian Shapiro and Will Kymlica (eds), *Ethnicity and Group Rights* (New York University Press 1997); Peter Jones, 'Human Rights, Group Rights, and Peoples' Rights' (1999) 21(1), *Hum. Rts. Q.* 80. Talbott argues for the recognition of group rights as a pre-emptive strike against the workings of power. Group rights, he argues, are 'a necessary evil to prevent a worse evil' because 'If a minority culture were not at risk of being dominated by [248] the majority culture, no such rights would be necessary.' William J. Talbott, *Human Rights and Human Well-Being* (Oxford University Press 2010) 247–8.

14 See Beitz (n 4) 21; John Mikhail, 'Moral Grammar and Human Rights: Some Reflections on Cognitive Science and Enlightenment Rationalism', in Ryan Goodman, Derek Jinks, Andrew Woods (eds), *Understanding Social Action, Promoting Human Rights* (Oxford University Press 2012) 172.

15 Robert A. Schapiro, 'The Consequences of Human Rights Foundationalism' (2005), 54 *Emory L.J.* 174.

16 Tom Obokata and Rory O'Connell, 'Ambition, Achievement and Potential: the UK and the Universal Declaration of Human Rights at Sixty' (2010) 14(3), *Intl J Hum Rts* 395.

explicit and may even occur in arguments that seek to establish foundations.[17] Nevertheless, 'human rights' is often understood to mean either, specifically, the set of rights articulated in the UDHR or, more generally, the spirit of the Preamble, its approach and the kinds of rights it is understood to endorse. In practice, this means that the negative rights, largely civil and political, are considered more important than the later rights in the UDHR.[18] This is reflected in the division of rights between the International Covenant on Civil and Political Rights (ICCPR) and the International Covenant on Economic, Social and Cultural Rights (ICESCR). In short, the substantive universality of human rights is often linked to the widespread signing and ratification of the UDHR and the related Covenants.

The international human rights paradigm depends on this official ratification as well as on acceptance of the related terms and discourse of human rights that have developed and, more importantly, the political purchase that the discourse has come to have.[19] Ultimately, however, a universality connected to the UDHR is necessarily contingent and relative: 'It depends on states deciding to treat the Universal Declaration and the Covenants as authoritative.'[20] It is political agreement, often driven by political concerns and motives rather than, perhaps, concern for individual citizens. That is, the decision to recognise these texts is as much a function of international politics, national foreign policy objectives and international image as it is about the inherent truth or persuasiveness of the UDHR itself. And while it is routine for states to at least pay lip service to the idea of human rights, this does not of itself guarantee their protection.[21] Moreover, because the sovereignty of the nation state is internationally recognised, outside intervention in what are considered domestic affairs are politically difficult. Even before violations occur, if a nation argues that a right conflicts with local culture, diplomatic advances can be extremely delicate. I will come back to the position of the nation state presently. First, it is necessary to say something about the relationship between rights and culture as it is here that the idea of universal human rights is under most pressure.

---

17 For example, Bryan S. Turner, *Vulnerability and Human Rights* (Penn State University Press 2006).

18 Thus, Articles 22 onwards in the UDHR are often considered more aspirational than those which come before it.

19 Donnelly, 'The Relative Universality of Human Rights' (n 9) 288–9. Although Freeman does point out that the UDHR is 'undoubtedly legalistic' in so far as it was 'based on a comparative study of national constitutions by a Canadian law professor, John Humphrey. Having been derived from national laws, it became a source of numerous international legal instruments' (51). In the same paper he also discusses its political character. Michael Freeman, 'Putting Law in its Place: An interdisciplinary evaluation of national amnesty laws' in Meckled-García, Saladin and Çali, Başak, *The Legalization of Human Rights: Multidisciplinary Perspectives on Human Rights and Human Rights Law* (Routledge 2006) 49–64.

20 Donnelly, 'The Relative Universality of Human Rights' (n 9) 289.

21 Brown (n 1) 53.

Culture and Human Rights

At the same time Maritain was distinguishing between the rights articulated in the UDHR and the reasoning behind them, the American Anthropological Association declared that to proclaim a set of universal human rights was to ignore and erase significant cultural differences.[22] Differences between human cultures are indisputable.[23] Whether such difference is fatal to specific rights or to human rights generally is more contested. As will be discussed presently, there are models of universal human rights that allow for local variation, as long as a core remains intact.[24] There has also been a great deal of work that seeks to demonstrate that even cultures apparently hostile to human rights have their own texts, values and traditions that are either compatible with or can be developed to conform with existing human rights norms.[25] This approach is particularly valuable when done from the 'inside' as it provides what is seen as a culturally authentic way of recognising rights, empowering individuals and yet respecting local tradition. My purpose here is not to examine the detail of arguments for and against particular rights, the particular phases of this dispute, or claims about local rights traditions. Rather, my concern is with the general issue of cultural difference, cultural relativism as it relates to human rights and the charge that 'universal' human rights are simply a case of Western imperialism.

When a discourse of 'culture' is used to resist human rights, it is discussed in terms of 'cultural relativism' or 'Western imperialism'. Lord Hoffman notes such objections in relation to the Universal Declaration,

> Some Asian and African writers and politicians say that their countries were not represented at the United Nations in 1948 and that the Declaration

22 Michael F. Brown, 'Cultural Relativism 2.0' (2008) 49(3), *Current Anthropology* 365–7; Samuel Moyn, *The Last Utopia: Human Rights in History* (The Belknap Press of Harvard University Press 2010) 67. Their position has now changed significantly, see http://www.aaanet.org/about/Policies/statements/Declaration-on-Anthropology-and-Human-Rights.cfm [accessed 30 January 2013].

23 It should be noted that 'cultural relativism' is used to refer to a number of more specific relativisms: linguistic, cultural, ethical, epistemological. Alison Dundes Renteln, 'Relativism and the Search for Human Rights' (1988) 90(1), *American Anthropologist* 59.

24 Such a view was endorsed by Vienna Declaration and Programme of Action (1993): 'The international community must treat human rights globally in a fair and equal manner, on the same footing, and with the same emphasis. While the significance of national and regional particularities and various historical, cultural and religious backgrounds must be borne in mind, it is the duty of the States, regardless of their political, economic and cultural systems, to promote and protect all human rights and fundamental freedoms'. http://www.unhchr.ch/huridocda/huridoca.nsf/(symbol)/a.conf.157.23.en [accessed 31 January 2013].

25 For example, see Abdullahi Ahmed An-Na'im, 'Human Rights in the Muslim World: Socio-Political Conditions and Scriptural Imperatives – A Preliminary Inquiry' (1990), 3 *Harvard Human Rights Journal* 13–52.

> reflects a peculiarly Western liberal tradition. Islamists say that it is a Judeo-Christian document.[26]

When nations seek to defend practices, ideas and values that are regarded as in some way incommensurable with the rights articulated in the UDHR, non-compliance is often justified by making reference to culture or tradition.[27] While Lord Hoffman declares he is 'not concerned with these disputes' they are of great concern to those who take the position that human rights are in fact universal.[28]

There is no shortage of arguments against cultural relativism in relation to human rights and they come from a variety of perspectives. Talbott argues that using relativism as an argument against the human rights promoted by the West (as is usually the case) is both contradictory and self-defeating.[29] His argument depends on understanding cultural relativism to mean that there is no objective basis, independent of culture, for determining truth and other related values. In the absence of a stable measure of truth or the good, there is nowhere to found the critique and hence no critique can be made. Arguments about culture may be invoked as a strategy of resistance to the imposition of norms and values, but according to Talbott's argument, it cannot go much further than this. Renteln disagrees, and suggests that rather than relativism ruling out critique, there are at least three ways it can take place. A practice may be inconsistent with internal norms, universal values or simply with one's own standard.[30] The last will of course be ethnocentric to some degree, but she points out that 'relativism blocks neither' internal nor external critique.[31] There seems to a distinction here between resources

---

26 Lord Hoffman, 'The Universality of Human Rights' (2009), *Judicial Studies Board Annual Lecture*, 19 March, http://www.judiciary.gov.uk/training-support/judicial-college/Annual+Lectures [accessed 16 May 2011] p. 20.

27 For a nice discussion of the Asian values question, see Fred Dallmayr, (2002) '"Asian Values" and Global Human Rights' (2002) 52(2), *Philosophy East and West* 173–89; Bhikhu Parekh, 'Non-ethnocentric Universalism' in Timothy Dunne and Nicholas J. Wheeler (eds), *Human Rights in Global Politics* (Cambridge University Press 1999) 128–59; Mark R. Thompson, 'Whatever Happened to "Asian Values"?' (2001) 12(4) *Journal of Democracy* 154–65.

28 Lord Hoffman (n 26) p. 20. Though see Judge Bonello in Al-Skeini and Others v. the United Kingdom (Application no. 55721/07) who takes an interesting position, 'For my part, I believe that those who export war ought to see to the parallel export of guarantees against the atrocities of war. And then, if necessary, bear with some fortitude the opprobrium of being labelled human rights imperialists' (p. 39).

29 William J. Talbott, *Which Rights Should be Universal?* (Oxford University Press 2005) 42.

30 Renteln, 'Relativism and the Search for Human Rights' (n 23) 64.

31 Renteln, 'Relativism and the Search for Human Rights' (n 23) 64. See also Parekh: 'We can ask whether their beliefs are coherent and hang together, and whether their practices match their beliefs'. Bhikhu Parekh (n 27) 135.

that may be marshalled for critique (Renteln's argument) and the viability of such arguments when measured against the claims of cultural relativism itself (Talbott).

While it may be rhetorically, logically and politically difficult to argue for non-compliance with human rights, there are many ready to dispute such arguments including the idea that human rights are simply an exercise of Western imperialism. Thus, Higgins notes that such points of view are 'rarely advanced by the oppressed, who are only too anxious to benefit from perceived universal standards'.[32] Goodhart concurs, observing that 'the language of universal rights has been seized by the oppressed and excluded as a weapon in the fight for freedom and dignity'.[33] Shestack argues that using cultural relativism as a way of resisting international human rights standards 'has scant claim to moral validity',[34] while Ignatieff's position is that the 'relativist case is actually a defense of political or patriarchal power'.[35] The charge here is that resistance to human rights is not about culture at all, but rather about maintaining power.[36]

Donnelly confronts the issue of cultural relativism and mounts a critique of what he calls 'cultural absolutism', that is the idea that 'culture provides absolute standards of evaluation; whatever a culture says is right is right (for those in that culture)'.[37] Donnelly argues that such a position confuses 'right' with 'tradition' and politics with culture. To use 'tradition' as a way of resisting human rights, he argues, would be to claim that cultures are infallible and to conceptualise culture as 'coherent, homogenous, consensual, and static'.[38] Such a position, he suggests, also ignores social change and political context and undermines the central claim of 'human rights', that they apply to all people equally. It is

---

32 Rosalyn Higgins, *Problems and Process: International Law and how we use it* (Clarendon Press 1994) 96.

33 Michael Goodhart, 'Origins and Universality in the Human Rights Debate: Cultural Essentialism and the Challenge of Globalisation' (2003) 25(4), *Hum. Rts. Q.* 959.

34 Jerome J. Shestack, 'The Philosophical Foundations of Human Rights' (1998) 20, *Hum. Rts. Q.* 228.

35 'Human rights intervention is warranted not because traditional, patriarchal, or religious authority is [77] primitive, backward or uncivilized by our standards, but by the standards of those whom it oppresses. The warrant for intervention derives from their demands, not from ours' (76–7). Michael Ignatieff, *Human Rights as Politics and Idolatry* (Princeton University Press 2001) 76, 76–7.

36 Ishay argues that cultural relativism is a 'recurrent product of a historical failure to promote universal rights discourses in practice, rather than a legitimate alternative to the comprehensive vision offered by a universal stand on justice'. Micheline Ishay, 'What are Human Rights? Six Historical Controversies' (2004) 3(3) *Journal of Human Rights* 365.

37 Donnelly, 'The Relative Universality of Human Rights' (n 9) 294; following Rhoda E. Howard, 'Cultural Absolutism and the Nostalgia for Community' (1993) 15, *Hum. Rts. Q.* 315.

38 Donnelly, 'The Relative Universality of Human Rights' (n 9) 295–6; see also Brown (n 1); Donnelly, *Universal Human Rights* (n 4) 86–7; Sen (n 8).

also profoundly ethnocentric.[39] In short, 'Culture is not destiny'.[40] Further, he points out that because cultures are neither homogenous nor stable, subjecting a particular practice to critique does not mean that an entire culture is denigrated. If this was the case, no cultures would be immune to critique.[41] Finally, to associate a practice only with 'culture' misrepresents the diversity of practices, values and perspectives found in any human society.[42]

Clearly not all cultural variation is incompatible with a commitment to human rights. As Schaefer's distinction between human rights and derived rights (above) shows, it is possible to set 'human rights' at a general level, and then derive, or construct, culturally appropriate instantiations of them. In this vein, Sen argues that the ethical demands of human rights are universal, even though there may be variability in their realisation.[43] This distinction between the right and its realisation is particularly valuable when it comes to intra-cultural variation.[44] For example, the model Donnelly provides to deal with such variation separates the concept (e.g. right to life) from both the conception and the implementation.[45] This allows for variation (as long as this is freely agreed and chosen by those concerned), while still retaining a core consensus. Donnelly argues that human rights need

---

39 Howard (n 37)

40 Donnelly provides a number of reasons for the persistence of cultural arguments, including experience of colonialism, cultural pride and their use 'by vicious elites as a way to attempt to deflect attention from their repressive policies' (100). Donnelly, *Universal Human Rights* (n 4) 88, 100.

41 In relation to the argument that human rights promote Western values, it has been noted that Western cultures are also vulnerable to critique. The West, 'no less than the rest of the world, [has been put] on permanent trial'. Ignatieff (n 35) 92. Donnelly points out that 'Some local traditions – both Western and non-Western – are antithetical to human rights and must be approached as such.' Donnelly, *Universal Human Rights* (n 4) 70. Indeed, what exactly Western 'culture' means is not always clear, especially if we consider the actions of governments and their executive arms. The UK's conduct in war and interrogation are not obviously 'cultural' nor was this sanctioned by her citizens or indeed by international law. See Ian Cobain, *Cruel Britannia: A Secret History of Torture* (Portobello Books 2012).

42 Shestack (n 34) 232; see also Donnelly, 'The Relative Universality of Human Rights' (n 9) 291.

43 Sen (n 8).

44 Donnelly, 'The Relative Universality of Human Rights' (n 9) 291.

45 Donnelly, 'The Relative Universality of Human Rights' (n 9) 299. 'Human rights are (relatively) universal at the level of the concept, broad formulations such as the claims in Articles 3 and 22 of the Universal Declaration that "everyone has the right to life, liberty and security of person" and "the right to social security"' (299). 'Particular rights concepts, however, have multiple defensible *conceptions*. Any particular conception, in turn, will have many defensible *implementations*. At this level – for example, the design of electoral systems to implement the right "to take part in the government of his country, directly or through freely chosen representatives" – relativity is not merely defensible but desirable' (299). Douzinas points out a similar distinction; between the abstract right and what it means in practice. Douzinas *The End of Human Rights* (n 4) 252.

only have a 'relative universality' or 'tempered universalism'.[46] This will help with some kinds of variation, but it may not be able to overcome significant ethical differences.

Models allowing for variation nevertheless depend on a core set of shared values and while they can accommodate some kinds of difference, they don't always solve problems related to, for example, the variable status of women. Moreover, if there is some relative agreement, it may be worth focusing on that, and trying to trace the basis of this agreement in order to generate rights that really would be universal. Adopting Renteln's definition of cultural relativism, that 'some evaluations are relative to the cultural background out of which they arise',[47] is useful as it acknowledges the variation we in fact find and yet doesn't rule out universal (as opposed to absolutist) values. Her approach is also productive in that it stresses the importance of enculturation in the way we perceive and understand the world. Relativism does not rule out the possibility of actual or emergent cross-cultural universals.[48]

Even if such universal are found, for better or worse, 'Cultural relativism is a fact' in so far as there is variation between, and indeed, within, different cultures and this variation does need to be taken into account.[49] This is difficult in itself. A further difficulty is introduced by the way 'culture' and 'cultural relativism' are used to mean a number of different things.[50] Moreover, implicit in arguments against the significance of cultural variation seems to be an anxiety that ceding too much ground to 'culture' would be to abandon the cause of human rights; that to acknowledge variation would be to relinquish any claim to universal standards

46 Donnelly, 'The Relative Universality of Human Rights' (n 9) 299.

47 Renteln, 'Relativism and the Search for Human Rights' (n 23) 59.

48 Renteln, 'Relativism and the Search for Human Rights' (n 23).

49 Donnelly, 'The Relative Universality of Human Rights' (n 9) 294.

50 There is a tendency to talk about relativism, though, as if it meant one thing only. However, Renteln identifies three kinds: 'apparent ethical relativism', 'the claim that peoples differ in their basic moral beliefs' (60); 'ethical relativism as descriptive (factual)', that there is no objective way of deciding the truth of value judgements; and finally 'ethical relativism as prescriptive (value)' or 'normative relativism' (61). The last is the idea that 'In every case the rightness of any act or goodness of any thing for a member of culture A is justified by reference to what in fact is considered right or good in culture A' (Schmidt 786 cited in Renteln, 61). In relation to normative relativism, Renteln notes that it is 'practically unintelligible to Western philosophers … because Western philosophers presume that the concept of morality makes no sense unless it is universally applicable' (61). This understanding of morality is central to debates about human rights as human rights are generally discussed in terms of ethical or moral standards. Thus, the search for universals tends to be at this level; a search for some kind of universal, if not absolute, morality. As it's far from clear that 'morality' itself is anything like a universal concept, this quest is problematic from the start. Renteln, 'Relativism and the Search for Human Rights' (n 23). Paul F. Schmidt, 'Some Criticisms of Cultural Relativism' (1955) 70, *Journal of Philosophy* 780.

or to the conceptual universality of human rights. There is one sense in which this danger is real, as too much attention to culture may reveal the ideological underpinnings of existing human rights systems.

I suggest that the central problem in this area is an unwillingness to treat the culture of the human rights system itself as culture. In all the arguments against cultural relativism, there is little recognition that the key elements of the human rights system (the nation, the human subject, the concept of rights) are cultural constructs. Rather, discussion of cultural difference is often conducted in terms of a comparison with the 'West' and a very particular understanding of 'human rights', as though these are entirely separate from culture. Failing to see the cultural aspects of these comparators will mean challenges to human rights on the basis of culture are likely to continue. Despite the difficulty of talking about 'Western culture' (or any singular culture) human rights as we know them are a cultural product. And while it seems to me that the concept of human rights can be defended on the basis of something that is universally shared, to do this, some of the cultural and historical baggage that comes with a great many theories of human rights needs to be questioned. This cannot happen unless we acknowledge its existence. In the following, I examine theories of human rights that claim to be anti-foundational. This shows two things. First, despite an explicit rejection of foundations, these systems nevertheless rely on something. Of itself, this is not problematic. Indeed, it is worth foregrounding the concepts on which they rely: the value of human life and the idea that human suffering should not be tolerated. At the same time, however, these models – at least implicitly – endorse the current human rights infrastructure, a system that first and foremost insists on the importance and inviolability of the nation state. This entity is a cultural construct. Moreover, it is a figure that displaces the individual human and necessarily leads to real human suffering.

(Anti) Foundations

There are, of course, those who argue that human rights either have foundations or need them. Understandably, these positions differ with respect to both what counts as foundations as well as to which substantive rights are supported by them.[51] Shestack documents the various sources of human rights including religion,[52]

---

51 Indeed, 'foundations' are often described as sources; see Chase's objections. Anthony Tirado Chase, 'Legitimizing Human Rights: Beyond Mythical Foundations and into Everyday Resonances' (2012) 11(4), *Journal of Human Rights* 505.

52 For discussion of the secular/sacred conflict, see Ari Kohen, 'The problem of Secular Sacredness: Ronald Dworkin, Michael Perry, and Human Fights Foundationalism' (2006) 5(2), *Journal of Human Rights* 235; Michael J. Perry, 'The Morality of Human Rights: A Nonreligious Ground?' (2005) 54, *Emory Law Journal* 97.

natural law (leading to natural rights theory),[53] the state (hence positivism), Marxism, the sociological approach (that attempts 'to line up the law with the facts of human life in society'), and utilitarianism.[54] Goodhart adds human capacities, moral agency and self-ownership to Shestack's list.[55] Other approaches identify a specifically human quality to be protected, such as dignity, agency[56] or equality. All are foundational in that they rely on a value, or set of values, that are either defended or presented as self-evident. This is not problematic, as human rights cannot do without some kind of foundation. If the crisis of authority that human rights faces is to be solved, an argument is required. As all arguments rest on something, foundations are unavoidable.

Cultural and social variation may suggest that any quest for foundations is doomed to fail. Differences between peoples may be so fundamental and so intractable that it would be better to simply stop trying to find any absolute common ground.[57] As long as there is agreement about substantive rights, one might argue that the question of foundations simply doesn't matter. But the reluctance to rely on foundations seems to have more to do with how 'foundation' is defined. Narrow definitions of this concept also lead to the claim that models are anti-foundational when they clearly rest on something. Here, I concentrate on the work of Donnelly, Ignatieff and Rorty as they are generally associated with the anti foundationalist approach. The way Donnelly and Ignatieff define 'foundation' shows a desire to protect human rights from particular interests but does not make

53 See Brown ((n 1) 44) who argues that human rights as new kinds of rights needed to rely on natural law; see Douzinas for a history of natural law ((n 4) 23ff). See Pagden for an argument that human rights comes from natural rights. Anthony Pagden (2003), 'Human Rights, Natural Rights and Europe's Imperial Legacy' (2003) 31(2), *Political Theory* 171.

54 Shestack (n 34) 211.

55 Goodhart (n 33).

56 Ignatieff identifies 'agency' as central in human rights. He also argues that 'rights language' 'presumes moral individualism and is nonsensical outside that assumption' (n 35) 67. Gewirth also takes agency or action as the 'common subject matter of all morality and practice' and then demonstrates that an agent cannot logically deny that he, or another person, has certain rights. Specifically, an agent must accept (as agent) that they have rights which function as necessary preconditions for that agency. The existence of human rights, then, is 'agent relative' and must be accepted by these agents (though this is logically necessary) rather than rights having an 'independent ontological status' (236). It is not a completely isolated view of the individual, however, as he also argues that there needs to be an ethical community, though this does not contradict individual rights. Freeman points out that this model prioritises rights that protect and promote moral action; it does not help when rights clash at this level (70). Michael Freeman, *Human Rights* (n 4); Alan Gewirth, 'Why there are Human rights' (1985) 11(2), *Social Theory and Practice* 235; Ignatieff (n 35).

57 '… the human rights phenomenon renders human rights foundationalism outmoded and irrelevant', Rabossi, cited in Richard Rorty, 'Human Rights, Rationality, and Sentimentality,' in *Truth and Progress: Philosophical Papers*, Vol. 3 (Cambridge University Press, 1998) 170.

clear that their understanding of 'human rights' also depends on cultural values. While their calls to action are compelling, the hidden foundations of human rights nevertheless need to be exposed and explored if human rights are to have a future. In both Igantieff's and Rorty's accounts we find a better basis for human rights; human suffering.

Donnelly takes the position that 'Overlapping consensus, rather than render human rights groundless, gives them multiple grounds.'[58] He argues that human rights has become the 'preferred option' for realising justice and equality,[59] and while he endorses a functional/consensus universality, he is pessimistic about finding a 'single transhistorical foundation'.[60] He identifies three problems with looking for such a foundation. First, there will never be agreement about the values proposed by 'adherents of a particular philosophy or religion'.[61] Second, 'all prominent comprehensive doctrines have for large parts of their history ignored or actively denied human rights'.[62] Finally, such a position implies 'that virtually all moral and religious theories through most of their histories have been objectively false or immoral'.[63] This is clearly a particular understanding of foundations as connected to religion or (moral) philosophy. It is also a particular understanding of 'human rights'. Donnelly locates the origin of human rights in the seventeenth century,[64] and while this is hardly an unusual position, it does have consequences for the rights that are recognised and for the construction of the subject who holds them. When he argues that 'claims to historical or anthropological universality confuse values such as justice, fairness, and humanity need with practices that aim to realize those values'[65] it seems clear that Donnelly understands human rights as a particular practice, with a distinctive, and distinctly non-universal, provenance.[66] Anything not exactly in line with this understanding does not, for Donnelly, count as 'human rights'.[67] This model of human rights, however, depends on cultural

58 This treats them as a 'Rawlsian political conception of justice'. Donnelly, 'The Relative Universality of Human Rights' (n 9) 293.

59 Donnelly, 'The Relative Universality of Human Rights' (n 9) 291.

60 'A single transhistorical foundation would provide what I will call ontological universality.' Donnelly, 'The Relative Universality of Human Rights' (n 9) 292.

61 Donnelly, 'The Relative Universality of Human Rights' (n 9) 293.

62 Donnelly, 'The Relative Universality of Human Rights' (n 9) 293.

63 Donnelly, 'The Relative Universality of Human Rights' (n 9) 293.

64 Donnelly, 'The Relative Universality of Human Rights' (n 9) 284, 286 ff.

65 Donnelly, 'The Relative Universality of Human Rights' (n 9) 284.

66 Alison Dundes Renteln, 'The Unanswered Challenge of Relativism and the Consequences for Human Rights' (1985) 7(4), *Hum. Rts. Q.* 514.

67 The terminology used is also not as illuminating as it might be. Donnelly calls a 'single transhistorical foundation' that which would provide ontological universality. He points to Talbott as an example of such a work. As will be evident when discussing Talbott below, the objections that Donnelly has to 'ontological universality' do not address the kind of argument Talbott is making. Rather, it seems that Donnelly is actually objecting

constructs. The nation, the individual and rights themselves are a product of a particular cultural history that will be interrogated below.

Like Donnelly, Ignatieff supports human rights, but he argues that it is impossible to find a universal foundation for human rights; nothing is, he contends, universal or incontestable. Relying on the dignity or sacredness of humans, he suggests, confuses what we want people to be with what we really are.[68] Moreover, he argues that these foundational approaches are dangerous and divisive. 'Foundational beliefs of all kinds have been a long-standing menace to the human rights of ordinary individuals.'[69] Rather, we should 'forgo these kinds of foundational arguments altogether and seek to build support for human rights on the basis of what such rights actually do for human beings'.[70] Like Donnelly, Ignatieff appears to understand foundations as religious, or at least, of that order. His treatment of foundations as similar to religion may be a reaction to the argument that human rights are a 'secular religion'[71] or 'values for a Godless age'.[72] It is also a clearly a response to the argument that only religion can provide an appropriate foundation for human rights.[73] Ignatieff, however, is insistent that treating human rights anything like religion risks 'idolatory'. His argument against foundations is at base practically motivated as a 'secular defence of human rights

---

to a deontological universality; this would explain the references he makes to religion and philosophical traditions. See also Brown (n 1) 45.

68 His understanding of 'dignity', however, links it to behaviour ('On occasion, men and women behave with inspiring dignity' (54)) which is not obviously the same as the UDHR assertion that all human beings are equal in dignity, which suggests equal worth. Ignatieff (n 35) 54.

69 Ignatieff (n 35) 86.

70 Ignatieff (n 35) 54.

71 Wiesel cited in Ignatieff (n 35) 53.

72 Klug cited in Gearty, *Can Human Rights Survive*? (n 7) 19.

73 Sachedina argues the foundation of the UDHR is secular and that this will not be acceptable to religious people; 'without a universal morality that speaks to each and every person on this earth, the Declaration will lack moral enforcement in the world community'. Abdulaziz Sachedina, 'The Clash of Universalisms: Religious and Secular in Human Rights' (2007), *The Hedgehog Review* 49, 52. Wolterstorff argues that in fact the UDHR is steeped in a Christian tradition. In a sense he agrees with Sachedina as he argues that 'whereas it is possible to articulate religious reasons for affirming human dignity, and thus for human rights, all non-religious attempts to do so have failed'. Nicholas Wolterstorff, 'Response: the irony of it all' (2007), *The Hedgehog Review* 63, 64, 67. Perry takes a similar position, arguing that only the language of religion can provide the vocabulary necessary for the value of people as people and, as such, necessary for human rights. He cites Raimond Gaita:

> The secular philosophical tradition speaks of inalienable rights, inalienable dignity and of persons as ends in themselves. These are, I believe, ways of whistling in the dark, ways of trying to make secure to reason what reason cannot finally underwrite. Religious traditions speak of the sacredness of each human being, but I doubt that sanctity is a concept that has a secure home without those traditions, cited in Perry (n 52) 129.

will necessarily leave religious thinkers unsatisfied. For them secular humanism is the contingent product of late European civilization and is unlikely to command assent in non-European and nonsecular cultures.'[74] The foundations that Ignatieff rejects are a very particular kind but it is not the case that his arguments rest on nothing. Specifically, in order to assess what human rights 'do' for people and in order to promote their protection, we need to have a sense of what humans are and what is good for them.

To make any kind of argument a perspective has to be taken. Foundations are needed; although this is clearly to provide a different definition of 'foundation' than that with which Ignatieff and Donnelly work. I share Ignatieff's trepidation about religion and idolatry but I am not convinced that all other possible foundations have yet been exhausted or that it is possible to do without foundations altogether (if one takes a broader, less religious definition). Indeed, adopting the broader definition, his own account is not as foundationless as it appears. For Ignatieff, human rights tell us when enough is enough; 'human rights as politics becomes a fighting creed, a call to arms'.[75] This relies not only on respect for human life but also on the ability to judge when a line has been crossed. For a line to be crossed, the line has to be drawn. As Schaefer argues,[76] Ignatieff's argument depends on valuing human life and recognising agency, as Ignatieff argues that when agency is protected people 'are less likely to be abused and oppressed'.[77] Politically, it also depends on the willingness of parties to engage in deliberation,[78] something that Schafer argues is 'surely too optimistic'.[79] In any case, it depends on a particular view of people and a particular kind of political context as Ignatieff's view of human rights is that they are not 'above politics' and need to work within the current international political order. While taking a pragmatic view about the current international political order may not seem to rely on foundations, it does at least leave intact the values on which this order relies. Specifically, it implicitly endorses the nation state and the model of the individual that this entails.

Like Ignatieff, Rorty is interested in what human rights can do. As he believes neither in human nature nor in any universal facts about human beings, he is suspicious of 'foundational moralisms' especially as they may simply work to

---

Raimond Gaita, *A Common Humanity: Thinking about Love and Truth and Justice* (Routeldge 2000).For a full discussion see Ari Kohen, *In Defense of Human Rights: A Non-religious Grounding in a Pluralistic World* (Routledge 2008).

74 Ignatieff (n 35) 91.

75 Ignatieff (n 35) 22.

76 Schaefer (n 11).

77 Ignatieff (n 35) 4. 'A minimalist liberal theory simply asserts the importance of human agency and dignity rather than offering what we might call a "thick" theory of common humanity'. Turner (n 17) 6.

78 Ignatieff (n 35) 84.

79 Schaefer (n 11) 47.

further cultural interests.[80] Rorty's approach is linked to how he understands the role of philosophy, which is to 'summarize our culturally influenced intuitions about the right thing to do in various situations';[81] these generalisations then increase 'the predictability, and thus the power and efficiency, of our institutions, thereby heightening the sense of shared moral identity that brings us together in a moral community'.[82] The role of philosophy is to help build a moral community. It should then be possible, he argues, to change behaviour by altering intuitions through a sentimental education. The rise of human rights culture, he notes, is not the result of increased knowledge but is rather the result of 'hearing sad and sentimental stories'.[83] In one sense, this sees rights as absolutely tied to socio-cultural context; the sentimental education is ultimately about promoting our own 'morally superior' culture. But, as it is tied to particular cultural contexts, the set of values promoted 'requires argument'.[84] In this way, it is no less cultural than the foundations that Ignatieff and Donnelly reject. It is also difficult to see how this is not simply our own 'foundational moralism', furthering our own cultural interests.

Rorty's laudable goal is in having all people recognised as human. The challenge is that for many people, identity 'is bound up with their sense of who they are *not*',[85] making an appeal to some human commonality pointless. How recognition of someone as 'human' can occur without some human commonality is not clear, though it appears to rely on something like empathy. Thus, despite his claims to be an antifoundationalist, Rorty nevertheless relies on a positive view of human nature and the value of human life. While his highlighting of the affective dimension of human community is welcome, the question of what counts as 'sad' and what these stories may then set in motion are crucial. Leaving value judgements about who is deserving of sympathy and who is not (as Rorty's account seems to do) to a 'moral community' relies rather too much on the worthiness of that community. Gearty appears to agree, and suggests that relying on 'sad stories' is not enough; 'We need truths – especially if they are true but also even if we have to make them up. It is not enough to leave everything to sentiment.'[86]

Despite the emphasis given to the sentimental education, there is more to Rorty's account than stories. Rorty understands that people do bad things to other people, thus his view of human nature is not thoroughly optimistic. His argument that we need to see human rights violators as rational and human rather than

80 Rorty (n 57). See also Douzinas *The End of Human Rights* (n 4) 253; Schaefer (n 11) 30; Turner (n 17) 40–41.

81 Rorty (n 57) 171.

82 Rorty (n 57) 171.

83 Rorty (n 57) 172.

84 Bhikhu Parekh (n 27) 141.

85 Rorty (n 57) 178.

86 Gearty, *Can Human Rights Survive*? (n 7) 56. Though see Rorty (n 57) 181–2. The argument that sentiment is somehow weaker than reason, he argues, is simply to do with resentment that there is no other way of controlling the powerful.

monstrous, leads to the conclusion that this bad behaviour is the result not of moral ignorance but of deprivation.[87] Thus, he suggests that we should see violators as lacking in security and sympathy; with security meaning that 'conditions of life [are] sufficiently risk-free as to make one's difference from others inessential to one's self-respect, one's sense of worth'.[88] This security is a necessary precondition for any educational project as 'Sentimental education works only on people who can relax long enough to listen'.[89] In this account, then, the foundations of human rights – the conditions necessary for even the conception of human rights – relate to basic security, to human needs, drives and desires. Humans, to be human, need to be secure. This concept of security is fundamental in Rorty's model and at least as powerful as his argument in favour of a sentimental education. As it relates to basic human needs it is also universal. It can also serve as a foundation. A universal foundation for human rights need not be a universal set of rights or a universal account of why some things are good and some are not. It is enough to find something about human life that is universally true. Rorty's attention to security is one candidate; Ignatieff provides another in his discussion of pain.

While acknowledging that what we share as people may be quite limited, Ignatieff observes that a basic intuition seems to be '… what is pain and humiliation for you is bound to be pain and humiliation for me'.[90] It then follows that the 'elemental priority of all human rights activism [is] to stop torture, beatings, killings, rape, and assault and to improve, as best we can, the security of ordinary people. My minimalism is not strategic at all. It is the most we can hope for.'[91] This account of pain can be reformulated so as to be more minimal and, at the same time, more concrete. That is, for pain to be relevant, it need not be the case that people suffer in the same way; it is enough to recognise that people feel pain and that this is (by definition) not good. This can then become more than an intuition; it can become a universal fact that, while minimal, is a potential universal ground. If pursued more fully, the common experience of pain can provide a very human model of human rights.

Accounts arguing against foundations are not as always foundationless as they claim. As it is impossible not to have some kind of foundation, this is not of itself problematic. The issue is that there is more than one foundation in these accounts

87 That he claims foundationalists would see the violator as deprived of truth or moral knowledge suggests a very particular kind of foundationalist. Rorty (n 57) 180.

88 Rorty (n 57) 180.

89 Rorty (n 57) 180.

90 Ignatieff (n 35) 95.

91 Ignatieff (n 35) 173. Ignatieff argues that the 'universal commitments implied by human rights can be compatible with a wide variety of ways of living only if the universalism implied is self-consciously minimalist' (56). This does not, however, translate into universal assent (68). In relation to foundations, Schaefer argues that this will not do by itself, as the 'intuition' that pain is bad for other people is not shared by all individuals with respect to all other people. Schaefer (n 11) 35.

and they are in conflict with each other. The suffering and real injustice that Donnelly, Ignatieff and Rorty want to stop are not compatible with the individual subject produced by the nation state. As the nation state underpins the international human rights system that Donnelly and Ignatieff accept, it is difficult to see how their calls to action can ever be properly heard. Moreover, the nation state itself is a construct, an entity that while dominant is not in fact self-evident.

I now consider the nation state and the individual it produces in order to reveal their outlines and limitations. In order to do this, a descriptive account of the current human rights system is discussed. This shows the centrality of the nation state to human rights as well as how the state constructs people.

The Current System

In *The Idea of Human Rights*, Charles Beitz provides an account of 'human rights' paying attention to the norms and practice of international politics.[92] Beitz argues that treating 'international human rights as a normative practice to be grasped *sui generis*' allows us to 'consider how the idea of a human right functions within it'.[93] Far from insisting on foundations or a single explanation as to why we have (or should have) a particular complement of rights, Beitz sees the variety of perspectives on human rights theory and practice as an advantage.[94] His final map of human rights has two levels and three elements.

1. 'Human rights are requirements whose object is to protect urgent individual interests against certain predictable dangers ("standard threats") to which they are vulnerable under typical circumstances of life in a modern world order composed of states'.
2. 'Human rights apply in the first instance to the political institutions of states, including their constitutions, laws, and public policies'.
3. 'Human rights are matters of international concern', that is, if a state fails to meet its obligations, others may come in and do things to help.[95]

As a result of this descriptive synthesis, the idea of human rights is necessarily both expansive and inclusive. It also allows us to see the foundations of existing human rights practice. Human rights in this account are really a matter for states and for politics; if an individual is present at all, she inhabits 'a modern world order composed of states'.

The subordination of the individual to the state can be seen in the procedure Beitz provides for identifying the 'urgent individual interests' of (1) and thus

92 Beitz (n 4); Chase (n 51).
93 Beitz (n 4) 12.
94 Beitz (n 4) 21.
95 Beitz (n 4) 109.

arguing for new rights. The interest should be, first, 'sufficiently important' to the people who desire its protection such 'that it would be reasonable to consider its protection to be a political priority', second, that 'it would be advantageous to protect the underlying interest by means of legal or policy instruments available to the state' and finally, that if the interest were not protected 'the failure would be a suitable object of international concern'.[96] While 'concern' appears to start with the individual interest, it quickly progresses to levels of national, international and political concern. Ultimately, human rights are concerned with what is advantageous to states. Given that the nation is the key actor in international human rights, this is hardly surprising.[97]

But Beitz draws attention to a rather more promising aspect of international human rights; human rights are 'emergent'. Rather than the substance of human rights being timeless and fixed, new rights can and will emerge as a response to new threats and risks, new conceptions of justice, and changes in infrastructure and authority.[98] The openness that Beitz identifies provides important room for critique and reformulation without reliance on 'foundations'.[99] Given that the recognition of new rights depends on political and national interests, this is not exactly utopian, but it does suggest that the current system is not quite as intractable as it appears.

Beitz's account draws attention to one of the most important aspects of contemporary international human rights: the nation state. The nation state is central to international politics and to the 'practical reasoning' that human rights involves.[100] As it is central, it is a sense foundational. More importantly, it is a cultural construct.

Nation State

Human rights and the nation state have long been bound together. In theory, human rights protect individuals from the state; at the same time, the state is the agent responsible for protecting its citizens: 'the contradictory role of the state is the great paradox of human rights theory'.[101] As should already be apparent, 'The

96 Beitz (n 4) 137.

97 As Weizman has argued, nation states make careful calculations which are clear in the distance maintained between human rights and a humanitarianism which 'unashamedly and impartially deals with the problems of "bare life"'. Eyal Weizman, *The Least of All Possible Evils: Humanitarian Violence from Arendt to Gaza* (Verso 2011) 54.

98 Beitz (n 4) 30. He argues that human rights are emergent in another respect, that is, they may be realised differently in different contexts without the right as such being threatened. Beitz (n 4) 204.

99 While the foundational approach has been ruled out, so has the idea that there needs to be actual agreement about what rights are; 'Actual agreement is, in general, too strong a condition to impose on critical standards, and therefore on human rights.' Beitz (n 4) 87.

100 Beitz (n 4) 212.

101 Turner (n 17) 33.

global human rights regime relies on national implementation of internationally recognized human rights.'[102] It is a reliance, however, rather than a compulsion; O'Neill draws attention to the fact that the Covenants 'do not assign states straightforward obligations to respect liberty rights ... but rather second-order obligations to *secure* respect for them' that is clearly not the same thing.[103] This is exactly why the political aspect of human rights is so important. The power of a nation over its citizens and its general inviolability with respect to other states makes the international political process crucial.

The power of nation states is, of course, key to the paradox. Perhaps only states are powerful enough to even begin to secure human rights. The problem is that power cannot always be compelled to the good,[104] especially because of the sovereign and inviolable status of nation states at international law; there is no one to compel them.[105] Just as the power to protect human rights could easily turn to their violation, entrusting the nation state with human rights protection also gives it power over individuals.[106] With every human right claimed by a people, state powers intrude further and further into the life of the individual.[107] But more importantly, in terms of the foundations of human rights, the nation state is hardly a natural entity; it 'is a socially constructed, historically specific identity, which has come to be universalized'.[108] And while a realist approach to international relations accepts the existence of the nation state, this does not of itself defend its status as 'a unit so uniquely solid and objective that it can fix the limits of our moral obligations'.[109]

---

102 'The few and limited exceptions – most notably genocide, crimes against humanity, certain war crimes, and perhaps torture and arbitrary execution – only underscore the almost complete sovereign authority of states to implement human rights in their territories as they see fit.' Donnelly, 'The Relative Universality of Human Rights', (n 9) 283.

103 Onora O'Neill, 'The Dark Side of Human Rights' (2005) 81(2), *Int'l Aff. (UK)* 427, 433.

104 O'Neill (n 103) 435.

105 Because of this, O'Neill suggests that perhaps some power over these second order obligations should be given to 'powerful non-state actors, such as transnational corporations, powerful non-governmental organizations, or major religious, cultural and professional and educational bodies'. O'Neill (n 103) 435.

106 It also means that states have a great deal of control over the meaning of human rights itself. See Conor Gearty, 'Is the Idea of Human Rights Now Doing more Harm than Good?' (2004) 12 October 2004. http://www2.lse.ac.uk/humanRights/articlesAndTranscripts/121004_CG.pdf [last accessed 27 January 2013].

107 O'Neill (n 103) 439; see also Douzinas *The End of Human Rights* (n 4) 101.

108 Carl F. Stychin, 'Same-Sex Sexualities and the Globalization of Human Rights Discourse' (2004) 49, *McGill L.J.* 951, 955.

109 Mary Midgley, 'Towards an Ethic of Global Responsibility' in Timothy Dunne and Nicholas J. Wheeler (eds), *Human Rights in Global Politics* (Cambridge University Press 1999) 171.

The specific contours of the nation state matter, especially in relation to the individual. As Beitz's account shows, the nation and its concerns are more important than those of the individual. Moreover, as the autonomy and inviolability of the nation state are akin to the agency and autonomy generally attributed to individuals, the nation is perfectly placed to displace the human individual. The way the nation effectively takes the place of the individual is clear in the figure of the national 'body'. Individual citizens are both subsumed in and erased by this entity. The body of the nation stands for, and yet erases, the bodies of individuals. It is not always possible to escape metaphors, and of itself, construing the nation as a body is not problematic. But in relation to human rights, the body and personhood of the nation displace the body and personhood of individuals. States are almost exclusively the only relevant persons on the international scene; and this means the individual human person is thoroughly backgrounded.[110] The displacement of the individual body by the national body can also be seen in the process through which the nation is formed; the social contract. Moreover, because of the central place of the contract in the formation of the state, the political community is understood in terms of rights and duties with the individual as a contracting party. That is, while it seems to be a truism to claim that it is not possible for there to be rights without someone owing a corresponding duty, this is (simply) a consequence of the formation of the nation state itself, the construction of the nation and the individual subject and the subordination of the individual person to the national body.

Rights and Responsibilities

Bentham's oft cited characterisation of human rights as 'nonsense upon stilts' argues that without a mechanism to enforce and uphold rights, they are meaningless.[111] This corresponds to one of the usual definitions of 'rights'. A right is generally thought to entail a corresponding duty on an identifiable person or entity.[112] Given the kinds of human rights in texts like the UDHR (and indeed in domestic and regional documents), this duty generally passes to the state. The duty is seen as a burden and this must be balanced in some way. This is one way of explaining why

110 There are some important exceptions to this and arguably some changes in process – see M.W. Janis, 'Individuals as Subjects of International Law' (1984) 17, *Cornell International Law Journal* 67.

111 'That which has no existence cannot be destroyed – that which cannot be destroyed cannot require anything to preserve it from destruction. Natural rights is simply nonsense: natural and imprescriptible rights, rhetorical nonsense, -- nonsense upon stilts.' Jeremy Bentham (1843), *The Works of Jeremy Bentham*, vol. 2, The Online Library of Liberty http://files.libertyfund.org/files/1921/Bentham_0872-02_EBk_v6.0.pdf [accessed 19 February 2013] 914.

112 Renteln writes, 'If Hart is right, then there is no necessary connection between right and duty.' Renteln, 'The Unanswered Challenge of Relativism and the Consequences for Human Rights' (n 66) 516.

there is wider acceptance of negative rights (that involve refraining from action) than for positive rights (that involve some positive contribution or action on the part of the duty bearer). Rights and duties, then, operate as a kind of trade; the benefits of the rights should be sufficient to justify the burden of protecting them; this is clear in Beitz's account above. This paradigm of rights generally requires that an entity, one with appropriate resources, can be identified to take up a duty before the existence of a right can be recognised and protected.

This contractual understanding of rights is ultimately a consequence of the social contract that founds the state. While the social contract is crucial in constituting the body of the state, it is also central in constructing the individual and her relationship with the state. Specifically, the social contract reduces the subject to 'an artificial construct of reason, a naked human being endowed only with logic, strong survival instincts and a sense of morality'.[113] The nakedness of the human being is not about corporeality but rather about the stripping away of any individual characteristics. The social contract subjects individuals absolutely to the power of the sovereign[114] with the only power left to people being over possessions.[115] The link of both the social contract and the model of the individual to capitalism is important and will be returned to in later chapters. For now, the focus is on the relationship between rights and duties.

Without the link between rights and duties, it is thought, all would be lost. Thus, O'Neill argues that 'the entire normative understanding of rights' depends on linking rights and obligations, as without this, rights can only be 'aspirational'.[116] This is not a universal view, however, and the necessary connection between rights and duties has been questioned in various ways. Griffin, for example, argues that particular rights and specific duties are not always co-extensive and that to talk meaningfully of a right, it is not necessary to identify a single responsible agent.[117] Rather, duty bearers need only be 'specifiable'; they don't actually have to exist.[118] Sen suggests that duties attach to those who are able to do something; thus, the particular entity responsible for the right may not be specifiable in advance of any rights violation; 'loosely specified obligations must not be confused with

113 'The fiction drew its power from the importance contract had acquired in early capitalism.' Douzinas *The End of Human Rights* (n 4) 65. The contract itself is founded on 'blood, suffering and sacrifice'. Pheng Cheah and Elizabeth Grosz (1997) 'The body of the law: noted towards a theory of corporeal justice' in Pheng Cheah, David Fraser and Judith Grbich (eds), *Thinking Through the Body of the Law* (New York University Press 1996) 15. See also Elizabeth Grosz, *Volatile Bodies: Toward a Corporeal Feminism* (Indiana University Press 1994) 123.

114 Douzinas *The End of Human Rights* (n 4) 78.

115 With the introduction of money, this too becomes abstract and limitless. This dynamic may also explain why bodily integrity is often discussed in terms of the body as property. Douzinas *The End of Human Rights* (n 4) 82–3. See also Goodhart (n 33).

116 O'Neill (n 103) 430.

117 Griffin (n 5) 85, 108.

118 Griffin (n 5) 110.

no obligations at all'.[119] These perspectives, however, are not compatible with a contractual understanding of rights. Indeed, at first it seems impossible to argue that there can be a right without a clear, corresponding duty. I suggest that this impossibility is linked exactly to the dominance of contractual models in understanding not only the relationship between rights and duties but also the relationship between the state and individuals. The dominance of the contractual model not only limits rights, the contract also constructs people in a particular way. The contractual person shares the same features as the individual constructed by the social contract; rational, logical and disembodied.

The subject of rights is a cultural construct. Like rights themselves, it is a Western invention. The idea that rights do have Western provenance is reasonably well settled. What is less often acknowledged is that the nation state itself and the individual it constructs should be understood as cultural constructs. It is the dominance of these entities that can be linked to cultural imperialism. I begin the next section by considering the Western origin of rights. And while this seems to confirm that human rights are in fact an example of Western cultural imperialism, there are grounds for optimism. Specifically, it has been argued that far from having a long history, human rights are in fact a very recent invention. This suggests that it may be possible to re-invent human rights in a new way.

The Origin of Human Rights

Human rights, Brown argues, '*is* liberal and western'.[120] Goodhart concurs: 'There is no debating the Western origin of human rights; it is a plain historical fact.'[121] This aspect of the provenance of human rights is, as Goodhart's assertion suggests, reasonably well settled. Whether the Western origin of human rights is problematic and what it means to claim they emanate from the 'West' are different issues. Thus, while acknowledging their Western origin, Ignatieff does not regard this as supporting claims that human rights are simply an instance of 'Western cultural imperialism' especially as the West also has to uphold these values.[122] Even if this is a case of imperialism, to call it 'Western culture' suggests that the values endorsed are uncontested in the West. But as Howard argues, human rights come from 'certain strands of Western political philosophy, mainly liberalism and social democracy' that are connected to capitalism, secularism and humanism.[123] That is, these values may be more properly connected to a political ideology and to power rather than what would normally be associated with the concept of 'culture'.

Donnelly writes:

119 Sen (n 8) 341.
120 Brown (n 1) 42.
121 Goodhart (n 33) 943. See also Griffin (n 5) 133.
122 Ignatieff (n 35) 91.
123 Howard (n 37) 335; see also Anthony Woodiwiss, *Human Rights* (Routledge 2005).

> Human rights ideas and practices arose not from any deep Western cultural roots, but from the social, economic, and political transformations of modernity. They thus have relevance wherever those transformations have occurred, irrespective of the pre-existing culture of the place.[124]

For Donnelly human rights development is linked to the 'spread of modern markets and states' and this near universal influence has at least the potential to lead to a 'functional universality' with respect to the substance of human rights.[125] However, the spread of modern markets and states takes with it certain ideas and values.[126] It is perhaps not necessary to call this 'culture' nor crucial to link it with the West, but these underpinnings need to be acknowledged.[127] As Douzinas points out 'Human rights were initially linked with specific class interests and were the ideological and political weapons in the fight of the rising bourgeoisie against despotic political power and static social organisation.'[128] And while this particular 'partiality has been transcended' that does not mean that all ideological baggage has been shed.[129] This is especially clear with respect to the influence of models of contract to the formation of both the state and the individual. The Western provenance of human rights, and accusations of their spread being a form of cultural imperialism, is not really challenged by the argument that human rights discourses spread because of modern markets. Indeed, the spread of economic models and related governance structures are arguably part of a more thoroughgoing process of Western imperialism that can be linked to economic globalisation.

Despite this broad agreement on the Western provenance of human rights, the history of human rights is not entirely settled. Perhaps the most dominant view sees human rights as emerging out of the French Declaration of the Rights of Man and the eighteenth century generally with our contemporary human rights framework originating in the post WWII period, with the development of the Universal Declaration of Human Rights.[130] There are, of course, other arguments that trace the values (if not the specific terms) of human rights back to natural law, religion and even the novel.[131] In *The Last Utopia*, however, Samuel Moyn argues

124 Donnelly, 'The Relative Universality of Human Rights' (n 9) 287.

125 Donnelly, 'The Relative Universality of Human Rights' (n 9) 287, 288.

126 Indeed, some argue that the spread of the modern state has led to widespread abuse of human rights (Marks, 58). As Klein argues in the case of Argentina 'the repression and the economics were in fact a single unified project' (cited in Marks, 59); the move to 'modern' politics and economics often has human casualties. Moreover, modernity beings with it new risks and threats and new vulnerabilities. Susan Marks, 'Human Rights and Root Causes' (2011) 74(1) MLR 57. See also Goodhart (n 33).

127 Donnelly, *Universal Human Rights* (n 4) 69.

128 Douzinas *The End of Human Rights* (n 4) 1.

129 Douzinas *The End of Human Rights* (n 4) 1.

130 Brown (n 1) 52; Michael Freeman, 'Universalism, Communitarianism and Human Rights: A reply to Chris Brown' (1998) 2(1), *Intl J Hum Rts* 79; Marks (n 126) 57.

131 Lynne Hunt, *Inventing Human Rights: A History* (Norton 2007).

that human rights are a very recent invention.[132] In the light of claims for a long and deep history of human rights,[133] Moyn's argument is provocative.[134] Nevertheless, his tracing of historical evidence around the emergence and development of human rights in the twentieth century suggests that understanding human rights as a 'transnational ideal and movement', the human rights discourse that has become so widespread in recent decades, only really emerged with the failure of political models, utopia, and the unfulfilled promise of the nation state.[135] It seems that 'the honest conclusion is that the phrase meant different things to different people from the beginning'.[136]

My interest in Moyn's argument is in the idea of re-invention.

> It is true that commitment to human rights crystallized as a result of Holocaust memory, but only decades later, as human rights were called upon to serve brand new purposes. What mattered most of all about the human rights movement of the 1940s, in truth, is not that it happened, but that – like the even deeper past – it has to be reinvented, not merely retrieved after the fact.[137]

Moyn's argument that human rights discourse is a recent invention suggests that human rights can be altered; they can be reinvented to 'serve brand new purposes'. Seeing human rights as an invention opens up new possibilities, and suggests that a new invention of human rights may be possible.

In order to explore these possibilities, I now consider two philosophical reinventions of human rights in some detail. Part of the reason for this is to show that that even accounts that start with what are ostensibly self-evident givens are nevertheless influenced by dominant views of what constitute both rights and individuals. This demonstrates how difficult it is to escape the figures of the nation and the individual when thinking about human rights. The more important reason for considering these models is that they provide room for real people, and pay attention to human needs and human suffering. They demonstrate that it is possible to re-imagine human rights in a human way.

---

132 Moyn (n 22). Midgley too notes that human rights is a recent addition to 'our moral vocabulary' (n 109) 160.

133 For example, Ishay, *The History of Human Rights* (n 4).

134 For a critical evaluation see Robin Blackburn, 'Reclaiming Human Rights' (2011) 69, *New Left Review* 126.

135 Moyn (n 22) 7, 123.

136 Moyn (n 22) 50.

137 Moyn (n 22) 83.

Humane Models

In *Which Rights Should be Universal*, William Talbott, relying on moral and empirical grounds, proposes a set of human rights that he argues should be universal.[138] His account is largely a consequentialist one, arguing 'that basic human rights can be justified by their contribution to human well-being' even though what 'well-being' means is not set out in detail.[139] Rather, his approach looks to human history in order to determine what constitutes a good life; it is an empirical question. His model is compelling and well balanced as evidenced in his care to avoid both moral imperialism and what he calls 'moral wishy-washiness'. The mode of reasoning is neither bottom up nor top down, but rather an 'equilibrium model',[140] that is able to take account of human fallibility, something that is central to his argument. Talbott holds that we do have a 'kind of moral perception which enables us to make directly justified particular moral judgements about what we are experiencing'.[141] Thus he argues for a moral standpoint, that appears to be similar to Rawls' conception of the original position. But Talbott's position differs in important ways. Crucially, the moral standpoint is 'a point of view from which we can reliably though not infallibly make important moral distinctions'.[142] This conception of moral sensibility allows for the development of new judgements about right and wrong, it does not dictate what these distinctions will be and it also takes account of human fallibility. The ground he relies on, and in a sense the conclusion that Talbott comes to, is autonomy. In short, humans have rights because of the capacity for autonomy; the rights we have should support the full development of this autonomy. The development of autonomy allows for feedback between citizens and their state, hence, 'Guaranteeing autonomy rights makes it possible for citizens to make reliable judgments about how well the government's policies are promoting their well-being.'[143] The universality he proposes is not 'strict universality', rather, it is 'an important kind of contingent universality'; the rights he proposes *should* be universal.[144]

138 Talbott, *Which Rights Should be Universal?* (n 29) 3. This work continues in Talbott, *Human Rights and Human Well-Being* (n 13).

139 Talbott, *Which Rights Should be Universal?* (n 29) 17. 'However, the exercise of good judgment in particular cases does not require a definition of "well-being". For example, it is not necessary to have a definition of "well-being" to recognize that typical cases of torture and coercion are bad for the person being tortured or coerced.' Talbott, *Which Rights Should be Universal?* (n 29) 206.

140 Talbott, *Which Rights Should be Universal?* (n 29) 29.

141 Talbott, *Which Rights Should be Universal?* (n 29) 63.

142 Talbott, *Which Rights Should be Universal?* (n 29) 109.

143 William J. Talbott, 'Reply to Critics: In Defense of One Kind of Epistemically Modest But Metaphysically Immodest Liberalism' (2008) 9 (2) *Human Rights Rev* 206..

144 Talbott, *Human Rights and Human Well-Being* (n 13) 19.

Talbott suggests a basic set of rights 'necessary for the development and exercise of autonomy'.[145] Because the moral standpoint is reliable and fallible at the same time, there are two kinds of rights in his model, '*development-of-judgment* and *exercise-of-judgment* rights'.[146] These are linked to both the development and exercise of autonomy and together are foundational and constitutive. He arrives at the following:

1. A right to physical security
2. A right to physical subsistence (understood as a right to an opportunity to earn subsistence for those who are able to do so and a welfare right for those who are not)
3. Children's rights to what is necessary for normal physical, cognitive, emotional, and behavioural development, including the development of empathic understanding
4. A right to an education, including a moral education aimed at further development and use of empathic understanding
5. A right to freedom of the press
6. A right to freedom of thought and expression
7. A right to freedom of association
8. A right to a sphere of personal autonomy free from paternalistic interference
9. Political rights, including democratic rights and an independent judiciary to enforce the entire package of rights.[147]

As Talbott points out, some of these look like classic liberal rights,[148] but there are important differences. For example, 'subsistence rights' include 'unpolluted air, unpolluted water, adequate clothing, adequate shelter, and minimal preventive public health care'.[149] In current frameworks, food and water are, at best, social and economic rights, while anything connected with the environment as such are at best third generation rights. The attention given to social practices in Talbott's work is also particularly useful. This allows consideration not simply of individual scenarios but also requires an assessment of the consequences of a social practice more generally. This approach is reflected in the 'main principle':

145 Talbott, *Which Rights Should be Universal?* (n 29) 113.

146 Talbott, *Which Rights Should be Universal?* (n 29) 128.

147 Talbott, *Human Rights and Human Well-Being* (n 13) 23. The rights under (8) are further detailed in Talbott's later work and five 'nonbasic' rights are added, including economic rights, negative opportunity rights, positive opportunity rights, rights to social insurance and privacy rights. Talbott, *Human Rights and Human Well-Being* (n 13) 350–51.

148 Talbott. *Which Rights Should be Universal?* (n 29) 137.

149 Henry Shue, *Basic Rights: Subsistence, Affluence, and U.S. Foreign Policy* (Princeton University Press 1980) 23 cited in Talbott, *Which Rights Should be Universal?* (n 29) 129.

> A change in or exception to status quo moral or legal practices is endorsed as an improvement by the main principle just in case the change, when evaluated as a substantive social practice and a practice of implementation, would not reduce the life prospects of bystanders and would make the overall system of social practices one that does a better job of equitably promoting life prospects of all participants, except those covered by the responsible noncompliance exclusion, than the status quo system of practices, and also does a better job than any of the relevant alternatives.[150]

As reasoned, balanced and (admirably) limited as Talbott's rights are,[151] the retention of the nation state (as (9) suggests) is potentially problematic.[152] I do not want to claim that democratic rights and an independent judiciary are not positive things; but it seems to me that they are not of the same order as rights to subsistence and physical security. Indeed, Talbott does distinguish between autonomy rights and political rights but with only the last (9) identified as political. Of course, Talbott's set of rights is entirely appropriate for the vast majority of the world's population and for the current political order. This is coherent with his aim, as for Talbott human rights are not about being human but rather, they are concerned with 'providing a framework in which we can live together, conduct experiments in living, and benefit from the experiments of others.'[153] Talbott's re-invention of human rights also provides a space for people. His attention to both human fallabilism and to what is good for people is extremely valuable and informs much of the thinking in this book.

The second argument for human rights from an ethical basis is equally impressive. In *On Human Rights*, Griffin argues that human rights need to protect 'normative agency'. The model he outlines does not *derive* from this concept of agency, rather he makes a 'proposal' that seeks to remedy the 'indeterminateness of the term' human rights.[154] Thus, the model can be understood as a response, and remedy, to the assertion that 'human rights' is 'nearly criterionless'[155] and that it is therefore necessary to 'stipulate' what it means; indeed, he points out that this should not be controversial as the meaning of 'human rights' was 'stipulated' from

---

150 Talbott, *Human Rights and Human Well-Being* (n 13) 66.

151 Although Reidy thinks the list is too long. David A. Reidy (2008), 'William Talbott's *Which Rights Should be Universal?*' (2008) 9(2), *Human Rights Rev* 181.

152 See Carole Gould (2008), 'The Theory of Universal Human Rights: A Comment on Talbott' (2008) 9(2), *Human Rights Rev* 157. Talbott notes that his account is 'institutional' as they are 'rights that all governments should guarantee to everyone everywhere'. Talbott, *Human Rights and Human Well-Being* (n 13) 326.

153 Talbott, *Human Rights and Human Well-Being* (n 13) 341.

154 Griffin (n 5) 4.

155 Griffin (n 5) 14.

the start.[156] His proposal is: 'Human rights can then be seen as protections of our human standing or, as I shall put it, our personhood.'[157]

In support of this stipulation, he writes:

> When I speak here of the 'derivation' of the human right to autonomy, I do not mean an entailment. I mean only that a reasonable person who recognises the prudential value of autonomy will also recognize the respect that it is due. And the reasonableness of that transition is enough to deny a relativist foothold here.[158]

In stipulating the meaning of human rights, Griffin focuses first on the concept of personhood, suggesting that this can be broken down into a right to autonomy, minimum provision (including education, information, resources and capabilities) and liberty,[159] describing his model as a trinist account. And while he expresses concern about whether 'all human rights can be derived from such a relatively slender base',[160] the rights that flow from the trinist conception include the right to life, the security of the person, having a voice in politics, free expression and assembly, a free press, freedom from torture and freedom of religion.[161] It is a proposal that allows for local variation in terms of how rights are realised and protected,[162] through consideration of 'practicalities'.[163] Thus, Griffin's model allows for different 'levels' of rights, not in terms of a hierarchy but rather in terms of their level of abstraction. Thus, rights can be 'basic' or 'applied and derived'.[164] In this sense, Griffin's reasoning is similar to Talbott's; it is neither absolutist nor inflexible.

Not everything qualifies as a human right, however. Interests that may be candidates have first of all to 'be *important* or *major* or *urgent*'.[165] Further, as the core in Griffin's model is personhood, an interest starts looking like a good candidate for a human right when its denial stops an individual from exercising their personhood. This leads to a rather small set of rights, but Griffin considers this to be an advantage in so far as a limited list is more likely to result in wide agreement.[166] Moreover, the limiting of human rights is not any kind of absolute brake on what should be considered valuable. Griffin takes great care to point out

---

156 Griffin (n 5) 5.

157 Griffin (n 5) 33.

158 Griffin (n 5) 135.

159 Griffin (n 5) 33.

160 Griffin (n 5) 51.

161 Griffin (n 5) 33.

162 Griffin (n 5) 38.

163 'According to my account, there are two grounds for human rights: personhood and practicalities. Personhood initially generates the rights; practicalities give them, where needed, a sufficiently determinate shape'. Griffin (n 5) 192.

164 Griffin (n 5) 50.

165 Griffin (n 5) 54.

166 Griffin (n 5) 92.

that in his view, the substance of human rights should not be the end of our moral vocabulary; justice and the good are not exhausted by human rights.[167]

Attention to justice and the good outside human rights are both necessary, in part because Griffin's definition of personhood is both highly bounded and agentive. Indeed, some people simply don't qualify for rights because they lack capacity for such personhood.[168] This does not mean that duties are not owed or that care should not be given, it simply means that no 'human rights' can be exercised by these individuals. The definition of personhood is more or less in line with liberal constructions of the subject and with traditional models of the political community. But there are important differences in the rights that flow from Griffin's model. The requirement for minimum provision, that at least at low levels has distributive consequences,[169] and the more expansive view of agency that includes at least some 'realisation' of goals are significant.[170] Finally, given that Griffin has only sought to stipulate a meaning for human rights his model is not ultimately open to any kind of fatal attack, at least not in the absence of a competing model that is at least equally likely to secure agreement. Describing his project as one of 'stipulation' also appears to take this into account suggesting that human rights are agreed rather than imposed. Thus, Griffin has an eye on the political reality and practical constraints on the enforcement of human rights.

The models that Talbott and Griffin propose include important features. First, their attention to the physical requirements of people, including food, water and the like, is significant as this pays attention to the physical, rather than the political, nakedness of the individual. Second, their approaches to generating a set of rights are attractive. Given the lack of agreement around substantive human rights, a definition based on consideration of people, and which human rights make sense when humans are considered, provides a realistic, tangible and ultimately defensible ground for human rights.

The model of human rights developed in this book follows Talbott and Griffin in paying attention to the individual human. In the chapters that follow I want to consider this individual human in some detail as it seems to me that consideration of real people, in terms of their physical and non-physical existence, can serve as a foundation to reinvent not only 'human rights' but the concept of 'rights' itself. The question, then, is not so much 'what are human rights' but 'what is a human'?

---

167 Griffin (n 5) 95; on rights inflation, see Ignatieff (n 35) 90.

168 'My belief is that we have a better chance of improving the discourse of human rights if we stipulate that only normative agents bear human rights – no exceptions: not infants, not the seriously mentally disabled, not those in a permanent vegetative state, and so on' (92). Griffin (n 5) 92.

169 Griffin (n 5) 64.

170 Griffin (n 5) 47.

The Human

Douzinas argues that 'human' is a floating signifier.[171] Ignatieff's attention to pain, however, suggests that there is something that tethers the idea of 'human' to something more specific. As a starting point, as something that human rights could be invented to prevent, pain may be appropriate. Far from constructing people as rational, bloodless beings, attention to pain asks us to consider human suffering. When confronted with pain, with human suffering, a response is required. But what is the right response?

In his argument for silence as central to human rights, Perrin focuses on 'responding to another who is suffering or who is dying. In this situation, the other's singularity is "presented" at the very point of its irreducibility: in the impossibility of suffering in the other's place or of sharing in his or her death.'[172] He argues that 'as there can be no adequate response to the other's suffering one should not respond at all'.[173] There is nothing one can say in such a situation that would be adequate. Language, in the face of suffering, fails. However, even though a common foundation for human rights 'could only ever violate the other',[174] because of suffering we are compelled to say something even while knowing that language will be inadequate. 'In the impossibility of ever finding the right words to say, one speaks *because* words are inadequate.'[175] One speaks because of a responsibility to the other. Human rights come out of this responsibility for the other, the response that will always be inadequate; the responsibility 'derives from the fact that human rights are and have to be made (up) *because* they are not given'.[176] The 'foundation' of human rights in Perrin's account is silence; but it is the silence that precedes the necessary response (responsibility) to the suffering of another. It is a silence full of meaning that cannot be adequately articulated but nevertheless needs to find a form.

In 'The Tragic Foundations of Human Rights', Wolcher also pays attention to the responsibility we have for the Other.[177] Dwelling on ethical distress as the companion of responsibility, he argues that 'In the sphere of international human rights, the passage from ethical responsibility to justice must always occur by means of a kind of bad faith.'[178] This is because it involves 'a certain evasive

---

171 Costas Douzinas (2002), 'The End(s) of Human Rights' (2002) 26, *Melbourne University Law Review* 445.

172 Colin Perrin, 'Breath from Nowhere: The Silent "Foundation" of Human Rights' (2004) 13(1), *Social and Legal Studies* 133, 134.

173 Perrin (n 172) 134.

174 Perrin (n 172) 134.

175 Perrin (n 172) 142.

176 Perrin (n 172) 136.

177 Louis Wolcher, 'The Tragic Foundations of Human Rights' (2006) 24, *Wis. Int'l L. J.* 523.

178 Wolcher, 'The Tragic Foundations of Human Rights' (n 177) 552.

turning-away, not entirely innocent, from the phenomenon of *universal* human suffering to the phenomenon of this *particular* Other's *particular* eruption of suffering'.[179] The attention given to the particular sacrifices everything else. Further, once the particular individual comes to the attention of existing human rights regimes, she too is subjected to violence in that her suffering is constructed according to the already invented definitions of both 'human' and 'rights'.

> Given that respect for human rights characterizes a kind of actual comportment in a real world, to seek foundations for that comportment outside the ways human beings just do and can comport themselves is to chase a mirage. While reason chases this mirage, universal human suffering continues. A human rights practice that does not open its eyes to the ubiquity of concrete human suffering in the here and now is neither fully human nor fully right. A human rights practice that does not put compassion in place of justice as its highest value threatens to sink to the level of ideology and to become an apology for the vast realm of human suffering that it ignores, condones, or causes.[180]

It may be tempting to read Wolcher as claiming that individual suffering doesn't matter; it seems to me that this is not his point. His argument, rather, is that suffering is universal. We should not be concerned simply with a rational justice for single instances of suffering, but instead realise that suffering is part of the universal human condition. While it is clearly impossible to alter the human condition, it should at least underpin our invention and understanding of human rights.[181] In other words, if justice is only ever to come, it makes sense to focus instead of compassion. Indeed, Wolcher's language, in his references to mirages and eyes, suggests that human rights be considered visually. We need to look in new places. We need to look differently.

The need to look in new places, to look differently, becomes clear when one considers the way law sees people in relation to human rights. Douzinas argues that if we consider human rights in terms of identity, desire and recognition, we realise

---

179 Wolcher, 'The Tragic Foundations of Human Rights' (n 177) 552. See also Louis Wolcher, *Law's Task: The Tragic Circle of Law, Justice and Human Suffering* (Ashgate 2008).

180 Wolcher, 'The Tragic Foundations of Human Rights' (n 177) 554.

181 One of the consequences of noticing the universality of suffering must also be to recognise the systematic causes of rights violations (as defined under current understandings). Just as human suffering is universal, it is also systemic. As Marks points out, 'Those who (directly or indirectly) live off the practices and processes that victimise others' are often ignored (76). The systematic nature of violence and violation calls for radical action while the universality of human suffering asks us to consider the human condition. It calls for recognition. Brown writes: 'Societies in which human rights are respected are more civilised and secure than those in which they are not, but rights are a symptom of this civilisation and security, not a cause.' Brown (n 1) 58. Marks (n 126).

that the subject of rights will never be satisfied, will never be whole:[182] 'the subject of rights tries incessantly to find in the desire of the other – the missing object that will fill her lack and turn her into a whole being'.[183] The desire can never be sated because 'this object does not exist and cannot be possessed'.[184] Rather than desire ceasing, it increases. Rights proliferate as the desire to be recognised, to be loved, increases.[185] This encodes more and more rights in an authoritative form and gives and more and more power to the state. Although this suggests a frustrated future for human rights, and for the subject who would be recognised, the specific terms and orientation of Douzinas's argument suggest another possibility.

He writes: 'Rights-claims proliferate because *legalised* desire is insatiable.'[186] This is the necessary result of the 'archaic traditions' of the law. Individual subjects are identified, and constructed, in a particular way and all that is left is negotiation and calculation. Nevertheless, Douzinas' focus on recognition and the desire to be loved reminds us that humans are not completely bounded and separate; we need the other. We desire recognition of who we 'really' are. However, this is not something the law can provide. Moreover, as Wolcher argues, the law itself is violent.[187] Legal recognition leads, of itself, to human suffering. The question is, then, can we do without the dismembering legal recognition, is there another space for desire and recognition? In short, what does it mean to be recognised as 'human'?

As it stands, the law is asked to recognise the human rights claims of individuals; to recognise them as individuals. As Douzinas argues, this desire can never be satisfied. But what if human rights, or indeed the law, asked us to recognise each other? As I will argue more fully in later chapters, we are not alone. Our human state means that we rely on other people in both straightforward and complex ways. While law and human rights discourses generally treat us as autonomous individuals, with our own personhood and agency, people are neither completely isolated nor completely rational. If we invent human rights in such a way that it takes account of who we really are and our connectedness with each other, it might be possible for us to recognise each other. If there is a duty in human rights, and it seems to me that there is, it is one of mutual recognition. Indeed, this is implicit in any account of human rights that relies on the values of equality and the worth of human life as to value human life it first has to be recognised as human. Human rights are, at base, about recognising the fact of each other's – each and every other's – suffering.

182 Douzinas *The End of Human Rights* (n 4) 320.

183 Douzinas, 'The End(s) of Human Rights' (n 171) 460.

184 Douzinas, 'The End(s) of Human Rights' (n 171) 460.

185 Ignatieff cautions against 'rights inflation – the tendency to define anything desirable as a right'. Ignatieff (n 35) 90.

186 Douzinas *The End of Human Rights* (n 4) 321; my emphasis.

187 Wolcher, *Law's Task* (n 179).

Suffering provides a universal morally relevant fact.[188] 'Suffering demands that the situation in which it finds itself be changed radically.'[189] It is part of what it means to be human. This is not about describing human nature, rather, it is about acknowledging the human condition, the nature of being human. To invent a human rights that takes suffering and pain into account requires close attention to the human condition; it requires that attention be paid to what people share, to what humans have in common.[190] Pain is an inescapable part of the human condition. It is also, crucially, linked with our embodiment. Wolcher observes:

> What is needed for human rights thinkers to awaken to the real problem of human suffering is a quasi-religious attention to universal human suffering, and a radicalized compassion that manages to let go of obsessive attachment to textual foundations.[191]

Radicalised compassion entails a radical reimagining of human rights, one that makes human suffering the focal point. This is not to make an idol of pain but rather to consider it fully, to let go of the invented textual foundations of human rights, the history that has been created to add weight to the idea. The weight of human rights is not in the 'rights' but in the 'human'. It is the human body that suffers. It is the human body that matters. It is the human body that we need to start looking at.

Conclusion

Human rights are an invention. As they are associated with law, international politics, the nation state and particular conceptions of 'rights' they are far from straightforward. This chapter has discussed only some of the controversies in the

---

188 Schaefer makes a distinction between a transcultural moral fact and a morally relevant transcultural fact (39). For a foundation of rights, he argues we need the former; moreover, their justification should be non-empirical (41). The problem is that it is not clear what these facts would be. Why the foundation should need to be moral of itself is not made clear; though an appeal is made to natural law, the UDHR and work in moral objectivism (41). Schaefer (n 11).

189 Illan rua Wall, 'On Pain and the Sense of Human Rights' (2008) 29, *A Fem LJ* 53, 64.

190 Drawing on Arendt's account of the human condition, Serena Parekh suggests,

Human rights are the conditions of the possibility of human life, understood in both its biological and existential sense. They are grounded in the conditions of human existence (not in the human being) since they are the rights which make an individual life possible. We have these rights not by virtue of being a certain kind of creature or agent or having a certain moral status, but by virtue of sharing the human condition.

Serena Parekh (n 2) 775

191 Wolcher, 'The Tragic Foundations of Human Rights' (n 177) 554.

field of the human rights. They were chosen as they seem to be most relevant to the quest for human rights that are both universal and human. At the moment, human rights are connected to, if not founded upon, a particular political context. The central presence of the nation state, its inviolability, and its power are all potentially advantageous for the protection of real human people. But it is only a potential and one that may easily be thwarted when the interests of the state are in conflict with those of individuals. This state of affairs, this political order, is cultural. However widespread it is, and however strongly defended by nation states themselves, it is neither self-evident nor inevitable. It seems to me that it is also particularly troubling for any understanding of human rights that would prioritise people in their individual and collective suffering.

The work examined here does not always have the wide human audience these matters should enjoy. For this reason, in the next chapter I discuss the meanings of 'human rights' that may be more familiar to more people; media representations of human rights. This data exhibit a similar preoccupation with law, politics and the state. However, in the margins of these representations a human being can be found. It is not a person involved in contractual obligations or in conversation with the law, it is not a person seen through the prism of the nation state and international politics, it is a person in pain.

Chapter 2
The Blinded Body

In the last chapter, some of the difficulties around finding a foundation for human rights were explored. While the lack of a universal foundation is regarded by some as a problem, others argue that foundations are unnecessary. But even anti-foundationalist arguments rest on something and the values and constructs on which they rely are not universal. Even though the international political order and the entity of the nation state are routine parts of the human rights landscape, they are nevertheless ideological constructs with particular histories and specific consequences. Moreover, there is very little space for the individual in this system because the nation state is regarded as the dominant entity in human rights models. If human rights are about people – as their name suggests they are – this is not entirely satisfactory. While the previous chapter examined what human rights means to academics and those active in the international political context, in this chapter, attention will be paid to what 'human rights' means to people more generally.

There has been research on lay understandings of 'human rights'.[1] Stenner's research, for example, concludes that there is 'a finite diversity of distinct ways of understanding human rights'.[2] His own work identifies a number of interpretations of human rights, including seeing them as 'rights and responsibilities', 'radical activist politics', a 'socio-political construction' and 'grounded universals'.[3] In this chapter I also explore lay conceptions of human rights. Rather than asking people, however, I examine the use of the term 'human rights' in the press in the UK and the USA. Media representations are important in producing and reproducing discourses. This is true in any number of areas and it would seem to hold in relation to human rights too. Indeed, the data examined here contains evidence of many of the interpretations Stenner uncovered. There is an important addition, however, the most common presence, and one not explicitly present in Stenner's data; law.

The data examined here show that the most dominant presence in representations of human rights is law. While the force of law ultimately rests with the courts and

1 Sam McFarland and Melissa Matthews, 'Who Cares About Human Rights?' (2005) 26(3), *Political Psychology* 365; Dario Spini and Willem Doise, 'Organizing Principles of Involvement in Human Rights and their Social Anchoring in Value Priorities' (1998) 28, *European Journal of Social Psychology* 603.

2 Paul Stenner, 'Subjective Dimensions of Human Rights: What do Ordinary People Understand by "human right"?' (2011) 15(8), *Intl J Hum Rts* 1215, 1227.

3 Stenner (n 2) 1228.

other agents of law enforcement, given the nature of politics and legal decision making, public opinion about laws is significant[4] and may even influence decisions in law itself. However, it is important at the outset to note that there is a distinction between the way 'law' is used in these representations and what the law actually is in relation to human rights. It seems to be the case that what lawyers understand by 'human rights' is not the same as the connections lay people make between law and human rights.[5] Thus, the normal meaning for 'law' in this chapter does not relate to human rights law as such, but rather, to more a general imagining of law.

While law is a dominant presence, there are other discourses in this data. Indeed, examination of the data shows that 'human rights' is polysemous. I therefore make a distinction between 'legal human rights' (LHR) and 'bare human rights' (BHR).[6] As with 'law' more generally in this data, the former is not about the actual law of human rights, rather, it is intended to capture lay understandings of the connection between the idea of law and the idea of human rights. And while I will suggest a meaning for BHR, finding evidence of its existence is difficult. This is exactly because of the dominance of LHR. Nevertheless, looking at the margins of the data here allows us to see these BHR and the human who bears them.

The polysemy of human rights may well be connected to different views about who should have human rights. While in theory all humans have human rights, the data show that there is a perception that they belong only to the other and are, in that sense, foreign. It seems that human rights are uncanny. They are both terrifying and familiar.[7] 'Human rights' as a concept, as a phrase, is familiar; but there is material in the data that suggests they are not welcome. It may be that human rights are perfectly agreeable in theory, but when it comes to their application, when certain classes of people argue for their human rights, human rights become horrific. In any case, we are not yet at home with human rights. The concept of the uncanny captures this duality that is more than simply a distinction between abstract and applied rights, as horror at particular realisations of human

---

4 Jennifer K. Robbennolt and Christina A. Studebaker, 'News Media Reporting on Civil Litigation and Its Influence on Civil Justice Decision Making' (2003) 27(1), *Law & Hum. Behav.*, 5.

5 Anne Lise Kjær and Lene Palsbro, 'National Identity and Law in the Context of European Integration: The Case of Denmark' (2009) 19(5), *Discourse and Society* 599.

6 Something like this distinction has been made by those working in the field, though not always in exactly such terms. For example, see Bryan S. Turner, *Vulnerability and Human Rights* (Penn State University Press 2006) 2–3. 5; Serena Parekh, 'Resisting "Dull and Torpid" Assent: Returning to the Debate over the Foundations of Human Rights' (2007) 29, *Hum.,Rts.,Q.*,754, 767. This is not surprising, given the 'lack of agreement about on what human rights are' as discussed in the previous chapter. Marie-Bénédicte Dembour (2010), 'What are Human Rights? Four Schools of Thought' (2010) 32(1), *Hum.,Rts.,Q.* 1, 2.

7 Sigmund Freud, 'The Uncanny' in James Strachey (trans.), Albert Dickson (ed.), *Art and Literature, vol 14* (Penguin 1985) 335–76.

rights renders the whole idea of human rights unpalatable.[8] Moreover, this turn against human rights may well be connected to negative media representations of them and of the people who claim them. It hardly needs to be said that these representations are both selective and ideological. The result of this is that human rights, in the breaching, the honouring and the balancing, belong to the other. *Our* rights, on the other hand, are defined in explicit or implicit contrast to 'human rights'. Specifically, the data show that our rights are 'civil liberties'. Moreover, our rights are apparently being eroded by the rights of criminals, who are represented as being aided by the law. As mentioned, what law actually is and what it looks like to non-lawyers are two radically different things. For the general public, legal human rights are uncanny; they are the rights of the monster in our midst.

I begin by briefly explaining the data collection and analysis of media texts undertaken before describing the fields that emerged from the 'human rights' corpora. The content of the fields reveals an overwhelming presence of LHR. Consideration of the data also shows that 'human rights' belong to the other; our rights are encoded as 'civil liberties' and are subject to 'balancing'. Attention is then paid to the singular 'human right' corpora. Here we find BHR. Finally, I argue that while LHR is the dominant presence in this data, BHR should be recognised as the proper meaning of human rights. BHR also allow us to see the proper bearer of human rights: the embodied individual. The body is the human frame and it is the appropriate frame for thinking about human rights.

Bodies of Data

> The cushions we probed with the fine long needles you have seen me employ. From the tables we removed the tops.[9]

My aim in what follows is to build a 'discursive profile' of the term 'human rights'.[10] For comparative purposes, when collecting and analysing data, I also examined 'civil right(s)', 'civil liberties' and 'human right' each term generating two corpora, one for the UK and one for the USA.[11] In all, eight corpora of varying

---

8 In the Hoffman story, *The Sandman*, that Freud discusses, there is also a link between law and sight. The Sandman is both the optician and the lawyer. More generally, the tale deals with sight and blindness, reality and dissimulation and different legal orders.

9 Edgar Allan Poe 'The Purloined Letter' in Andrew Barger (ed.), *Edgar Allan Poe's Annotated Short Stories* (Bottletree Books LLC 2008) 465.

10 Gerlinde Mautner, 'Mining Large Corpora for Social Information: The Case of *elderly*' (2007) 36, *Language in Society* 51, 54.

11 Using Nexis UK, searches of news media were conducted for both the UK and the US. A year's worth of data was collected for 'human rights' (11 August 2008–11 August 2009). For all data, this was restricted to articles with 'three or more mentions'; for the US, news wires were excluded. The same parameters were used for 'civil rights', 'civil liberties' and 'human rights'. Data were analysed using AntConc 3.2.1w (Windows) for

sizes were built and analysed. I look specifically at 'semantic preference', that is, whether collocates of the keywords constitute 'a class of words which share some semantic feature'.[12] This approach considers 'macro-level phenomena, both social and discursive, and their micro-level linguistic manifestations' as well as taking advantage of methods from both critical discourse analysis and corpus linguistics.[13]

One might argue that analysis of newspaper coverage is rather analogue in a digital world.[14] However, given the wide range of political views apparent in such mass media, as well as the opportunity for lay contribution in the form of letters, short comments and discussion sections, newspapers include a wide variety of genres, views and topics. They also tend to reveal dominant discourses. Moreover, the decision to include marginal, which were usually negative, discourses was taken exactly to reflect the broad range of public views on human rights. Some of these are discussed below to make clear that while some people are enthusiastic about human rights, others do not see human rights as having any positive relevance whatsoever.

The Fields

Of the eight corpora built, the largest are the two 'human rights' corpora.[15] Most of the fields coded are common to both corpora, although there are two fields, disparaging and association with criminals, which did not emerge for the US data. These are dealt with last. First, the fields laws, legal processes/actors, institutions

---

collocations and frequency data (http://www.antlab.sci.waseda.ac.jp/antconc_index.html). Each corpus was ordered according to the search phrase and sorted first for right collocates and then left. Collocations were examined by eye and with AntConc before being manually coded into fields. The size of the 'human rights' corpora were such that not all data was coded; one-off collocations without an obvious theme were discarded. The coding was undertaken only by the researcher and as such is not as reliable as it would be had there been cross coding. Further, some significant collocations were included even if these were not numerically strong. The judgement about significance was influenced by familiarity with discourses around human rights, especially those with negative affect and judgement. For full details see Annabelle Mooney, 'Human Rights: Law, Language and the Bare Human Being' (2012) 32, *Language and Communication* 169.

12 Michael Stubbs, *Words and phrases: Corpus studies of Lexical Semantics* (Blackwell 2001) 88, cited in Mautner, 'Mining Large Corpora for Social Information' (n 10) 56.

13 Gerlinde Mautner, 'The Entrepreneurial University: A Discursive Profile of a Higher Education Buzzword' (2005) 2(2), *Critical Discourse Studies* 95, 99.

14 See Gerlinde Mautner, 'Time to get Wired: Using Web-based Corpora in Critical Discourse Analysis' (2005) 16, *Discourse and Society* 809.

15 In the UK 'human rights' corpus, there are 14,395 instances of the keyword 'human rights'. In the US 'human rights' corpus, we find 14,204 instances of the keyword.

and activists, activism and advocacy are discussed. Common to both corpora, these four fields can be grouped under a macro-category of LAW.

Law

Law is the most dominant presence in the human rights corpora. In this section, four fields that are understood as falling into the macro category of LAW are described. These four fields together constitute half of the coded data for the UK corpus (50.6 per cent; see Table 2.1). The first field, laws, captures those collocations concerning either particular laws (e.g. The Human Rights Act) or legal instruments, whether domestic or international (e.g. legislation, treaty). The recurring right collocate 'policy' was also included here as these are often connected with national governments and may well precursors to the hard law of legislation. The second field, legal processes/actors, contains left and right collocations related to litigation. Here we find 'courts', 'appeals', 'claims' and 'barristers'. The third field, institutions, relates to the first in that it contains the authors of laws, treaties and conventions. Thus, human rights bodies from domestic and international organisations are grouped here, for example, 'committee', 'council' and 'minister'.

Table 2.1 Fields in macro-category of LAW (UK)

Field	% of total corpus	Examples
Laws	14	Human Rights Act, Human Rights treaty, human rights and humanitarian law
Legal processes/actors	9.9	Appeal, claims, barrister, court
Institutions	10.8	European Human Rights Commission, United Nations Human Rights Committee, Quango, centre for human rights
Activists, activism and advocacy	15.9	Activist, body, advocacy, Human Rights Watch, campaign

The fourth field, activists and advocacy, also belongs in the macro category of LAW on the basis that activist work is generally connected with campaigning for legal change or legal recognition.[16] Thus, human rights bodies and campaigns are very often set up in response to a legislative proposal or policy lack. For example, Liberty, a British Human Rights organisation, 'campaigns to protect basic rights and freedoms through the courts, in Parliament and in the wider community'.[17] They work to 'protect civil liberties and promote human rights for everyone'. As they were established in 1934, before the European Court and Convention of Human Rights (1950/1953)[18] and before the recognition of human rights in domestic law (1998/2001), the inclusion of 'civil liberties' is historically explicable.

The incorporation of the European Convention into UK domestic law through the Human Rights Act (1998) does make campaigning on legal issues even more effective. Indeed, one need not even argue for legislative change through Parliament as the judiciary have an obligation to construe domestic legislation to be 'compatible with the Convention Rights', at least 'so far as it is possible to do so'.[19] Whether such arguments are effective depends on the 'plain meaning' of the legislative words used and how far the judiciary is willing to 'stretch' this meaning.

In the US 'human rights' corpus, of the 14,204 instances of the keyword 49.5 per cent relate to the same four law-related fields (see Table 2.2). The lexicalisation of laws as 'legislation', 'conventions' and 'treaties' is the same in the US as in the UK. Because of different nomenclature in the American legal system, however, the legal processes/actors contains 'attorney' in addition to 'lawyer' and 'court'. Likewise, the presence in the US corpus of 'committee' and 'office' in the field institutions is a consequence of institutional structures and naming practices.

Table 2.2 Fields in macro-category of LAW (USA)

Field	%	Examples
Laws	7	Convention, Human Rights Act, international law and human rights
Legal processes/actors	4	Attorney, lawyers, case, court
Institutions	11.4	Department of, commission, committee, office
Activists and advocacy	27	Campaign, agencies, bodies, groups, Human Rights Watch

16 Spini and Doise (n 1) 605.

17 Liberty, http://www.liberty-human-rights.org.uk/about/ last accessed 25 June 2013.

18 The first date indicates when the text was finalised; the second when the *convention/law* came into force.

19 Human Rights Act s. 3(1).

In both the UK and US corpora, the macro category of LAW accounts for about half of the data altogether. This shows the connection between 'human rights' and 'law'. Nevertheless, even this macro category of LAW does not exhaust all fields that are related to law.

Abstract Values

A category of abstract values was coded to capture the ideas and ideals associated with 'human rights' (see Tables 2.3 and 2.4).[20] Given that human rights is itself an abstract noun, other abstract nouns in close collocation were considered significant. While concepts like 'social justice', 'dignity' and 'peace' reflect concerns connected with human life and society generally, others are more politically inflected. 'Civil liberties' and 'civil rights' sit somewhere in the middle of this distinction, as they are connected to ideas about rights and citizenship and thus have some link with the concept of the nation state. Even so, 'civil liberties' is not a very common collocate of 'human rights'. Why this may be the case is discussed below. For the moment, it is worth noting that in the US corpus we find a higher incidence of 'civil rights' in close proximity to 'human rights'. Given American social and legal history, the linking of these two concepts is not unexpected.

Table 2.3 Examples of abstract values in 'human rights' corpus (UK)

Abstract Values	**N=329**
Civil liberties	7
Civil rights	2
Democracy	51
Dignity	3
Equality	216
Justice	16
Peace	7
Rule of Law	14
(Social Justice)	0

20 Where a term is common in one corpus, its incidence is also given for the other. Thus, 'civil rights' is enumerated for the UK corpus even though it only occurs twice, as it scores more highly in the US corpus.

Table 2.4 Examples of abstract values in 'human rights' corpus (USA)

Abstract Values	n=387
Civil liberties	23
Civil rights	84
Democracy	191
Equality ('Equality and human rights')	9 (7)
Justice	19
Liberty	3
Peace	6
Rule of Law	24
Social justice	5

Looking at the most common collocates in this field, for both corpora, suggests that that LHR has at least some purchase here. There are concepts in the abstract values field (such as 'peace' and 'social justice') that indicate the presence of something like BHR, but these are greatly outnumbered by those that are more politically, or indeed legally, inflected. While the most common collocate in the abstract values field for each corpus is different, they are both related to ideas about law. However, the most significant collocate in the field for the UK is 'equality' (Table 2.3). On the face of it, this is not a legal, or even political, term. However, on closer inspection, its presence can be understood as connected to LHR. The high level of occurrence in the UK data (216 times) contrasts with the US corpus, where it only occurs nine times with 'human rights'. This incongruence is resolved when one notes the 735 instances of 'Equality and Human Rights Commission' in the UK corpus. These were coded under institution, as it is a statutory body (established in 2006).[21] The existence of this body, and its presence in the corpus, together with the low levels of 'equality' in the US corpus, suggests that 'equality' as an abstract value may be connected to the Equality and Human Rights Commission. Indeed, seven of the nine US examples are references to the UK body. 'Equality' is a common collocate of 'human rights' because of this institutional presence.

21 The Equality and Human Rights Commission was established by statute in 2006, and came into existence in 2007. We see the same kind skewing of the data, and arguably a 'contamination' but in a less legalistic way, for the US data in relation to Civil Liberties, as the Civil Liberties Union accounts for 43.5 per cent of the data, making activists/groups the largest category at 60 per cent (n = 631).

The most significant presence in the US data is 'democracy' (Table 2.4). This may indicate a national preoccupation with the concept or perhaps be linked to US foreign policy discourses (e.g. 'humanitarian interventions' that, among other things, argue for the benefits of democracy). Certainly 'democracy' is about governance, but it is also an important American export. Democracy is associated with politics, but democracy is also associated with a political structure and system, rather than simply with partisan politics or policy. Indeed, when contrasted with some other forms of governance (e.g. monarchy, oligarchy) democracy is about equality in relation to government, rights and law.[22] The presence of 'democracy' may suggest a third sense of human rights, that is, political human rights, is warranted. In short, the precise relevance of 'democracy' here requires more in depth, qualitative investigation. It may also simply be about self-identification particularly in contrast with other forms of government, specifically communism; this emerges in the field as abuse in other countries and is discussed below.

In both corpora, the macro law category accounts for very nearly half the data. As a consequence, the idea that there could be something other than LHR becomes more difficult to grasp. The paradox, or rather the quandary, is that any discourse adopted in relation to human rights will inevitably become appropriated by the mechanisms, or the least the shadow, of law. I am not suggesting that law has no contribution to make to human rights. The specific point here is that it may be too much of a presence in popular representations of human rights. Nor is it my intention to make an argument about what or how the media should report on human rights.[23] Rather, the point is simply that the face of human rights that is presented in the mass media is a legal one. The problem, then, is not that 'the law' is a dominant presence; the issue is about what kind of presence it is. Given that some legal cases are apparently more newsworthy than others, the image of LHR in the media does not represent how lawyers and courts define human rights. The media are more likely to report on monsters receiving human rights than real people searching for justice. Certainly human rights violations are reported, but this is done in a particular way.

Breaching, Balancing and the Monster

The field of Breach/Violation includes collocates of 'human rights' such as 'breach', 'abuse' (both of these as noun and verb), 'violate', 'infringe', 'crime', 'atrocities' and 'ignored' (see Table 2.5). While these collocations denote negative

22 See OED 'In mod. use often more vaguely denoting a social state in which all have equal rights, without hereditary or arbitrary differences of rank or privilege' http://www.oed.com [accessed 1 July 2011].

23 Although, see Annabelle Mooney, 'Citizens, Immigrants, Anarchists and Other Animals', in Anne Wagner, Tracy Summerfield and Farid Samir Benavides Vanegas (eds), *Contemporary Issues in the Semiotics of Law* (Hart 2005). 35.

event and affect, they are also related to law and hence LHR. Naming an action as a 'breach' or 'violation' of human rights has legal significance, as it is only if such naming occurs in a sanctioned way that redress is possible. While this category constitutes only 2.8 per cent of the overall data for the UK,in the US corpus, this category amounts to 8.5 per cent of the data, with 'abuse', 'violation' and their related verbs a majority of this.

Table 2.5 Breach/violation in UK and US 'human rights' corpora

Country	Field	% of corpus	Examples
UK	Breach/violation	2.8%	Abuse, breach, violate, infringe, crime, atrocity
US	Breach/violation	8.5%	Abuse, violation, violate, victims, crime

Table 2.6 Abuse in other countries in UK and US 'human rights' corpora

Country	Field	n	% of corpus	Examples
UK	Abuse in Other Countries	74	0.53	Afghanistan, China, Russia, Palestine
USA	Abuse in Other Countries	472	3.3	China, Cuba, Iran, Russia, North Korea

Related to the field of breach/violation, though coded separately, is the field of abuse in other countries (Table 2.6). This emerged as a significant field for the US corpus, thus collocates of this kind were subsequently identified for the UK. For the UK, the countries in this field (n = 74) represent areas with significant conflicts either at the time of data collection or in the past few years, for example, Burma, Chechnya, China, Darfur, Kosovo, Sri Lanka, Saudi Arabia, Zimbabwe and so on. In the US corpus, the field abuse in other countries accounted for 3.3 per cent of the data (n = 472). In contrast to the UK, 44 per cent of this category concerned Communist regimes (China, North Korea and Cuba). This suggests a continuing preoccupation with communism and can be understood in relation to the high levels of 'democracy' in abstract values (discussed above). Indeed, it strengthens the argument for a further sense of human rights, political human rights.

Realising an action as a 'violation' or 'abuse' presupposes that there is an actor, as will be discussed below. But events and actions with human rights dimensions are not always lexicalised in this manner. This is seen in the field less than abuse (Table 2.7), which was coded separately from breach/violation but is obviously related to it. This field was used to code collocates that denote events that may be human rights violations, but cannot be lexicalised as violations because of a lack of severity or information. Thus the field includes terms such as 'problems', 'complaint', 'concerns', 'reports' and 'issues'. In the US data, this field constituted 6.4 per cent of the data (n = 916). In the UK data, the same category was smaller at only 3.5 per cent (n = 506). All items in this field are related on the basis of their negative prosody as well as connotations of an emerging or developing human rights situation. That is, 'concerns' are expressed and 'issues' noted when it is thought that abuse of violation of human rights is likely in the foreseeable future.

Table 2.7 Less than abuse in UK and US 'human rights' corpora

Country	Field	n	% of corpus	Examples
UK	Less than Abuse	506	3.5	Concerns, issues, record, situation, disregard, lack of, monitor
USA	Less than Abuse	916	6.4	Problem, complaint, concern, allegation, report, issue, monitoring, conditions

The distinction between breach/violation and less than abuse is significant in two ways. First, the terms in the breach/violation field have a legal flavour; that is, in the case of violations, a legal line (as well as a moral line) has been crossed. Second, it is not that the category (less than abuse) necessarily deals with less horrible events; the difference is rather the stripping out of agency. 'Violations' need a violator; 'crises', 'conditions' and 'reports' are less attached to individual actors. When an actor has been identified, action can be taken against them. When a violator has been identified, it may be possible to bring a legal case. Thus, without an agent the breach cannot be recognised as a 'breach'. There is another instance when breaching is not recognised as such. This occurs when a human right is sacrificed to more 'important' concerns. This kind of erosion of human rights is often framed as a 'balancing' of rights.

Balancing

In the United Kingdom in 1997, the then Labour government introduced a white paper called 'Rights Brought Home'. The concept of 'home' is thus potentially salient for UK discourses around human rights; but it is also problematic in that when our rights are under threat they are not lexicalised as 'human rights'.[24] In this

24 Given the current push for a British Bill of Rights, this discourse remains.

context, it is important to note that threats to rights take many forms. They may be breached and violated alternatively, 'problems' and 'concerns' may be identified. Another way rights are compromised is when they are in competition with something else. Commonly, this is phrased as 'balancing' a right with something else. It is in this balancing that we can discern an uncanny presence, as it seems the other has to be made undeserving of rights in order that we can retain ours. The threat to human rights here is a lexical one.

Discussion of balancing more often than not concerns specific rights, thus it did not emerge as a common collocate for the phrase 'human rights'. Nevertheless, the data suggest that 'balancing' is used as a euphemism for 'erosion' of human rights. When politicians talk about 'balancing' privacy with, for example, national security, the rights at issue are clearly not absolute. What is interesting is that when such 'balancing' occurs with human rights, they are lexically realised as 'civil liberties'. To show this, reference will be made to the 'civil liberties' corpora.

In the UK, the 'balance between' civil liberties and something else is 0.68 per cent, while the balance between human rights and something else is 0.05 per cent. In the US the situation is similar; balancing something with human rights occurs five times, 0.03 per cent. Balancing with civil liberties occurs ten times, but as civil liberties corpus is much smaller, the percentage is 0.93 per cent (see Table 2.8).

Table 2.8 Balancing: in UK and US 'civil liberties' and 'human rights' corpora

	UK	US
balance x and civil liberties	0.68%; n = 2	0.93%; n = 10
balance x and human rights	0.05%; n = 8	0.03%; n = 5

Instances of specific rights being balanced include the 'right to privacy', 'right to free speech' and even 'rights of the individual'. Clearly these are small sets; however they do suggest a fundamental difference in the way the terms are used, especially in relation to *our* rights. Close attention to the difference between how 'civil liberties' and 'human rights' are rhetorically deployed when an erosion of rights is at stake suggests a single influential variable. The data show that *our* rights are more often realised as 'civil liberties', while *others* rights are expressed as 'human rights'. When taken together with the balancing of rights, this also means that 'our' rights, civil liberties, are represented as being subject to erosion while 'their' rights, human rights, are not.

The use of 'civil liberties' for our human rights can be seen in a newspaper text that provides a summary of questions and issues around access to personal data and the right to privacy.[25] At issue is a European Court of Human Rights ruling about the way DNA information is held in the UK. Two individuals successfully appealed to the European Court of Human Rights arguing that their rights had been breached by the retention of their DNA and fingerprints on a police database, despite the fact they had never been found guilty of any crime. While the phrase 'human rights' occurred, it was only used in the name of the court and for institutional figures, such as 'the Council of Europe's Commissioner for Human Rights'. When the breached right itself was discussed, or indeed rights in general, this was realised as 'civil liberties'.

The results in Tables 2.9 and 2.10 provide further evidence that human rights tend to belong to 'them' and civil liberties to 'us'. This in line with Klug's observation that while we are hearing less and less about our human rights, we are hearing more about our civil liberties.[26] The preference for civil liberties in the UK is partly explicable in terms of historical circumstances. Traditionally, instead of having positive rights, citizens in the UK have had liberties, that is, actions unaffected by the law. Thus, instead of rights being protected by the state, citizens were free to do what the law did not prohibit.[27] This may go some way in explaining the figures, but as the same pattern is found in the US data it would seem that 'civil liberties' and 'civil liberty' are rather more comfortable and familiar than 'human rights'. It also suggests a turning away from 'human rights'. That is, it seems to be the case that human rights do not belong to us, but to the other.

Table 2.9 Collocations of possessive pronouns with civil liberties and human rights (UK)

Civil liberties, n = 293	Our civil liberties (5.4%; n = 16)	Their civil liberties (1.7%; n = 5)
Human rights, n = 14,395	Our human rights (0.3%; n = 41)	Their human rights (1.9%; n = 284)

25 Archie Bland, 'Should Government Be Allowed to hold So Much Data on its citizens: The Big question' (2008) 5th December *The Independent*, 46.

26 Francesca Klug, 'The Human Rights Act: Origins and Intentions' Tenth Anniversary of the Human Rights Act Symposium 24 September 2010, St John's College, Durham University.

27 Gary Slapper and David Kelly, *The English Legal System*, 7th ed. (Cavendish 2004) 23.

Table 2.10 Collocations of possessive pronouns with civil liberties and human rights (USA)

Civil liberties, n = 603	Our civil liberties (2.3%; n = 14)	Their civil liberties (0.66%; n = 4)
Human rights, n = 14,204	Our human rights (0.07%; n = 11)	Their human rights (0.28%; n = 40)

That human rights belong to the other may explain the uncanny nature of human rights. The other is to be feared. That which belongs to the other is also tainted. That we do not feel 'at home' with human rights is explicable in this way. How this estrangement has come about is clear when the association between criminals and human rights is mapped.

Criminals, Money and Monsters

There are some instances in the corpora of human rights belonging to 'us' in the sense that human rights are discussed in relation to individuals in the country. Looking at some of these cases demonstrates that 'human rights' are generally LHR and that they largely belong to the other. Two fields in the UK data capture this in particularly negative ways: association with criminals (n = 16) and disparaging (n = 50). The field association with criminals contains terms such as 'prisoner' (10), 'paedophile' (2) and 'charter for criminals' (4).

Paying close attention to the assumptions that inform the discourses here reveals a particular construction of human rights as transactional and only available to the worthy. That is, some individuals are said to be undeserving of human rights because they have broken the law in particularly egregious ways. The logic underlying this position is that human rights are 'earned' by good citizens and hence can be taken away from bad citizens. It hardly needs to be said that those not part of the national body, non-citizens, deserve few if any rights. [28] First and foremost, an individual must have been included in the national body as a citizen. The citizen will only be protected by rights if she has upheld her

28 This attitude is apparently common in the UK. A viewer survey on Sunday Morning Live (BBC) asked whether 'Immigrant criminals should have human rights?' Ninety two per cent of respondents thought they should not (broadcast 26 June 2011). The same kind of approach is seen in a proposal made by a member of a recent UK Commission. The Commission was asked to consider the possibility of a new UK Bill of Rights to replace the Human Rights Act, which incorporated the European Convention of Human Rights into domestic law. A draft Bill was proposed, written by one member of the Commission and included in the final report. Article 26 proposes that:

> '1. The rights and freedoms in this Bill of Rights shall be enjoyed by individuals who are citizens of the United Kingdom.

end of the bargain, by performing whatever duties are required. This transactional element is given further significance when money enters into the equation, as will be discussed presently. The view of human rights as conditional and transactional is also salient in discourses that associate human rights with criminals.

The connection between human rights and criminals is clearly made by one letter writer to *The Sun* (UK) who attests 'I DO feel that my right NOT to be blown up should count for far more than simply pandering to the crazy demands of all those wishy-washy human rights idiots out there.'[29] A similar kind of opposition is found in another letter, complaining that police violence against a 'thug' has been recognised as a breach of human rights.[30] 'The justice system protects and defends the criminal and we the law-abiding public, along with the police, just don't stand a chance.'[31] Aligning with the visible and forceful arm of the law makes sense; we only have rights in so far as they are effectively policed. What is significant here, in terms of the discussion above, is that 'the justice system', the abstract realisation of law, is understood as protecting the criminal other. Further, the 'thug' is essentially stripped of humanity and thus undeserving of human rights.

This argument is also taken up in an article from the UK corpus on the sixtieth anniversary of the Universal Declaration of Human Rights.[32] Here, the focus is on some recent 'tough' talking by then Home Secretary Jack Straw. Straw acknowledges the perception of the Human Rights Act as a 'villain's charter'. This is the theme taken up by the journalist, Owen Amos, who argues that 'We only see the Human Rights Act protect those who don't deserve it.' He laments that once the concept of 'human rights' 'stood for the power of law; now it stands for the power of the loophole'. Detailing the crimes and human rights claims of various 'scoundrels', he writes: 'They didn't respect others' rights – why should we respect theirs?' While acknowledging the inherent and unconditional nature of rights recited in the Declaration, Amos nevertheless argues that the original ratifiers 'couldn't possibly imagine the twisted minds that spawned' the scoundrels' cases.

In a sense, none of these laments are particularly interesting and are easily disposed of. But there are two arguments embedded here that are worth bringing to light. The first is the rights and responsibilities paradigm, which is simply a particular instantiation of the transactional/conditional model already mentioned.

> 2. Citizens of other Member States of the European Union shall be entitled to those rights to the extent provided for by or under the Treaty on European Union or the Treaty on the Functioning of the European Union.
>
> 3. Non-citizens shall be entitled to the rights and freedoms in the Bill of Rights save for those set out in Articles [....]; and nothing in this Bill of Rights shall prevent restrictions being placed on the political activities of non-citizens.'

Commission on a Bill of Rights (2012) http://www.justice.gov.uk/about/cbr vol 1: 214. Accessed 8 January 2013.

29 *The Sun*, Letters (2009), 15 April, 41.

30 *Evening Chronicle (Newcastle, UK)*, Letters to the Editor (2009), 12 June, 28 9.

31 Ibid.

32 Owen Amos, 'Rights and Wrongs' (2008), 10 December, *The Northern Echo*, 18.

While circling around the issue by paying lip service to the universality and inherent nature of rights, the desire that seems to be expressed is only to award rights to those who are deemed worthy.

> No one, of course, argues that right to a family, or right to a hearing within a reasonable time, are not human rights. Lose them, and we're sliding down a slippery slope to Zimbabwe, or – dare we say it – China. But why should Chindamo and Mellors, convicts in the middle of sentences, have such rights?[33]

Thus a distinction is made between who should have human rights and who should not. Implicit here, though not fully made, is a distinction between rights that are not absolute and those that should be. Without making such a distinction it is not clear how one avoids sliding down the 'slippery slope'. In short, arguments like this may be understood as suggesting that these criminals are in fact not human and therefore not deserving of even the most basic human rights. Such a separation of people into human/not human is often the first step in the most horrific abuses.

The second argument he makes relates to the meaning of 'human rights'. The argument is that these 'scoundrels'' cases, one by one, diminish the concept of 'human rights' itself. Thus, as well as rights being conditional and transactional, the very concept of 'human rights' is under threat.[34] It seems to me that there is another threat. The idea that human rights should only protect 'good' people presents a very real difficulty; it does violence not only to the idea of human rights but also to real human bodies. Moreover, continuing to focus only on human rights cases involving criminals presents a distorted view of the way human rights law actually operates. Given his lament that we 'only *see* the Human Rights Act protect those who don't deserve it' it may be that other cases should be brought into view.

The argument appears to be that if some people have their rights protected, we lose something as a consequence. This kind of reasoning is deployed in relation to criminals' rights in yet another way. Specifically, what is lost is quantified in monetary terms in order to make this loss seem tangible. The compensation of 'criminals' is a recurring topic in the association with criminals field. The damages awarded by the European Court of Human Rights are used as a quantifiable indication of how much citizens have been 'short changed'. This payment of money to criminals is said to be a 'humiliation' and a cause of 'shame'.[35] The Leader from the same day makes the same argument, stating that 'The losers, so often, are taxpayers.'[36] Again, one letter writer complains: 'No prisoner should

33 Ibid.

34 This can also be seen in the turning of arguments about the criminal's charter to a call to secede from the EU. See *Western Morning News* 'Abusing our right to our own legal system', *Western Morning News*, 9 April 2009, 10.

35 *The Sun*, 'Rights Wrong', Editorial (2009), 20 February, 8.

36 Ross Clark, 'So what about the human rights of the law-abiding?' Leader (2009) 20 February, *The Express*, 10. The Leader is the leading editorial.

be allowed to make money in this way' (i.e. through damages from the courts) especially when 'this obscene act', the legal trial, is funded by 'the taxpayer'.[37] The focus on money as legal damages is simply a particular instantiation of the more general argument that rights are conditional, that they are somehow scarce and must be hoarded. It results in some individuals being considered less than human so that their rights can be taken away. It is the individual person I now consider.

Particular Human Rights

The overwhelming presence of LHR in the material examined so far may well be due to the abstract nature of 'human rights' pluralised. I turn to close analysis of the two 'human right' corpora presently; first, I consider the particular human rights that emerge in the large corpora. In the UK 'human rights' corpus we do find evidence of specific rights (privacy, sanctity of life, environmental and ecological concerns) and rights bearers (women, soldiers, children, travellers, immigrants, workers and the disabled).[38] For the US, a similar list of rights bearers emerges: women, terrorists, war criminals, workers.[39] There is also mention of particular kinds of rights: environmental, free speech, religion, abortion, freedom of the press, freedom of expression, energy, torture, sexuality. The issues and groups here are not surprising. The former are largely consistent with the rights encoded in documents like the UDHR. Likewise, some of the groups of people mentioned are protected (in theory) by specific treaties or organisations.[40] Other groups identified are included because of their 'monstrous' status.

Distinguishing different rights-bearers does foreground concerns that may not have counted as rights before. In this sense, it is a positive thing to do. But there is also a risk in treating individuals as members of a group. That is, it is possible to read the mention of these rights-bearers as a way of limiting by particularising rather than as extending rights to the named people. I'm not suggesting that soldiers, older people, the disabled or any other group that may be mentioned don't have human rights; how they have these rights, that is, the (lexical) terms under which they have these rights is crucial. Specifically, to mark people as members of groups may suggest that their human rights are a gift rather than the entitlement of people who simply happen to be soldiers, older, disabled and so on. Feminist scholars have made the argument that identifying rights specific to women has distinct disadvantages.[41] Articulating a set of rights for women, as a marked case, may be a

37 *Daily Mail*, 'Human Rights Scandal', Letter (2008), 16 October, 72.

38 See Table 2.1.

39 See Table 2.2.

40 The Convention on the Elimination of All Forms of Discrimination Against Women (CEDAW) for women and the International Labour Organisation (ILO) for workers.

41 See Ursula A. O'Hare, 'Realizing Human Rights for Women' (1999) 21(2), *Hum. Rts. Q.* 364.

way of foregrounding concerns, but it may also be a way of indicating that women are not 'human'. It is important to be clear that women (or any other people) have human rights because they are human rather than for any other reason.[42] This does not rule out paying attention to structural and political inequalities; I do not want to suggest that these are insignificant. But if human rights attach to an individual (*qua* individual), there should be no need for any other marking to be done. I return to this issue in later chapters. For the moment, it is perhaps enough to say that all individuals, as particular people, have particular claims. That is, it is not possible to adequately address the human rights of individuals unless they are treated exactly as individuals rather than simply instances of a more generic kind of whatever kind. For this to work, however, existing definitions of human rights need to be revised. Such revision, the invention of human rights, needs a frame of reference. This frame can be found by looking in the margins of the singular human right.

The Singular Human Right

If human rights are to protect individuals, it makes sense to first look at single people and their singular rights. The singular 'human right' will clearly focus on particular issues, if only because of its non-plural form. But it also makes it possible to extend this singularity to 'human'. This singularity is itself marginal because the plural, 'human rights', is far more prevalent. The problem is that in the plural form of 'human rights', 'human' may also be pluralised, and understood as abstract, general and ultimately adjectival. In contrast, if one considers the singular 'human right', it may be easier to imagine that a specific person is involved as in the singular form, that is, it may be easier to parse 'human' as a noun rather than an adjective.[43]

Looking at marginal instances in marginal corpora does need some defence. Britain helps in this respect when he reminds us of the importance of the outlier, that which is found in the margins, in sociolinguistics.[44] His subject matter is rather different from the data considered here, but he argues that 'Analysis of outliers … has taught us considerably more than might ordinarily be warranted by this small number of reported instances.'[45] The same is true in the case of representations of human rights in the media.

42 Catherine A. MacKinnon, *Are Women Human? And Other International Dialogues* (The Belknap Press of Harvard University Press 2006).

43 See Jennifer Coates, 'Denominal Adjectives: A Study in Syntactic Relationships between Modifier and Head' (1971) 27. *Lingua* 160.

44 David Britain, 'Exploring the Importance of the Outlier in Sociolinguistic Dialectology' in David Britain and Jenny Cheshire (eds), *Social Dialectology: in honour of Peter Trudgill* (John Benjamins 2003) 191.

45 Britain (n 44) 191.

The two 'human right' corpora are small (n = 589 for the US and n = 142 for the UK) especially when compared to the 'human rights' corpora (n = 14,204 for the US; n = 14,395 for the UK) but they nevertheless provide useful insight into the kinds of particular rights that are considered important. In the UK human right corpus, the two largest fields are basic right and specific right. Forty one per cent of the coded data for the UK 'human right' corpus is captured by the field basic right (see Table 2.11). The distinction between what is basic and fundamental is not entirely clear. The incidence of 'basic human right' does exceed that of 'fundamental human right' in the UK corpus, but this is also the case in the UK 'human rights' corpus.[46] The difference between the two corpora is in the ratio of difference. In the UK 'human rights' corpus, 'basic human right' occurs exactly twice as much as 'fundamental human right'. In the UK 'human right' corpus, however, 'basic human right' outnumbers 'fundamental human right' by a factor of over 7.

Table 2.11 Dominant fields in the UK 'human right' corpus

Human right UK (142)	Number of instances	Examples
Basic right	41%; n = 59	Basic human right (51), fundamental human right (7); universal human right (1)
Specific right	43%; n = 61	Privacy (4), freedom of speech (3), sexuality (11)

The field specific right is somewhat easier to make sense of, as most relate to familiar rights including voting, education, freedom of speech, privacy, housing, religion, sexuality and abortion. These specific rights are often about autonomy of a particular kind, around start and end of life issues, but they are also connected to consumption and identity. They are rights normally attributed to the classical liberal subject[47] and as such suggest a particular ideological construction of the individual.[48]

46 Basic human right = 59; fundamental human right = 28.

47 Martha Albertson Fineman, 'The Vulnerable Subject: Anchoring Equality in the Human Condition' (2008) 20(1), *Yale Journal of Law and Feminism*, 1–23.

48 As seen in Chapter 1, it is exactly this kind of implicit ideological construction that has been noted in arguments about the inapplicability of Western models of human rights to other parts of the world. See Rosalyn Higgins, *Problems and Process: International Law and How We Use It* (Clarendon Press 1994) 96, Lord Hoffman, 'The Universality of Human Rights' (2009) Judicial Studies Board Annual Lecture, 19 March http://www.judiciary.gov.uk/training-support/judicial-college/Annual+Lectures (accessed 16 May 2011).

This subject appears to have become even more neo-liberal, being associated with explicitly capitalist activity. That is, the language of rights is being used to make arguments about individual autonomy and choice in the context of consumer behaviour. While there was only one mention specifically of the human right to buy something, among the rights in specific right we find one example of the 'right' to home ownership, two to access to credit and six for texting (though only to question their existence as 'human rights'). However, some other acts of consumption and capitalist behaviour were suggested to be human rights. For example, one letter writer claims that 'Tax avoidance is a human right',[49] co-opting the language of rights for an argument that is really about fine edges of legality and a particular view of the relationship between capitalist activity and the state. That is, 'human right' is here deployed simply to insist on a personal freedom that is technically allowed within the law.

In one sense the wider use of 'human rights' is positive in that it links the concept to freedoms generally. Moreover, some rights that at first seem to be diametrically opposed to any concept of BHR are, on closer consideration, connected to bare life. Access to credit, for example, is of great importance for anyone living in a modern economy as it allows a certain standard of living and indicates a level of social capital. Access to credit has very real consequences in terms of satisfying basic needs.

Table 2.12 Dominant fields in the US 'human right' corpus

Human right USA (589)		Examples
Basic right	36.7%; n = 216	Basic (143), fundamental (52); inalienable (3); inherent (4)
Specific rights	40%; n = 238	Right to marry (18); freedom of speech and expression (10); education (3); religion (2); health care/insurance (84; 14%); water (25); environment (11); abortion (8)

In the US data, a great number of the examples in specific right are familiar (see Table 2.12). These include the right to marry (18), freedom of speech and expression (10), education (3) and religion (2). There are two specific rights, however, that are not quite so familiar and that provide a way of thinking about what a bare human right is. They are the right to health care and the right to water. While a great number of the particular rights found in the US data are specific, already legally recognised rights such as the right to marry, freedom of speech and

49 *Sunday Times*, Message Board: 'Are Protestors right to target the band for channelling their funds through the Netherlands' (2009), 8 March, *Sunday Times*, 21.

expression, education and religion,[50] these two specific areas are worth attention. Both are closely connected to bare human life. I deal first with health care as a human right. This field includes 'health insurance' (which in the US is closely bound to health care) and accounts for over a tenth of the data.[51] If the data is searched for 'health care' such as to include instances that are not close collocates of 'human right', the figure increases by a factor of more than ten.[52] It should be noted that this data is from a period before President Obama's legislative proposals with respect to health insurance and thus are not a response to this campaign. The concern with health care and health insurance signals the importance of life certainly, but also of care for the body. This is also true in the case of water.

While there was not an overwhelming presence of water as a close collocate of 'human rights', it does appear to be significant in the corpus overall.[53] The presence of water is a surprising result in two ways. In many jurisdictions, water is not recognised as a human right. Second, one would think that in the United States water would not be scarce, not likely to be withheld from people and thus would be unlikely to be invoked in the context of human rights. Indeed, the other rights that occur in the 'particular rights' field in this data tend to be rights that are subject to fierce debate; such as abortion and the right to life (especially around end of life decisions). While water is marginal in terms of the data overall, it is fundamental. Without it, any 'right to life' is insensible. At the very least, the right to life presupposes access, if not a right, to water. Without water there is no life. Without a suitable environment, there is no life. If there is no water it simply makes no sense to talk of a right to life or even life itself. Water is a bare human right.

BHR, then, are those human rights that come into focus when we are confronted with a single, bare individual. They are the rights that any body has. It is also only possible to see them if we pay attention to the condition of the singular person. That is, these rights are found not by thinking about rights in the plural, but by thinking about a single person. However, to argue that the proper meaning of human rights is in fact 'bare human rights' is – at the very least – to argue for language change. I deal with this presently. In the chapters that follow I flesh out what bare human rights are by paying attention to the body and arguing for a particular way of looking at it. This shows that BHR include what is basic to the human: water, food, shelter and sleep. While these are bare rights, which attach to individual people, they nevertheless have to be looked at in a more global context. Just as the human body presupposes food and water, these goods presuppose a functioning environment. This means the most basic individual human rights need to be conceived of in a global sense. However, even in a global frame the focus remains on any and every individual human.

50 Right to marry, n = 18; freedom of speech/expression, n = 10; education, n = 3; religion, n = 2. See Table 2.14.

51 n = 84; 14%.

52 n = 1038.

53 n = 25 in the former; n = 466 for the latter.

Frames

The concept of the frame is crucial and will be explored here in two ways. I deal first with how frames help to argue that there is a proper meaning of human rights, bare human rights. Relying on the concept of bare human rights, I then turn to the question of how human rights should be framed more generally.

Understanding the meaning of a term is to understand how it is used. As use changes, so does meaning. The workings of power, however, should not be forgotten. Language does always change by itself; it also changes because of the actions of the powerful.[54] Remembering this not only permits language reclamation but also helps identify instances of when this may be necessary. Uncovering the effect of power on the meaning of a term or on a discourse can license language reform. Indeed, it is exactly the effects of power that preoccupy scholars working in areas like critical discourse analysis (CDA). They seek to identify power by analysing the linguistic contours and effects of the ideological position endorsed.[55] Looked at another way, the critique that CDA engages with can be used to argue for the 'proper' meaning of a term, a meaning freed from the influence of powerful ideological interests. It is precisely this kind of attention that allows, for example, feminist language reform without threatening the fundamental values of linguistics.[56] This leads to a more general conclusion. When power has been exercised in a discursive field in order to promote a particular ideology, it is permissible (indeed to it may be obligatory) to argue for reform.

The dominance of LHR in the data here suggests that language reclamation may be appropriate. Human rights have been placed in a frame that is not related to law as such; rather it is related to ideas about law. This kind of framing is often motivated by particular interests. Discourses, including the meaning of terms like 'human rights', are not neutral. Of course all language and all discourse are to some degree ideological and the power that motivates such language change may not be linked to any particular group or concern; it may well be a confluence of interests and accidents. That is, I am not claiming that the overwhelming presence of LHR in the media is itself the result of conscious planning. However, seeing only some human rights cases as newsworthy, labelling our rights as 'civil liberties' and only reporting on human rights violations in other places seems to be motivated by something. These choices appear to be underpinned by an understanding of human rights as foreign, 'legal' and completely unrelated to the concerns of 'normal people'. This is an ideology that is conducive neither to the needs of real people nor to any positive future for human rights.

54 Deborah Cameron, *Verbal Hygiene* (Routledge 1995).

55 Norman Fairclough, *New Labour New Language?* (Routledge 2000).

56 See Sara Mills, *Language and Sexism* (Cambridge University Press 2008); Anne Pauwels, 'Linguistic sexism and feminist linguistic activism', in Janet Holmes and Miriam Meyerhoff (eds.), *The Handbook of Language and Gender* (Blackwell 2003) 487.

Ochoa insists 'It is essential to retain a "plain language" with respect to human rights … The language of human rights, in order to be understood by those it aims to protect, must, above all, be intelligible and accessible.'[57] The marginal presence of BHR suggests that the current framing of human rights is not appropriate for individuals. The language and meaning of human rights need to be re-centred on the figure in the margin, the bare human. The bare human is the holder of bare human rights. The bare human, the naked person, needs water to survive. The bare human needs food to eat and air to breathe. The bare human is any person, each individual body. This bare form, this individual any and every person, is the figure on which we need to focus. It is the ultimate bearer of human rights.

This reframing, a refocusing, is required because at the moment, definitions of human rights are lacking something. What we are lacking can be found in the margin, in what the frame obscures. The frame, in discourse and in visual terms, delimits what is seen. While the frame shows us something, it also hides something. What is shown, what is foregrounded, depends on pushing something else to the margins. What is hidden in these media representations of human rights, what is pushed to the margins, is the singular human, the body that needs food and water, the person who lives and dies. In the data here, people are presented only in some forms. We are shown only criminals, monsters and the other. What we lack is an understanding of what we ultimately depend on. The borders, the margins, are both fundamental are hidden. But they are also close by. In the margins we find what we depend on, the bare human rights of the bare human being.

Paying attention to margins does question the value of talking about 'foundations' when it comes to human rights. Foundations are fundamental and hidden. And while I want to claim that the body is fundamental, both for humans and for human rights, it should not be hidden. To treat the body as foundation would be, in a sense, to bury it. It needs to be kept in sight if it is to provide a frame for human rights. The body of human rights is a living body rather than a corpse. To treat the body as foundation would be to seek to build something on top of it. But this will not allow us to understand what the human of human rights is. We first need to pay attention to what the body presupposes. To do this, we need to see it and understand what the body enables us to see.

The human frame is our shape, our body. Our body frames our experience of the world, as our lines of sight frame what we can see. The concept of a frame also suggests an incompleteness that while formed is nevertheless not determinate. While 'foundation' suggests solidity, a frame is more flexible while still providing shape. A frame can also be moved. Given that risks may be emergent,[58] and that new rights may need to be invented, it is well to have some room to move. This also makes clear that there is more than one way of seeing, that our vision will never be perfect, and that something is always hidden.

57 Christiana Ochoa, 'Advancing the Language of Human Rights in a Global Economic Order: An Analysis of a Discourse' (2003) 23(1), *B.C.Third World L.J.* 57, 114.

58 Charles R Beitz, *The Idea of Human Rights* (Oxford University Press 2009).

Chapter 4 sets out a way of reading the body. For the moment, it is well to remember that the body is also uncanny. As Nancy argues, 'Nothing's more proper, nothing's more foreign to our old world.'[59] We are of course familiar with bodies but these tend to be clothed, hidden in some way. The bare body, the naked body, is of a different order; it is found in art, sexual intimacy and in looking after those not able to clothe themselves. But we are all bare humans; we are all naked under our clothes. While it may not be possible to find a language to express the naked vulnerability that we all share, it may be possible to see it.

Conclusion

In the corpora examined in this chapter, the presence of LHR is overwhelming. Close attention, however, reveals the body in the margins. The body needs to be seen; it is the human frame and should not be buried. The body needs to be brought into the light, to be looked at, to be considered. Having met with darkness and monsters, a little light is perhaps needed.

The Australian poet Simon West has written two poems called 'The Dark'.[60] They are the mirror image of each other; the first a question, the second a response. The first asks 'Why does it grow, the dark?' while the second answers, 'That it grow, the dark .' The first poem asks:

> How from a lack can it bud
> and blossom, branching thicker until
>
> it menaces (the dark)
> and must be warded off (the dark)
> with words and lights
> and little voices saying I?

The second poem confirms this budding, blossoming and branching. This is how the dark emerges; this is how it grows. The dark is always there and must be 'warded off'. And with what? With light and words – little voices saying 'I'.

For human rights to make any sense, it is first of all the body that needs to be guarded. Moreover, the ability to say 'I' depends in complex ways on relationships with others. The saying of 'I' only makes sense if there is a 'you' to hear it; others need to be present for our voices to be heard. Words are required, but light is also needed to see. We need to see if we are to say.

---

59 Jean-Luc Nancy, *Corpus*, Richard A Rand (trans) (Fordham University Press 2008) 5.

60 Simon West, *First Names* (Puncher and Wattmann 2006) 47, 55.

Chapter 3
The Body

The body can serve as a universal frame for human rights; it just needs to be looked at in the right way. It is important, then, to consider work on the body in human rights, law and philosophy to understand how the body has been constructed with a view to finding a new way of doing so. Like the body in law more generally, the body of human rights is merely a 'pale outline of the "human"' lacking in 'flesh blood and sex'.[1] Examination of the body in law makes clear that the pale outline is male rather than female. This, of course, presents a challenge to feminist legal scholars and to feminism more generally as this male body is not only found in legal context; it is a broader cultural figure. What becomes clear is that the body in all these fields is a particular kind of construction. The specific features it is given and the fact that it is a construction are both problematic. However, attention to the details of this body, noticing what it lacks as well as what attributes it is given, suggests another way of seeing the body. I first examine the body in the context of human rights and law before turning to work from feminist philosophers.

Where is the body in rights? 'everywhere and nowhere'.[2]

Even though the law depends on the body, the body is not recognised by law; it is simply used, written on, dismembered. The body is an uncanny presence in law, a necessary haunting that can never be fully present. This is especially clear in the case of human rights. As the Law is 'first and foremost, a linguistic form', in the process of articulating and bestowing rights the Law writes 'the body through a language which is a *righting* of the body'.[3] This righting does not involve any kind of restoration of the body, rather, 'The utterance of the name, "rights", effects a cut which severs from the individual which it "hails" as a signifier, that individual's signified: specifically, his or her *body*.'[4] MacNeil argues that law cuts the body

1 'To defend human beings, we must attack humanism – a banal combination of classical and Christian metaphysics'. Costas Douzinas, 'The End(s) of Human Rights' (2002) 26, *MULR* 455, 447. See also Chris Brown, 'Universal Human Rights: A Critique' (1997) 1(2), *Intl J Hum Rts* 41, 43.

2 William MacNeil, 'Law's Corpus Delicti: The Fantasmic Body of Rights Discourse' (1998) 9(1), *Law & Crit.* 37.

3 MacNeil, 'Law's Corpus Delicti' (n 2) 40, 44.

4 MacNeil, 'Law's Corpus Delicti' (n 2) 52. Wall also uses the verb 'righting' in relation to human rights; although this is related to a verbing of the noun, linking it to Levinas's 'Saying' and Nancy's Sense. 'Right-ing would be a transformation of the sense of human rights from "having" to "being".' Illan rua Wall, 'On Pain and the Sense of Human Rights' (2008) 29, *A Fem LJ* 53, 75.

itself from rights,[5] leaving the language of rights to bring the body back in, not in a real way but only in a representational and ultimately metonymic sense.[6] In law, the body can never be '*the body itself*'.[7] While law depends on bodies, it does not (and cannot) recognise them as such.

Douzinas's psychoanalytic reading of human rights law confirms the dismemberment of the body.[8]

> Human rights societies by compartmentalising group characteristics, personal traits and individual entitlements split the imaginary wholeness of self and body. They recognise some aspects of self (formal equality and dignity), withhold recognition from others (the necessary material preconditions for the effective enjoyment of dignity), finally, devalue or dismiss still others (sexual orientation and identity is a prime example).[9]

This is a consequence of the subject coming into existence only through language or the symbolic realm.[10] The body is then castrated a second time when it moves into law.[11] The legal subject becomes a bundle of attributes; not actually a whole person.

> Rights by their nature cannot treat the whole person; this is the reason why no right to rights exists. Such a right would be the right of a person to be himself or herself, a unique human being in common with others, a right that would defeat the whole purpose of having rights.[12]

Human rights both dismember the body and provide for an imaginary wholeness. However, as MacNeil points out, it is only the male body that is righted. Further, it is only a particular kind of male body that survives in law, waiting for 'judicial and/or legislative reassembly'.[13] This is problematic for any kind of corporeal presence in law. Keeping this body would not only essentialise the male body but also preclude the feminine and other bodies.[14] Thus, MacNeil suggests a 'different conception of the body and its politics – one which neither "essentialises" the

---

5 William MacNeil, 'Taking Rights Symptomatically – Jouissance, Coupure, Objet Petit a' (1999) 8(1), *GLR* 134.

6 MacNeil, 'Law's Corpus Delicti' (n 2) 45.

7 MacNeil, 'Law's Corpus Delicti' (n 2) 50.

8 Costas Douzinas, 'Human Rights and Postmodern Utopia' (2000) 11, *Law & Crit.* 219, 231.

9 Douzinas, 'Human Rights and Postmodern Utopia' (n 8) 232.

10 Douzinas, 'Human Rights and Postmodern Utopia' (n 8) 227.

11 Douzinas, 'Human Rights and Postmodern Utopia' (n 8) 233.

12 Douzinas, 'Human Rights and Postmodern Utopia' (n 8) 233.

13 MacNeil, 'Law's Corpus Delicti' (n 2) 46.

14 MacNeil, 'Law's Corpus Delicti' (n 2) 46.

former nor "totalises" the latter'.[15] MacNeil ultimately suggests a postmodern theory of rights, one predicated on a 'fantasmatic body'.[16] But given that human rights is found before the law, it may be possible to see a body after all, even if it can't be immediately recognised as such by law; 'the fact that there is some*thing* of the body which is not discursive, which is not reducible to language, which words fail to *see*'.[17] As shown in the previous chapter, the body is only found in the margin. It cannot be fully signified. However, just because words fail to see the body this does not mean the body cannot be seen in other ways. While law rests on bodies, the body is outside law; while language depends on the body, the body is not reducible to language. Nevertheless, the reliance of language and law on bodies suggests that there is something there. The question is how this something can be seen.

Real Bodies

The reliance of both law and the concept of human rights on the body have been construed in other ways. A rather more tangible corporeal presence is found in the work of Turner and Grear who argue that the vulnerability and corporeality of humans is intimately connected to human rights. Sociologist Bryan Turner in *Vulnerability and Human Rights* starts from the perspective that 'vulnerability defines our humanity and is … the common basis of human rights'[18] while Anna Grear, in *Redirecting Human Rights,* argues that the legal subject of human rights needs to be understood as an embodied person. While this position is a direct challenge to the encroachment of other legal persons, like corporations,[19] into the area of human rights, Grear's argument also has significant consequences for issues like environmental protection. While their approaches are distinctive, coming as they do from different disciplinary backgrounds, they both arrive at similar conclusions in so far as they both accept significant parts of the existing human rights model, both in terms of content and in terms of institutional frameworks. Significantly, they both insist that the body be given proper attention.

Turner focuses on the vulnerability and precariousness not only of the human body but also of social institutions. He undertakes a 'a sociological study of rights as they are inscribed in national forms of citizenship and human rights as they are

---

15 MacNeil, 'Law's Corpus Delicti' (n 2) 47.

16 MacNeil, 'Law's Corpus Delicti' (n 2) 56.

17 MacNeil, 'Law's Corpus Delicti' (n 2) 46.

18 Bryan S. Turner, *Vulnerability and Human Rights* (Penn State University Press 2006) 1.

19 See also Grear on corporations and their non-equivalence with bodies. Anna Grear, 'Challenging Corporate "Humanity": Legal Disembodiment and Human Rights' (2007) 7, *H.R.L.Rev.* 511.

manifested globally in legal declarations, conventions and institutions'.[20] As such, his work takes the existing set of international human rights and seeks to justify them through a sociological consideration of rights and the body.

> This study of human rights places the human body at the center of social and political theory, and it employs the notion of embodiment as a foundation for defending universal human rights. My argument is based on four fundamental philosophical assumptions: the vulnerability of human beings as embodied agents, the dependency of humans (especially during their early childhood development), the general reciprocity or interconnectedness of social life, and finally, the precariousness of social institutions.[21]

In his wide-ranging work, Turner defends cultural rights as essential to modern human identity, argues for the importance of recognition of and engagement with the Other, insists on the importance of sexual and reproductive rights, discusses the welfare state and its connection to human rights and the body, considers the effects of advances in medical science on corporeal vulnerability, and examines both multiculturalism and xenophobia in modern life.

Turner argues that individuals have human rights simply by virtue of their 'shared vulnerability'.[22] 'Human rights can be defined as universal principles, because human beings share a common ontology that is grounded in a shared vulnerability.'[23] This universal condition allows for a claim to a universal set of human rights, and, as a consequence, is also a ground for intervention when human rights abuses take place.[24] As vulnerability is universally shared, it provides an excellent basis of human rights. Moreover, if the body is the basis of rights, some rights should be understood as more salient than others.[25] In line with this, Turner regards 'torture' as the most 'fundamental denial of human rights'.[26] The prominent position given to torture underlines Turner's concern with corporeality and pain. Clearly it also aligns with Ignatieff's argument about what humans share. Turner, however, grounds his argument in corporeality and thus is concerned not only with torture but with all aspects of embodied experience.

While the existing set of UDHR rights are considered, shown to be closely linked to vulnerability and generally endorsed, Turner does make a distinction between

20 Turner (n 18) 2.

21 Turner (n 18) 25.

22 Turner (n 18) 3.

23 Turner (n 18) 6.

24 Turner (n 18) 6.

25 These include both social and economic rights 'to reproduce, to family life, to health care, to a clean environment and protection from pollution, and to protection from medical and technological exploitation'. Turner (n 18) 9.

26 Turner (n 18) 9.

human rights and the 'social rights of citizens'.[27] Social rights, or contributory rights, are related to duties with 'effective claims ... associated with contributions that citizens have made to society through work, war (or a similar public duty), or parenting'.[28] It is not always clear which rights belong where.[29] This is not problematic, however, as Turner takes into account both the protection available to citizens and those areas in which protection is not yet adequate. In the case of the latter, human rights discourse (as it exists through treaties and conventions and the work of NGOs) can step into the breach. In the final analysis, it would seem that existing human rights and citizenship rights have at least the potential to protect our vulnerability, even though Turner makes clear that attention to other aspects of society may be necessary. This holistic approach, which could be read as a kind of 'mainstreaming' of human rights, is important. Turner points out that while law can provide 'a formal juridical safety net against abuses', he also argues that 'in order to flourish as ethical beings we need to cultivate and protect a set of virtues' as taking 'account of the psychological, sociological, and biological features of human beings' requires a virtue ethics approach.[30] This approach fits well with Turner's identification of institutional precariousness, that is, recognising that it is necessary to repair and redesign institutions, including human rights institutions because as human constructions they are ultimately fragile and contingent.[31] And while law may be a safety net, it is certainly not enough.

Turner's argument is important in that it pays attention to the body, our vulnerability and the fragility of our social institutions. However, even taking into account the distinction between human rights and social rights, and the recognition of the importance of economic rights, it seems to me that the argument does not go far enough. Wall provides an elegant and insightful critique of Turner's position, arguing that it is based on a Hobbesean model of human life. This means that pain is something we need to be protected from, that ultimately we need to be protected from others. As Wall puts it, Turner's position is that:

> we *must* be protected *from* the world; pain and suffering is something we can be protected from; pain is a problem which must be solved. Human rights, in this

27 Turner (n 18) 2.

28 Turner (n 18) 2–3.

29 For example, cultural rights are discussed in terms of human rights (67) but also in terms of 'cultural citizenship' (50) which suggests a more contributory facet. Likewise, the right to a 'safe environment, clean water, and an adequate food supply' are detailed under 'health citizenship' which suggests a contributory aspect (112). In relation to reproductive rights, Turner observes that they 'straddle the distinction between individual human rights and the rights of citizens' (70). Conversely, 'the language of human rights is ultimately the only plausible language for expressing the needs of people with impairment and disability ...' (90). Turner (n 18).

30 Turner (n 18) 23, 22.

31 Turner (n 18) 32.

> perspective, are *a manner of turning away from our vulnerability*, away from pain and suffering, so that we do not have to consider them.[32]

Wall insists that we must consider them. 'We are looking for nothing less than a politics which begins from our vulnerability but which refuses the conservative instinct to flee from it.'[33] We can't escape our vulnerability.

Taking existing human rights and related discourse and explaining how these are connected to embodied vulnerability is useful in finding an immediate space for the body, but if the body is the basis of human rights, human rights need to fully consider our corporeal vulnerability. If our embodied vulnerability is the basis of human rights, these rights need to be reinvented. Indeed, Turner's attention to institutional precariousness, which includes identification of emerging risks, as well as urging the constant review of human rights, suggests precisely the possibility of completely reinventing human rights. While he argues that 'vulnerability is a collective condition, which can only be addressed or moderated within a shared world',[34] as I have tried to show, the current human rights system depends on something which is not shared. It relies on cultural models which are far removed from the human condition.

Like Turner, Grear pays close attention to the embodiment of people not only in relation to law and human rights but also in a more wide-ranging manner. A central concern of her argument is that human rights need to be protected from colonisation by non-human legal entities like corporations. Human rights belong to humans and as corporations are not 'reducible, in any straightforward way, to the human sub-stratum beneath it' they should not be able to claim human rights.[35] To stop this incursion, Grear argues that the legal subject of human rights should be the embodied person. Grear first shows that the legal subject is not constructed with the human person in mind. This is done by tracing the history and the current conception of the legal subject showing it to be masculine, rational and disembodied.[36] It becomes clear that the legal subject 'has historically taken a reductive form: that of the quasi-disembodied, rational, acquisitive actor' and so matching 'to a high degree, the template of the corporate actor'.[37]

32 Wall (n 4) 66.

33 Wall (n 4) 67

34 Turner (n 18) 127.

35 Anna Grear, *Redirecting Human Rights: Facing the Challenge of Corporate Legal Humanity* (Palgrave 2010) 33.

36 Grear, *Redirecting Human Rights* (n 35) 41 ff. See also Costas Douzinas, *The End of Human Rights* (Hart 2000) 97 and MacNeil, 'Taking Rights Symptomatically' (n 5) 143.

37 This is hardly surprising given prevailing values and ideologies in the seventeenth and eighteenth centuries when individual rights of all kinds underwent a period of transformation. The market, property, rationality and individualism were key concerns at this juncture (81). Grear, *Redirecting Human Rights* (n 35) 48, 81. MacNeil writes: 'Finally, within the fantasy frame of bourgeois-liberalism, rights have become equated with, indeed identical to the fetish of property, reduced (*ad absurdam?*) to the rights of ownership and

> [I]t needs to be emphasised that the full significance of the fact of human material embodiment, on which law ultimately rests for its effect, has been systematically supressed in law and legal theory.[38]

Grear argues that the law presupposes the body and then erases it.[39] Indeed, once taken into the realm of law, human rights 'become subject to law's closures' to its writing/righting.[40]

> First, there is a closure invoked by the *abstraction* of the 'universal' possessor of right. Secondly, a related set of closures are invoked when human rights become positivised as law and the human being becomes the human *legal* subject.[41]

In contrast to this bloodless form, Grear argues that the UDHR was a response to the 'inescapable materiality of human existence'.[42] Human rights, she argues, need to be directed back to the body they started with. The redirection of human rights then 'will hinge on reconstituting the "universal" of human rights in terms that do full justice to the embodied complexity and vulnerability of human beings, and in a way that is capable of being genuinely inclusive'.[43] This is done by taking 'human embodied vulnerability as the basis of a legal theoretical approach to the reinvigoration of human rights as constructs uniquely concerned with the legal, quasi-legal and trans-legal protection of human beings'.[44] The legal subject here is a concrete universal, embodied vulnerability.[45] Grear argues that the body can and should be understood as the foundation of human rights we now have. In so far as the UDHR is predicated on consideration of embodiment, the existing UDHR rights can protect the body.[46] Rights to freedom of assembly, to life, freedom from

---

contract, thereby trivialising free speech, association and belief as marketplace functions.' MacNeil, 'Taking Rights Symptomatically' (n 5) 144. See Nedelsky for the history of property rights in the USA and the link of these to other 'basic human goods, in particular liberty and security'. Jennifer Nedelsky, 'Law, Boundaries, and the Bounded Self' (1990) 30 *Representations* 162, 165. See also Upendra Baxi, 'Voices of Suffering and the Future of Human Rights' (1998) 8 *Transnational Law & Contemporary Problems*125.

38 Grear, *Redirecting Human Rights* (n 35) 41.

39 Grear, *Redirecting Human Rights* (n 35) 123.

40 Grear, *Redirecting Human Rights* (n 35) 48.

41 Grear, *Redirecting Human Rights* (n 35) 96.

42 Grear, *Redirecting Human Rights* (n 35) 41.

43 Grear, *Redirecting Human Rights* (n 35) 113.

44 Grear, *Redirecting Human Rights* (n 35) 129.

45 Grear 'Challenging Corporate "Humanity"' (n 19) 540. This means that all humans must have protection, that none should simply be considered '"bare life", judged unworthy of protection, life or flourishing, regardless of citizenship status' (155). Grear, *Redirecting Human Rights* (n 35) 155.

46 Grear argues that Turner's model only makes an indirect connection between the body and human rights, while her link is direct.

torture and so on all 'presuppose both a physical body inhabiting geographical space – and vulnerability'.[47]

There are good reasons for trying to defend the human rights that are already recognised, especially where there is existing legal protection of rights. Finding a place for an embodied subject in legal regimes is also clearly desirable; it is also logical if the human rights we have were always concerned with embodiment. As Grear's argument suggests, a thoroughgoing critique of existing legal subjects may help to reconceive the legal subject in a more human and corporeal way. Once the legal subject is reconceptualised in the way Grear suggests, this entity can then be read back into the text.

The work of Turner and Grear allows an important shift in the understanding of human rights. The argument I make in this book can be read as an elaboration of the arguments they make. Indeed, both call precisely for more work on the connection between embodiment and human rights. Grear concludes her work with a call to consider 'our embodied particularity' and notes that the body 'awaits further and fuller theorisation' to realise the 'possibility of a truly universalist conception capable of embracing the *entire* "human family" at the heart of the inaugural text of international human rights law'.[48] Turner also argues that 'We need arguments that flesh out the commonalities of the human, especially social, experience.'[49] These are the calls I seek to answer here as it seems to me that at the heart of the problem is our understanding of the body. We need not only a theory of embodiment but a way of seeing this. If we manage to see that something of the body which escapes language, it may be possible to invent a *human* human rights.

The Absent Body

The body in law is a difficult presence, as law both depends on and erases the body. This legal body, so far as it is recognised, is male, rational and bounded. As such, it has received the attention of feminist legal scholars. The body outside law is no less constructed and has received attention from feminist philosophers. Here, I examine first feminist analysis of the body in law before turning to the approaches of feminist philosophers, though neither examination can be exhaustive or do justice to the range of work in this field.

The body for feminists, within law and outside it, is difficult as feminism wants to pay attention to the embodiment of women without essentialising. Moreover, while law constructs bodies as male, more generally in Western culture the body is associated with the feminine and in this connection, not usually understood as particularly positive or powerful. Further, examination of thinking about the body makes clear that more often than not, the body is understood as textual; it is either

47 Grear, 'Challenging Corporate "Humanity"' (n 19) 542.

48 Grear, *Redirecting Human Rights* (n 35) 206.

49 Turner (n 18) 63.

constructed by texts or it is written on. Nevertheless, this area of work sets out the challenges that need to be met as well as suggesting, in their calls for a new body, how it might be found and what it might look like.

It is well settled that the legal subject is constructed, at least in part, through a reliance on a mind/body split, with the former taking precedence over the latter such that that the body is at least repressed but more generally erased.[50] The human body of flesh and bone is not the body of law. As Grear puts it, law 'creates a gap between living persons and the legal subject, a gap which, in the case of the embodied human being, has ethical implications ...'.[51] In relation to rights in particular, legal subjects 'do not reflect our material selves but merely give the illusion of freedom'.[52] Subjects are attributed a degree of autonomy, freedom and agency, but these are nevertheless determined and defined in a way that does not take full account of a real person. For law, the body can never be '*the body itself*'.[53] That is not to say that there are no bodies in law, as a 'normal' body is constructed and recognised. Attention to these 'normal' bodies shows how many other, real, bodies are erased. As such, the 'normal' body may provide some clues about what the body itself may be.

The particular body constructed by law is the 'normal' body. Only a normal body can claim rights and the characteristics of this 'normal' construction determine which rights are available.[54] The normal body is not properly corporeal at all, being a rational, liberal, male subject it is rather less fleshy and certainly less female than one might like.[55] Experiences (and bodies) that can't be mapped onto this normal body are erased; only that which is containable within the normal body, a bordered space, is relevant. Moreover, as the concept of border suggests, the normal body is connected to ownership, control and autonomy.[56]

The boundedness of the legal subject has a variety of consequences. Nedelsky argues that constructed the body as boundary, or bounded, is both a source and result of power, exclusion, separation and rules.[57] For example, while the normal body is seen as bounded and hence inviolable, bodies that don't fit this form,

---

50 See Cheah Pheng and Elizabeth Grosz, 'The Body of the Law: Notes Towards a Theory of Corporeal Justice' in Cheah Pheng, David Fraser and Judith Grbich (eds), *Thinking Through the Body of the Law* (New York University Press 1996) 3–25; Grear, 'Challenging Corporate "Humanity"' (n 19); Ngaire Naffine, 'Who are Law's Persons – From Cheshire Cats to Responsible Subjects' (2003) 66, *MLR* 346.

51 Grear, 'Challenging Corporate "Humanity"' (n 19) 524.

52 Patrick Hanafin, 'Refusing Disembodiment: Abortion and the paradox of reproductive rights in contemporary Italy' (2009) 10(2), *Feminist Theory* 227, 238.

53 MacNeil, 'Law's Corpus Delicti' (n 2) 50.

54 Nicola Lacey, 'Unspeakable Subjects, Impossible Rights: Sexuality, Integrity and Criminal Law' in *Unspeakable Subjects: Feminist Essays in Legal and Social Theory* (Hart 1998) 98–124.

55 Lacey (n 54) 115–16.

56 Nedelsky, 'Law, Boundaries, and the Bounded Self' (n 37).

57 Nedelsky, 'Law, Boundaries, and the Bounded Self' (n 37) 175.

including women and children's bodies, are not. As well as being violable and tradable, the female body has long been constructed as inferior and irrational, that which the male, rational, mind must rule over. Before the female body can be incorporated into a legal order, these readings need to be revised so that a way of presenting a properly female body, including the injustices that women suffer because of their particular embodiment, can be found. But as Lacey explains, finding an appropriate female body is difficult: while feminism would want to reject the idea that women are *determined* by their bodies, because gender is written so indelibly on our bodies – as a result of cultural and legal norms – it seems that feminists can't do without the body.[58]

Exactly because of the erasure of women's bodies from law and from positions of power and autonomy more generally, Bottomley outlines ways that the body (TB), and women's bodies in particular, may be brought back into view in a way that is neither essentialist nor simply critical of existing constructions. Even though the death of the subject in postmodern theory may be thought to work against such a project, Bottomley argues that 'the reclaiming of TB in post-modernist thought presents a possibility for overcoming the binaries which reproduce sexual difference'.[59] That is, the death of the subject opens a space with the potential 'for conceiving new modes of thinking and representing "ourselves"'.[60] Lacey concurs, noting that as it is now possible to treat everything (even sex) as a social construct, there must be a way of recognising the materiality of bodies without essentialising, fixing or excluding. Nedelsky too calls for a 'rethinking of the role of the body with all its difference and particularity'.[61] As the body has been repressed in law, the argument is that paying attention to embodiment, recovering both vision and voice, may help to 'give body' to law.[62] While important, this is also risky, as the current normal body may simply be replaced with a new normal body that continues to exclude any other that does not fit its form. Thus, Nedelsky suggests that 'we need to find the modern equivalent of the soul',[63] a new mythology, 'a

58 Lacey (n 54).

59 Anne Bottomley, 'The Many Appearances of the Body in Feminist Scholarship', in Andrew Bainham, Shelley Day Sclater and Martin Richards (eds), *Body Lore and Laws* (Hart 2002) 135.

60 Bottomley (n 59) 136.

61 She argues this may be possible if we collapse the rational/irrational binary and acknowledge that emotion is always part of decision making; it is a call to acknowledge that judgements are always partly affective and that this needs to be properly accounted for in understanding (legal) decision making (see fact value distinction in chapter 4). She also points out that judgments, at least implicitly, point to a (judging) community (1997: 107). Jennifer Nedelsky, 'Embodied Diversity and the Challenges to Law' (1997) 42, *McGill L.J.* 91, 106, 107.

62 'By playing with vision/voice in academic law, we can begin to challenge our own discipline by understanding how our work has been predicated on the use of disembodied voices and a lack of vision.' Bottomley (n 59) 145.

63 Nedelsky, 'Embodied Diversity and the Challenges to Law' (n 61) 115.

new vocabulary, new metaphors to invoke if we are not to be sucked back into the forms we are resisting even as we argue against them'.[64] This will have to 'combine rather than mediate antinomies' and will allow us 'to find new ways of comprehending and responding to our responsibilities'.[65]

In order to find this equivalent of the soul, to find the new vocabulary for the unthought corporeality of the flesh, it is necessary to examine what has said about the body in other places as this may allow the emergence of a body outside of law. This is far from certain, however, as the bodies erased, repressed and oppressed by the normal legal body are strikingly similar to the bodies ignored outside law. As Cavarero notes, the body politic itself is 'modeled upon the natural body of an exemplary rational and political man'.[66] She argues that this is a consequence of the exchange that constitutes the state, the pact required to quell the violence produced by '[m]en's bodies, [which] left to the mechanical law of their actions, produce war and death'.[67] This exchange turns all bodies into one, constituting the state.[68] What is exchanged here is the body proper; individuals are left only with a mechanical body, the normal body that the state allows. Like the normal body of law, it proclaims itself sexless and banishes the female and the other from the polis. It is, however, crucial to remember that the male associated with the normal body is very narrowly drawn and thus only serves the interests of a small group.[69] This is not just about sex; it is about power.

The parallels between the formation of the legal subject and the construction of the body outside of law are not accidental. As both are closely connected to the conventional distinction between male and female (that is then mapped onto mind/body, rational/irrational and so on) it may be time that this particular binary was discarded. This cannot happen until the historical and cultural gendering of bodies has been appreciated, in order that similar injustices are avoided. In the following, I gather some strands of feminist thinking about the body in order to show that there may be a body that transcends these distinctions. Before the body can be given to law, or to rights, or even to ourselves, it has to be found.

---

64 Nedelsky, 'Law, Boundaries, and the Bounded Self' (n 37) 181.

65 Nedelsky, 'Law, Boundaries, and the Bounded Self' (n 37) 184.

66 Adriana Cavarero, *Stately Bodies: Literature, Philosophy and the Question of Gender*, Robert de Lucca and Deanna Shemek (trans) (University of Michigan Press 2002) 113.

67 Cavarero, *Stately Bodies* (n 66) 163.

68 This resonates with Agamben's discussion of the social contract. See chapter 4.

69 'I have been concerned with the ways in which a corporeal "universal" has in fact functioned as a veiled representation and projection of a masculine that takes itself as the unquestioned norm, the ideal representative without any idea of the violence that this representational positioning does to its others – women, the "disabled", cultural and racial minorities, different classes, homosexuals who are reduced to the role of modifications of the (implicitly white, male, youthful, heterosexual, middle-class) human body.' Elizabeth Grosz, *Volatile Bodies: Toward a Corporeal Feminism* (Indiana University Press 1994) 188.

Searching for the Soul of the Body

Given the diversity of women and their long history as the other, a theory of body suitable for feminism may also be fit for others excluded by the 'normal' body. In *Volatile Bodies*, Elizabeth Grosz searches for a theory of the body appropriate to the aims of feminism. Surveying various philosophical perspectives, Grosz uncovers the theories of the body in psychoanalysis, phenomenology, Nietzsche and neurophysiology. This produces a detailed picture of a feminine body that it is either erased or made subordinate and insignificant. Describing the body as 'site of contestation, in a series of economic, political, sexual, and intellectual struggles' she argues that it is at least possible to bring the body back into sight, if not to revive it completely.[70] Like the feminist legal scholars discussed above, she calls for 'understanding of *embodied subjectivity*, of *psychical corporeality*' that 'refuses reductionism, resists dualism, and remains suspicious of the holism and unity implied by monism ...'.[71]

It seems to me that this could be done by focusing on the materiality of the body and questioning how it is usually understood. While I want to insist on the importance of the physicality of the body, approaching this fleshiness has been made difficult because of the way the matter of body has been signified. It is precisely in the 'signification' that the central tension in conceptions of physical materiality can be found. For example, a recurring trope in Grosz's survey (exactly because it is a persistent idea in philosophical consideration of the body) is the body as written upon.[72] The discourses that operate here can be (and have been) critiqued. However, often the solution to this is to provide an alternative discourse, to re-write the body in another way. This is, of course, not only valuable but also liberating as it allows identities and subject positions that might otherwise be invisible to have a language. But even this re-writing relies on understanding the body as something that is writable. Grosz questions this in one way when she writes:

> I am suggesting that, in feminist terms at least, it is problematic to see the body as a blank, passive page, a neutral 'medium' or signifier for the inscription of a text. If the writing or inscription metaphor is to be of any use for feminism – and

70 Grosz (n 69) 19.

71 Grosz (n 69) 22.

72 Psychoanalysis sees the body as 'literally written on, inscribed, by desire and signification, at the anatomical, physiological, and neurological levels. The body is in no sense naturally or innately physical, sexual, or sexed. It is indeterminate and indeterminable outside its social constitution as a body of a particular type. This implies that the body which it presumes and helps to explain is an open-ended, pliable set of significations, capable of being rewritten, reconstituted, in quite other terms than those which mark it, [61] and consequently capable of reinscribing the forms of sexed identity and psychical subjectivity at work today'. Grosz (n 69) 60–61.

> I believe that it can be extremely useful – the specific modes of materiality of the 'page'/body must be taken into account: one and the same message, inscribed on a male or a female body, does not always or even usually mean the same thing or result in the same text.[73]

In these lines, Grosz foregrounds the way in which the body is commonly construed as a writing surface. And while important attention is paid to sex here, the body remains a surface, still to be inscribed even though it is always and already marked. This shows clearly how dominant the view of the body as surface is.

My point here is not to argue that 'readings' (or indeed 'writings') of the body are simplistic; quite the reverse.[74] The way the body is written should be described and critiqued but it seems to me that this does not allow us to think or see the body itself. I agree that the 'specific modes of materiality' matter. But bodies are more specific, more individual, in their materiality than the categories of sex allow for. Indeed, even anatomical sex is written onto the body. Culturally, this marking is somehow fundamental. But this need not be the case.

The contingency even of the originary marking of sex is made clear in Butler's *Bodies that Matter*, where she looks to cultural norms in order to understand how bodies come to have meaning. Butler shows that gender is produced corporeally and discursively and these cannot be separated. Moreover, neither appears to be primary, and not even anatomy is stable.[75]

> The anatomical is only 'given' through its signification, and yet it appears to exceed that signification, to provide the elusive referent in relation to which the variability of signification performs. Always already caught up in the signifying chain by which sexual difference is negotiated, the anatomical is never given outside its terms, and yet it is also that which exceeds and compels the signifying chain, that reiteration of difference, an insistent and inexhaustible demand.[76]

---

73 Grosz (n 69) 156.

74 For Grosz, the central concept is alterity. 'Bodies themselves, in their materialities, are never self-present, given things, immediate, certain self-evidences because embodiment, corporeality, insist on alterity, both that alterity they carry within themselves (the heart of the psyche lies in the body; the body's principles of functioning are psychological and cultural) and that alterity that gives them their own concreteness and specificity (the alterities constituting race, sex, sexualities, ethnic and cultural specificities). Alterity is the very possibility and process of embodiment: it conditions but is also a product of the pliability or plasticity of bodies which makes them other than themselves, other than their "nature" their functions and identities.'

Grosz (n 69) 209.

75 Judith Butler, *Bodies that Matter: On the Discursive Limits of 'Sex'* (Routledge 1993) 65.

76 Butler, *Bodies that Matter* (n 75) 90.

The body, then, is always and already constructed and it is always and already gendered.[77] The way the construction takes place explains why some bodies matter and some don't.[78] My concern, however, is that there seems to be no way out of the 'signifying chain' as 'there is no reference to a pure body which is not at the same time a further formation of that body'; even to refer to something is to constitute it.[79] The body, the materiality and sex of the body, is always constituted; the body cannot be present, cannot be referred to otherwise.[80] Whatever means are used to signify or constitute the body, whatever discourse is deployed, some bodies will be excluded. This seems to be unavoidable as Butler argues that for the body to appear at all, it has to be intelligible; this necessarily subjects the body to power. The matter of bodies can never be affirmed in a neutral way.[81]

If the body is understood as being constituted according to the logic of the signifier/signified relationship, it is necessarily caught up in chains of signification. The body as a surface is marked originally and subsequently with discourses that ultimately depend on arbitrary conventions. Once this model is invoked, once the body is understood as a writable surface, it is inevitable that chains of signification, the effects of discourse, become paramount. Clearly critique, deconstruction, reconstruction and refiguring are endlessly possible; but once the analytic choice of signification is made, there is no way back. To be sure, the idea of writing (on) the body is a powerful one and it certainly captures the social, cultural and discursive effects, identification and violence that bodies (and the subject) are subjected to. As Grosz and Butler make clear, focusing on signification does allow a critical foothold; and bodies that didn't figure before can be made to matter.

While I do not want to claim that the body is simple or singular, there are two fundamental points where the theory of the body I present here differs from Butler's. First, I seek to break the chains of signification she identifies not by critiquing or rewriting them, but by arguing that we need to *see* the body rather than to write on it. Second, it seems to me that in very significant ways, the body is not intelligible and should not be comprehended. I think Butler is correct in stating that once a body is intelligible it is subject to power. However, I think that the body can appear in a way that does not involve signification. This will result in the body not being intelligible, and thus not immediately subject to the power involved in

77 'Subjected to gender, but subjectivated by gender, the "I" neither precedes nor follows the process of this generating, but emerges only within and as the matrix of gender relations themselves.' Butler, *Bodies that Matter* (n 75) 7.

78 Butler, *Bodies that Matter* (n 75) 8.

79 Butler, *Bodies that Matter* (n 75) 10–11.

80 'The body posited as prior to the sign, is always *posited* or *signified as prior*. This signification produces as an *effect* of its own procedure the very body that it nevertheless and simultaneously claims to discover as that which precedes its own action.' Butler, *Bodies that Matter* (n 75) 30.

81 Butler, *Bodies that Matter* (n 75) 67.

signification, but the body will nevertheless be able to appear. Doing this requires that attention be given to the matter of bodies.

This is not straightforward. In Butler's account, materiality and language are closely linked. Language itself is a mode of materiality.[82]

> Language and materiality are fully embedded in each other, chiasmic in their interdependency, but never fully collapsed into one another, i.e. reduced to one another, and yet neither fully ever exceeds the other. Always already implicated in each other, always already exceeding one another, language and materiality are never fully identical nor fully different.[83]

Just as the body needs language, language requires the body.[84] The subject is constructed by discourse, always and already marked; discourse is necessary for the construction of the body and yet inadequate, it cannot access the real. It seems that all we can do is 'learn a double movement: to invoke the category and, hence, provisionally to institute an identity and at the same time to open the category as a site of permanent political contest'.[85] This double movement is clearly trying to perform acrobatics in Saussurean space. It is a strenuous activity and it is exactly the consciousness of the instability of identity and the danger of making this too stable that are important. As soon as stability is established, power emerges, some bodies matter and some cease to matter.

In her discussion of the chiasmic relationship between language and materiality, Butler does note that neither is reducible to the other. At some level there is what we might call an incommensurability (as this can neither be about reduction nor exceeding). In relation to the materiality of the body, this suggests that there is something more than language that is, of course, dangerous if not impossible to name. It may, however, be feasible to see it and think it without naming it. This is exactly what Merleau-Ponty's concept of the flesh suggests.

> … not the union or compound of two substances, but 'thinkable by itself', an elementary or foundational term, which 'has no name in any philosophy' (139, 147), an '*exemplar sensible*'. While it does not displace perception as

82 Butler, *Bodies that Matter* (n 75) 68. See also Judith Butler, 'How Can I Deny That These Hands and This Body Are Mine?' in: Tom Cohen, Barbara Cohen, J. Hillis Miller, Andrzej Warminski (eds), *Material Events: Paul de Man and the Afterlife of Theory* (University of Minnesota Press 2001).

83 Butler, *Bodies that Matter* (n 75) 69.

84 This includes writing; thus leading to Butler's reading of Descartes. As the meditations must take place through language the body is clearly present. 'When we consider Descartes's efforts to think the mind apart from the body, we see that he cannot help but use certain bodily figures in describing that mind' (266). Butler, 'How Can I Deny That These Hands and This Body Are Mine?' (n 82) 258, 266.

85 Butler, *Bodies that Matte*r (n 75) 222.

> the thematic object of investigation, it is a more elementary and prior term, the condition of both seeing and being seen, of touching and being touched, and of their intermingling and possible integration, a commonness in which both subject and object participate, a single 'thing' folded back on itself.[86]

As the flesh is an exemplar sensible it *presents* itself even though it is nameless. To acknowledge the flesh is to show that it is possible to think the matter of bodies without subjecting them to the potential violence of discourse. Precisely how this might be possible and what the consequences of it might be are taken up in the next chapter. For the moment, the singularity of the flesh needs to be noted; the flesh is not a way of thinking about bodies in general, rather it is way of encountering any body in particular. Merleau-Ponty's definition suggests that the flesh is *seen*, that this is a visual encounter. However, there are other ways to meet the Other.

Cavarero, for example, focuses on the voice as that which stands for the singularity of the Other. The connection she makes between the voice and the body here is compelling. The connection between the voice and the body is intimate:

> A voice means this: there is a living person, throat, chest, feelings, who sends into the air this voice, different from all other voices … A voice involves the throat, saliva.[87]

The voice is not a disembodied sound. The voice indexes the body and means more than simply what is said. Consideration of the voice in this way provides space for a human encounter. In *For More than One Voice* Cavarero looks for the voice that is before, outside of language; voice stripped of semantics.[88] This is a voice that communicates its presence, rather than any specific message. This is not simply about the connection between body and voice, Cavarero is concerned with how the Other is met. The hearer should be willing to hear the voice of the Other, even if it 'says' nothing. The relationality that Cavarero insists upon[89] is

86 Grosz (n 69) 95 citing Maurice Merleau-Ponty, *The Visible and the Invisible* (Northwestern University Press, 1968).

87 Cavarero, *For More Than One Voice Toward a Philosophy of Vocal Expression*, Paul A. Kottman (trans) (Stanford University Press 2005) 4, citing Italo Calvino, 'A King Listens' in *Jaguar Sun*, William Weaved (trans) (Harcourt Brace 1988) 33–64.

88 Cavarero, *For More Than One Voice* (n 87) 180.

89 This relationality can also be received through the sense of sight. While Cavarero treats sight and voice differently, Malabou writes that 'the eye is the eye of discourse itself, an optical arrangement that language brings up to its edge through its structure, so that talking gives birth to the visibility of its subject matter' (17). She thinks about it what it would be like to see a thought; it is the Levinasian face (24). Nevertheless, like Butler and Grosz, Malabou also identifies 'an originary violence at work in language, causing an irremissible schism between discourse and figure, sense and sensible, the idea and flesh' (18). Catherine Malabou, 'An Eye at the Edge of Discourse' (2007) 17, *Communication Theory* 16.

crucial. I want to suggest that this relationship, this encounter, can be described in terms of the phatic function of language. In this mode, what matters is not what is communicated (the semantic content) but the relationship brought about through the act of communication; it is not the said but the saying that matters. The phatic function of language is concerned with relationships, recognition and simply speaking with someone.[90] Such relationality, exemplified in the greeting, is local, particular and corporeal. It is an interaction based on something shared.

Conclusion

We all have bodies but we share more than this. As Butler argues in *Precarious Life*, we are bound to each other through our vulnerability but also through our very personal experiences of loss. Butler points to the inevitably common experience of loss in order to argue for a kind of universal 'we' (2006: 20). Our shared experience of loss, shared in so far as we have all lost something, can found a relationship with others. This relationality has a profound influence on identity and the self, showing that the 'I' is never separate:

> It is not as if an 'I' exists independently over here and then simply loses a 'you' over there, especially if the attachment to 'you' is part of what composes who 'I' am. If I lose you, under these conditions, then I not only mourn the loss, but I become inscrutable to myself. Who 'am' I without you? When we lose some of these ties by which we are constituted, we do not know who we are or what we do. On one level, I think I have lost 'you' only to discover that 'I' have gone missing as well. At another level, perhaps what I have lost 'in' you, that for which I have no ready vocabulary, is a relationality that is composed neither exclusively of myself nor you, but is to be conceived as *the tie* by which those terms are differentiated and related (2006: 22).

Seeing 'I' as implicated in the 'you' thoroughly undermines any conception of the subject as bounded or autonomous. The absolute reliance of the self on the other aligns with Butler's turn to Levinas; it is a turn to ethics, the face and responsibility for the Other. And while Butler opines that 'one would need to hear the face as it speaks in something other than language to know the precariousness of life that is at stake' what this would be cannot be articulated.[91] As mentioned above, it seems

90 Cavarero, *For More Than One Voice* (n 87) 169, 175, 195.

91 Judith Butler, *Giving an Account of Oneself* (Fordham University Press 2005) 151. At times, Butler seems to treat the Levinasian face as a 'real' face which subjects this figure to exactly the modes of signification which would totalise the other. 'If my face is readable at all, it becomes so only by entering into a visual frame that conditions its readability. If some can "read" me when others cannot, is it only because those who read me have internal talents that others lack? Or is it that a certain practice of reading becomes possible

to me that the central impasse, the line that cannot be crossed (but that Butler clearly wants to gesture beyond) is that drawn by signification. There does seem to be something outside this realm, but how it should be indicated is not clear. The prevalence of the arbitrary sign relationship, of the desire for a particular kind of meaning can be seen in discussion of the body and its relationship to language. But it is particularly visible in Butler's discussion of Cavarero's question 'Who are you?'. Butler writes that the question 'assumes that there is an other before us whom we do not know and cannot fully apprehend'.[92] The terms of apprehension are crucial; this question asks for a name; 'who?'.

I want to suggest that to ask 'who are you' is the wrong question as it asks the other to give up their singularity by responding with a name, an identity, a sign. It asks the other to commit a violent act and so is a violent question. Butler makes the point in *Frames of War* where we find a clear articulation of the difference between recognition and apprehension:

> precariousness itself cannot be properly *recognized*. It can be apprehended, taken in encountered, and it can be presupposed by certain norms of recognition just as it can be refused by such norms. Indeed, there ought to be recognition of precariousness as a shared condition of human life (indeed, as a condition that links human and non-human animals), but we ought not to think that the precariousness masters or captures or even fully cognizes what it recognizes.[93]

Rather, we need a frame; one that allows us to see others, one that makes their lives grievable. Butler calls for a framing that 'will bring the human into view in its frailty and precariousness, that will allow us to stand for the value and dignity of human life, to react with outrage when lives are degraded and eviscerated without regard for their value as lives'.[94] This is a framing that allows the apprehension of the other as a singular person. A question is needed that nevertheless allows the other to be ungraspable in her singularity. This is surely not 'who' are you, but 'How are you?'. [95] This is the phatic question, a question of an absolutely open hospitality. It is the greeting that does not seek to categorise the other but simply to meet them, to address them with language, to simply respond to their presence.

---

in relation to certain frames and images that over time produce what we call "capacity"? For instance, if one is to respond ethically to a human face, there must first be a frame for the human, one that can include any number of variations as ready instance. But given how contested the visual representation of the "human" is, it would appear that our capacity to respond to a face as a human face is conditioned and mediated by frames of reference that are variably humanizing and dehumanizing' (29).

92 Butler, *Giving an Account of Oneself* (n 91) 31.

93 Judith Butler, *Frames of War: When is Life Grievable* (Verso 2010) 13.

94 Butler, *Frames of War* (n 93) 77.

95 Justine Coupland, Nikolas Coupland and Jeffrey D. Robinson, (1992) '"How Are You?": Negotiating Phatic Communion' (1992) 21(2), *Language in Society* 207.

This has always been the challenge for human rights; responding to the other as a person, seeing all people as people. The tendency to write the body of the other (or indeed the self) in such a way that 'human' is erased is so prevalent as to be universal. The stranger is not met openly; the stranger is considered to be radically other.[96] The stranger is not met with open hospitality, but rather, she has been framed as a knowable other; knowable only in the threat she poses to us.[97]

The stranger is human and the human needs to be rethought.[98] To apprehend the human, because this is not a meaning that can be fully known or grasped, we need to allow ourselves to be exposed in new ways. We need to listen, to ask questions, to pay attention to the voice and the body, to every possible mode, to ask without any expectation of a response. We need to see the body in a new light; not just the idea of the body, but a body, any body, every specific body. This is the task to which I now turn.

---

96 Turner argues that the stranger is now both close and far away 'an anonymous and placeless person without citizenship or rights, a member of an underclass that is seen by the state to form a recruiting ground for criminals and terrorists'. Turner (n 18) 132.

97 'In Latin, the *hostis* is always bound by a set of exchanges, or gifts, that create mutual obligation through reciprocity, but the problem is that gifts can also be competitive and aggressive.' But this is already a particular kind of relationship; a gift economy which is contractual in essence. Turner (n 18) 129.

98 Judith Butler, *Precarious Life: The Powers of Mourning and Violence* (Verso 2006) 91.

Chapter 4
The Body, the Index and the Other

The body found in the margins of human rights discourses is any body. For human rights that will be good for people, the body needs to be a more explicit presence. As has been discussed, while human rights presuppose the body, the body is not found in human rights as they are currently constituted. However, given that embodiment is common to all people, and given that human rights should belong to all people, it makes sense for the body to have a central position in conceptions of human rights. A truly human conception of human rights is one that focuses on the body. But a human rights that begins with the body results in radical changes to what we understand by 'human rights'.

In this chapter, I continue to consider the body. While it is obvious that humans are embodied, as shown in Chapter 3, with important exceptions, this fact has been largely neglected in relation to human rights. Thus, it is worth considering what embodiment means and how the body itself can be more productively, and inclusively, seen. While the body has been endlessly written upon, freighted with all manner of meaning, these discourses do not come from the body; rather, they are imposed on it. Here, I consider the body itself. As embodiment makes perception, meaning and existence possible, I argue that the body is our zero institution. The zero institution is what makes meaning possible. Our corporeal state not only has consequences for being in the world, it is also how we come to be in the world. We are bound to the world, we experience the world, through our bodies. I do not mean to suggest that humans are only physical, in the sense of somehow being determined by our biology. I simply want to argue that embodiment is where we start.

Here, I draw on Nancy's conception of the body as corpus, as that which shows itself. While Nancy argues that we must not, we cannot, stop talking about the body, the body is found at the limits of writing. The body cannot be understood in terms of writing or signification. The body shows itself. The body is exposed. Because of this, it is appropriate to see the body as an index rather than as a sign. Such an approach to the body seeks to find what the body shows rather than to use the body as a surface upon which to write. Further, seeing the body as an index suggests an entirely different set of human rights than those we are used to. An argument needs to be made, however, for moving from an understanding of the body as index to a new conception of human rights. As this involves moving from an 'is' to an 'ought' I engage with Hume's prohibition.

The consequences of seeing the body as index are then considered in relation to the environment and to how bodies might exist together. These issues will be explored in more depth in later chapters. Here, I simply want to suggest that because the body relies on the natural world, and because human activity has had profound effects on the world, attention needs to be given to the environment. Indeed, given what the body needs to exist, and to continue to exist, environmental rights are human rights. It seems to me that the reason these have not been connected until relatively recently is due to two things. First, it is only in the last few decades that we have started to properly appreciate the impact that human activity has had on the world. As Dipesh Chakrabarty argues, humans now wield a geological force. Second, the social contract underpinning the nation state has distanced the citizen from the human. The founding of the state involves banishing the body and excluding bare life. The human rights we have are generally more concerned with protecting the political existence of the citizen rather than existence as such. In order to find an alternative to the social contract, however, consideration of how bodies might exist together needs to take place. For this to work, it is crucial to understand that we should not seek to understand the Other; this is not our task. Rather, we are required to be responsible for the Other, to respond to her. This is not a relationship of contractual equality, but one in which the self is already in debt to the Other.

The Body and the World

'The body is our general medium for having a world.'[1] The body is the frame through which and with which humans experience the world. The body touches itself and allows us to interact with the world we inhabit. It is self-reflexive in the sense that the body is experienced in terms of the body. Language already fails at this point as to talk of 'the body' and 'I' is to suggest a separation that does not in fact exist. It suggests that the body is a foreign body. Even calling the body a 'frame' may suggest that we are 'inside' the body. 'We' are not 'in' our bodies – this suggests a false separation – but neither are we equivalent with our bodies. The relationship between the 'self' and the 'body' – if these terms must be used at all – is one of interdependence; though even this suggests a division. This relationship is difficult to articulate. It may be easier to see.

In Chapter 2 I argued that it was appropriate to think of the body as a 'frame' in order to draw attention to the state of human existence and to the perspective embodiment brings. Our bodily existence frames our experience of the world. Human embodiment is simply a fact of physical existence, but it also has consequences for how we interact with others, how we engage with the world, how we come to know things. All knowledge 'is gained from my particular point

1 Maurice Merleau-Ponty, *Maurice Merleau-Ponty: Basic Writings*, Thomas Baldwin (ed.) (Routledge 2004), 123.

of view, from some experience of the world'.[2] Embodiment is not incidental to knowledge and perception, it is absolutely fundamental to it. Levinas writes:

> Meaning, as an illuminating totality necessary to perception itself, is a free and creative arrangement: the eye that sees is *essentially* in a body which is also hand and [80] phonetic organ, a creative activity in gestures and language. The 'position of the one that is looking' does not introduce a relativity into that allegedly absolute order of the totality that would be projected on an absolute retina. *Of itself* a look would be relative to a position. Sight would be *by essence* attached to a body, would belong to an eye. *By essence* and not only *in fact*. The eye would not be the more or less perfected instrument in which the ideal enterprise of vision, capturing, without shadows or deformations, the reflection of being would be realized empirically in the human species. Both the fact that the totality overflows the sensible given and the fact that vision is incarnated would belong to the essence of sight. Its original and ultimate function would not consist in reflecting being as in a mirror. The receptivity of vision should not be interpreted as an aptitude to receive impressions. A philosophy such as that of Merleau-Ponty, who guides the present analysis, was able to be astonished by the marvel of a sight essentially attached to an eye. In such a philosophy the body would be conceived as inseparable from the creative activity, and transcendence as inseparable from the corporeal movement.[3]

Sight and the body; the body and touch; being and knowing; they are reflexive relationships. They presuppose each other; they are exposed to each other. For us, neither can be primary. Flesh is 'the inauguration of the *where* and the *when*'.[4] The body is our base, the basis of being. This is not to say we are determined by the body, constructed only out of biological features, it is simply to observe that the body places us in the world. Even when we are not thinking, even when our eyes are closed, we are placed in our body. Even asleep the body is in a position.

2 Merleau-Ponty, *Basic Writings* (n 1) 65.

3 Levinas, Emmanuel, 'Meaning and Sense' in *Collected Philosophical Papers*, Alphonso Lingis (trans) (Duquesne University Press Pitts, 1998) 79–80. 'Once again, the flesh we are speaking of is not matter. It is the coiling over of the visible upon the seeing body, of the tangible upon the touching body, which is attested in particular when the body sees itself, touches itself seeing and touching the things, such that, simultaneously, as tangible it descends among them, as touching it dominates them all and draws this relationship and even this double relationship from itself, by dehiscence or fission of its own mass.' Merleau-Ponty, *Basic Writings* (n 1) 26.

4 Merleau-Ponty, *Basic Writings* (n 1) 256. 'For reality can only be given to us through the multiple moving and moved perception of embodied being and the potentiality of our being with others.' Helen A Fielding, 'Multiple Moving Perceptions of the Real: Arendt, Merleau-Ponty, and Truitt' (2011) 26(3), *Hypatia* 518, 532.

> What does sleeping consist in? To sleep is to suspend physical and psychic activity. But an abstract being, hovering in the air, lacks an essential condition for this suspending: a place. The summoning of sleep occurs in the act of lying down. To lie down is precisely to limit existence to a place, to position.
>
> A place is not an indifferent 'somewhere', but a base, a condition ... Sleep re-establishes a relationship [70] with a place qua base.[5]

Our base is that we are in a position; this is not something 'added to consciousness like an act that it decides on; it is out of position, out of an immobility, that consciousness comes to itself'.[6] The body 'is the very advent of consciousness ... It is not posited: it is a position.'[7]

Being means being in a position. Being means being (in) a body.

Our embodiment means that humans exist physically, in a physical world. Humans are not abstract beings, 'hovering in the air'. Nancy describes the world of bodies as 'a world where *bodies initially articulate space*. The world is spacing, a tension of place, where bodies are not in space but space in bodies.'[8] The connection between space and bodies, as Nancy's chiasmic construction suggests, is interdependent. Neither can be thought of as primary; they touch each other. 'We grasp external space through our bodily situation.'[9] According to Merleau-Ponty the body 'is not merely one expressive space among the rest ... It is the origin of the rest, expressive movement itself, that which causes them to begin to exist as things, under our hands and eyes.'[10] The body is our base, our mode of being in the world, it places us in space, it is the origin of meaning and experience. It is our zero institution.

Before the Zero Institution

Lévi Strauss coins the term 'zero values' that are then referred to as 'institutions'.

> These institutions have no intrinsic property other than that of establishing the necessary preconditions for the existence of the social system to which they

5 Emmanuel Levinas, *Existence and Existents*, A. Lingis (trans) (Matiinus Nijhoff 1978) 69–70.

6 Levinas, *Existence and Existents* (n 5) 70.

7 Levinas, *Existence and Existents* (n 5) 71.

8 Jean-Luc Nancy, *Corpus*, Richard A. Rand (trans) (Fordam University Press 2008) 27.

9 Maurice Merleau-Ponty, *The Primacy of Perception: And Other Essays on Phenomenological Psychology, the Philosophy of Art, History, and Politics (*Northwestern University Press, 1964) 5.

10 Merleau-Ponty, *Basic Writings* (n 1) (Routledge 2004), 123.

> belong; their presence – in itself devoid of significance – enables the social system to exist as a whole.[11]

The zero value is the base, the idea, that allows everything else to be meaningful. It can be understood as a kind of semiotic or cultural Archimedean point. As it allows the 'social system' to exist, it is a cultural construct. Lévi-Strauss introduces the figure of the zero institution in order to understand the structure of societies and the geographical layout of villages in particular. Zero values are a way of articulating a kind of deep structure, the concepts, lines or divisions around which a society constitutes itself. Žižek, following Lévi-Strauss, describes it as:

> a kind of institutional counterpart to the famous mana, the empty signifier with no determinate meaning, since it signifies only the presence of meaning as such in opposition to its absence: a specific institution that has no positive, determinate function. Its only function is the purely negative one of signalling the presence and actuality of social institution as such, in opposition to its absence, to presocial chaos. It is the reference to such a zero-institution that enables all members of the tribe to experience themselves as such, as members of the same tribe. Is, then, this zero institution not ideology at its purest, that is the direct embodiment of the ideological function of providing a neutral all-encompassing space in which social antagonism is obliterated, in which all members of society can recognize themselves? And is the struggle for hegemony not precisely the struggle for how will [sic] this zero-institution be overdetermined, colored by some particular signification?[12]

If the zero institution is that which allows individuals to see themselves as part of the 'same tribe', then it follows that it is in some sense a shared point of view. The use of 'tribe', however, and the link Žižek makes between the zero institution and hegemony points to the exclusionary function that the zero institution can have, or, more precisely, the exclusion that occurs as the consequence of the zero institutions that cultures choose. In Lévi-Strauss's account, and indeed in Žižek's, the zero institution is an arbitrary foundation. It is the point at which one stops, or starts, for no good reason except for the excellent reason that one needs such a point. In both accounts, the zero institution functions according to

11 Lévi-Strauss devotes only a short paragraph to the concept, though in a footnote he links it to his earlier definition of 'mana'. He does identify the zero institution as a problem, however, remarking that it is one anthropology shares with linguistics. 'This is the problem posed by the existence of institutions having no function other than that of giving meaning to the society in which they are found' (159). Claude Lévi-Strauss, 'Do Dual Organizations Exist?' in *Structural Anthropology*, Claire Jacobsen and Brooke Grundfest Schoepf (trans) (Basic Books 1963) 159.

12 Slavoj Žižek, *Enjoy your Symptom! Jacques Lacan in Hollywood and Out*, 2nd ed. (Routledge 2001) 222.

the logic of the sign, it is 'the empty signifier with no determinate meaning'.[13] It is a signifier.

The empty signifier is not left unspecified. Žižek makes clear that it is fully and extensively read. This is the hegemonic struggle. He names the nation as an example of 'zero institution'[14] and wonders whether 'sexual difference is ultimately a kind of zero-institution of the social split of humankind'.[15] The point here is that the zero institution, as signifier, is constructed.

The nation, sexual difference, a line in the sand; all may function as zero institutions. But the line can be drawn elsewhere. As the zero institution is an empty signifier, anything can be chosen. I want to argue that there is a better candidate than sex or the nation. As embodiment is what we all have in common, as corporeality is how we are in the world, it seems more reasonable for the body to be *recognised* as our zero institution, that which is linked to being itself. In a sense, the body is actually prior to the zero institution. It is what makes any zero institution possible. It is the absolute zero value. The body is that without which nothing else makes sense. The body is our zero institution, but it is not an empty signifier. The body is an index that shows us something. But before considering the body as index, I want to show how the body cannot be signified, how the body is sense itself. This is the reality that we have closed our eyes too perhaps because we did not know how to look.

This is My Body

My body is absolutely mine and absolutely strange. It can be touched, but it cannot be spoken.

> If *hoc est enim corpus meum* says anything, it's beyond speech. It isn't spoken, it's exscribed – with bodily abandon.[16]

---

13 Žižek, *Enjoy your Symptom!* (n 12) 222.

14 'To provide a concrete example: Is not the modern notion of nation such a zero-institution that emerged with the dissolution of social links grounded in direct family or traditional symbolic matrixes, that is, when, with the onslaught of modernization, social institutions were less and less grounded in naturalized tradition and more and more experienced as a matter of "contract"? Of special importance is here the fact that national identity is experienced as at least minimally "natural", as a belonging grounded in "blood and soil," and as such opposed to the "artificial" belonging to social institutions proper (state, profession etc.): pre-modern institutions functioned as "naturalized" symbolic entities (as institutions grounded in unquestionable traditions), and the moment institutions were conceived as social artifacts, the need arose for a "naturalized" zero-institution that would serve as their neutral common ground.' Žižek, *Enjoy your Symptom!* (n 12) 222.

15 Žižek, *Enjoy your Symptom!* (n 12) 222–3.

16 Nancy (n 8) 7.

In *Corpus*, Jean-Luc Nancy considers the body, bodies, what they are and what they mean. 'Body is certitude shattered and blown to bits. Nothing's more proper, nothing's more foreign to our old world.'[17] He argues that we invented the body, that is absolutely ours and absolutely strange. While the body can be touched, it cannot be understood simply by writing (on) it. This is because the connection between writing and the body occurs at 'the border, at the limit, the tip, the furthest edge of writing';[18] this limit is touch. This is not inscription. This is not the writing of signification.

> The body is neither a 'signifier' nor a 'signified'. It's exposing/exposed: *ausgedehnt*, an extension of the breakthrough that existence is. An extension of the *there*, the site of the breakthrough through which *it* can *come in from the world.* A mobile extension, spacings, geological and cosmological displacements, drifts, sutures and fractures in archi-continents of sense, in immemorial tectonic plates shifting under our feet, under our history. *The body is the architectonics of sense.*[19]

The body, then, cannot be accounted for with the singular logos. Instead, Nancy suggests that the body is a corpus.[20] The body is a collection of things, but a collection that cannot be ordered in any way. The single body is a corpus and there is a corpus of such bodies.

> There would have to be a *corpus* of such infinite simplicity: a drop-by-drop nomenclature of bodies, a list of their entries, a recitation itself enunciated out of nowhere, and not even enunciated, but announced, recorded, and repeated, as if I say: foot, belly, mouth, nail, wound, hitting, sperm, breast, tattoo, eating, nerve, touching, knee, fatigue …[21]

Such a corpus, without order, with an abundance of sense, cannot be catalogued. Sense cannot be made of this corpus; it cannot be signified. 'There's nothing here to discourse about or communicate *but bodies, bodies and bodies*. A community of bodies … .'[22] But because there is nothing 'more proper' or 'more foreign' to the world than bodies,[23] we are faced with 'a twofold failure … a failure to speak about the body, a failure to keep silent about it'.[24] We must, he insists, not stop talking about the body. The struggle between language and the body must continue

17 Nancy (n 8) 5.
18 Nancy (n 8) 11.
19 Nancy (n 8) 25.
20 Nancy (n 8) 53.
21 Nancy (n 8) 57.
22 Nancy (n 8) 57.
23 Nancy (n 8) 5.
24 Nancy (n 8) 57.

even if the body forms a 'black hole' as it 'retreats into its own depth – to the depth of Sense'.[25] There 'is nothing to decipher in a body – except for the fact that the body's cipher is the body itself, not ciphered, just extended'.[26] The body is Sense.

The body, 'declares outside-language' it declares itself.[27] Nancy's lists, his corpora of bodies, his accumulation of the details of physical existence, invoke a specifically corporeal world where we might try to see the body as though for the first time. The phrase with which he begins *hoc est enim corpus meum*, this is my body, is specific to a person and a place; the grammatical indices ('this', 'my') point us in this direction. Every body is unique but also 'substitutable for every other as *unsubstitutable*'.[28] All bodies are the same in their singularity. 'This is my body' invites the gaze, it centres (on) an image and the image shows 'each and every time again an "each one", is suffering'.[29]

Each one is suffering. Each and every body is suffering. This is the human condition, the condition of corporeality. This is the trauma, the antagonism, that cannot be captured by the signified. All ideology, all over-determination of the zero institution could be explained as a way of trying to make sense of this pain. The pain is the fault of the Other; the pain can be overcome if the Other can be vanquished. But this is delusion. We are in bodies and we feel pain. This is the condition of the body. And like the body, pain resists signification.

As the body is the base, we find our most basic relationship to it when the body itself is under stress.[30] In pain there is no signification. In extreme physical pain, language deserts us.

> Physical pain does not simply resist language but actively destroys it, bringing about an immediate reversion to a state anterior to language, to the sounds and cries a human being makes before language is learned.[31]

Anterior to language; before language. While the cries and sounds mean something they are not arbitrary signs. The cries of pain do not need to be translated; they do

25 Nancy (n 8) 75.

26 Nancy (n 8) 47.

27 Nancy (n 8) 115.

28 Nancy (n 8) 93.

29 Nancy (n 8) 101.

30 'Tell me your relation to pain, and I will tell you who you are.' Ernst Jünger, *On Pain*, David C. Durst (trans) (Telos Press 2008) 1. Wierzbicka writes: 'From a certain point of view, pain can be seen as a human universal: Presumably, all people sometimes and in some ways feel what speakers of English call "pain". Does this mean that in all cultures and societies people think and talk sometimes about pain? Here, the answer must be: no. Pain is not a universal [315] human concept and the English word *pain* does not translate very easily across all languages.' Anna Wierzbicka 'Is Pain a Human Universal?' (2012) 4(3), *Emotion Review* 4(3) 307, 314–15.

31 Elaine Scarry, *The Body in Pain: The Making and Unmaking of the World* (Oxford University Press 1985) 4.

not signify. These sounds resist transcription; they are pre-linguistic but they are not pre-social. While a cry of pain resists signification, cannot be fully captured in language, it nevertheless communicates something in so far as it shows something. Cries of pain point to a suffering body. Scarry writes:

> ... for physical pain – unlike any other state of consciousness – has no referential content. It is not *of* or *for* anything. It is precisely because it takes no object that it, more than any other phenomenon, resists objectification in language.[32]

The cries do not refer to an object, or even a meaning, but communicate (rather than refer to) an experience. To put it properly: cries of physical pain are an index of the experience of physical pain. We cannot know another's pain, and we cannot know what it is to experience someone else's embodiment. All we know is that we all have bodies even if we're not yet sure what this means. Our body is our base. The body is the zero institution. It cannot be read like a signifier or a text, but it can be looked at.

The Body as Index

As the base of existence, as the zero institution, the body shows itself, if only we would look. With the body, we are not dealing with inscription, but exscription. The body shows itself. The body is exposed. I propose that it is possible to see the body as an index.

Charles Saunders Peirce's division of signs into three kinds is well known. While the icon stands for an object because of a quality or because it bears a resemblance to its object, and the symbol is analogous to de Saussure's sign, the index is different. In contrast to the arbitrary relationship of the symbol, in the case of the index there is a motivated connection, a 'real reaction'. 'An index is a sign fit to be used as such because it is in real reaction with the object denoted.'[33] There is a necessary connection between the index and what it indexes. 'It is something which, without any rational necessitation, is forced by blind fact to correspond to its object.'[34] While this seems to be reasonably straightforward, the examples of an index given by Peirce are 'a mixed bag' and it is important to be clear about what kind of index the body is.[35] I deal first with pronouns, as these are often treated

---

32 Scarry (n 31) 5.

33 'New Elements', EP 2:307, 1904?. All Peirce's work taken from Charles Saunders Peirce (2003), *The Commens Dictionary of Peirce's Terms*, Mats Bergman and Sami Paavola (eds), http://www.helsinki.fi/science/commens/dictionary.html. Citations given in that source are included here.

34 'Telepathy', CP 7.628, 1903. *The Commens Dictionary* (n 33).

35 Thomas A Goudge, 'Peirce's Index' (1965) 1(2) *Transactions of the Charles S. Peirce Society* 52, 53.

as indexes when they are in fact symbols. The five features of an index that Atkin identifies will then be discussed. Finally, I argue the body is an authentic index; it shows us something.

Peirce describes the index as follows:

> This is a real thing or fact which is a sign by virtue of being connected with it as a matter of fact and by also forcibly intruding upon the mind, quite regardless of its being interpreted as a sign. It may simply serve to identify its object and assure us of its existence and presence. But very often the nature of the factual connexion of the index with its object is such as to excite in consciousness an image of some features of the object, and in that way affords evidence from which positive assurance as to truth of fact may be drawn.[36]

The definition begins by insisting on the real connection between the index and the object, 'quite regardless of its being interpreted as a sign'. This is the index proper. The real connection is fundamental and helps explain why pronouns are not actually indices.

Burks deals precisely with the question of pronouns and argues that a distinction needs to be made because of the different functions that pronouns have. He points out that while some pronouns refer directly to the objects they index (as when one says 'I' of oneself); others point back to a noun (as in, 'Peter came. He said he was coming'). The difference leads Burks to suggest a revision to the definition of index such that both kinds of pronouns are included:

> an index is a sign which signifies its object through an existential connection to this object or to a sign of this object.[37]

The first part of the definition is a precise account of the index, a sign that signifies through an existential connection. The second part, however, describes the symbol. If the index is an index because of a 'real reaction with the object denoted', 'something which, without any rational necessitation, is forced by blind fact to correspond to its object', there can be no intervening sign or sign system. Pronouns only mean because of their position in a linguistic system. Pronouns are not indices. Even the pronoun that points to a person (a speaker saying 'I' of herself, or 'you' to another) requires comprehension of the language in which it is spoken. Certainly it only requires a basic comprehension, and this may be conveyed through other signals (by pointing, for example). But the point remains.

---

36 'Logical Tracts, No. 2', CP 4.447, c. 190. *The Commens Dictionary* (n 33). Peirce then provides the example of a photograph as an index. But as Burks argues, a photograph does not have the necessary factual connection with its object that the index requires. Arthur W. Burks (1949), 'Icon, Index and Symbol' (1949) 9(4), *Philosophy and Phenomenological Research* 673.

37 Burks (n 36) 678.

The connection between 'I' and the speaker is not, strictly speaking, an existential one therefore, a pronoun is not an index. In short, if the existential connection is not maintained, the very distinction between index, icon and sign loses its explanatory force.[38]

The necessary, existential, connection between the index and its object is fundamental. This may not be enough, however, to understand how the body is an index. To try and be clear about what seeing the body as index means, I draw on the five features of an index identified by Atkin.

1. Indices use some physical contiguity with their object to direct attention to that object.
2. Indices have their characteristics independently of interpretation.
3. Indices refer to individuals.
4. Indices assert nothing.
5. Indices do not resemble, nor do they share any law-like relation with, their objects.[39]

The body is a clearly an index, as it displays all the features Atkin identifies. In relation to (1), the body, as an index of itself, is absolutely physically contiguous with its object. The exact contiguity may be why the body has not tended to be read as an index. Of course, attention has been drawn to the body; this is made clear by the various ways the body is read. The desire to want the body to mean may be exactly why it is not read as an index. We have been more willing to see the body in terms of, for example, sexual difference and nationality than we have to see the body as it is. Trying to understand the human condition in terms of these zero institutions, we have been blind to the characteristics that the body has independent of interpretation. Atkin calls this the 'independence feature' pointing out that the 'existence [of an index] is independent of our interpretative practices'.[40] Smoke indexes fire without interpretation being required (except in so far as interpretation is a necessary part of ordinary perception).[41] This is important in relation to the body. Seeing the body as index requires that all interpretative schemas, all other ideologies and zero institutions be put aside; it is a call to de-familiarise the body

38 Of course, it may be appropriate for the term 'index' to be used differently in other contexts. For example, Silverstein's work on the indexical order has been very important for recent work in sociolinguistics. Michael Silverstein, 'Shifters, linguistic categories, and cultural description' in K. Basso and H. Selby (eds), *Meaning in Anthropology* (Albuquerque University of New Mexico Press 1976) 11–55; Michael Silverstein, 'Indexical Order and the Dialectics of Sociolinguistic Life' (2003) 23, *Language and Communication* 193.

39 Albert Atkin, 'Peirce on the Index and Indexical Reference' (2005) 41(1), *Transactions of the Charles S. Peirce Society: A Quarterly Journal in American Philosophy* 161, 163–4. See also Goudge (n 35) 53–4.

40 Atkin (n 39) 165.

41 John Berger, *Ways of Seeing* (Penguin 2008); R.L. Gregory, *The Intelligent Eye* (Oxford University Press 1971).

and look at it afresh. We want the body to mean, but in wanting this the body has been overdetermined, written upon and inscribed in ways that distract us from what the body shows. Seeing what the body shows simply involves looking at it. I return to this below.

Atkin calls the third feature the 'singularity feature'; an index points to something particular. The body, each body, 'refers' to an individual in so far as each body is an index of itself. Thus, seeing the body as index is not about treating all bodies in the same way in all respects; rather, it is to realise that all bodies, all individuals, are the same *in their singularity*. The fourth feature, that indices assert nothing, appears at first to be a problem. If an index asserts nothing, how is it possible to 'read' the body as anything at all? Atkin calls it the 'indicatory feature' and offers a more positive framing, 'all indices show or indicate their objects rather than describe them'.[42] Indexes show their object. It is 'by definition an informational sign which enables the interpreter to identify what it represents'.[43] The body is thus an index that shows itself. It is exposed.

The final feature needs some clarification, as 'law-like' suggests exactly a necessary connection between index and object. However, as Atkin explains, 'law' here refers to convention; a symbolic relationship. Thus, this feature simply claims that the index is not like the icon (which resembles) or the symbol (which is related in a conventional – law like – way to its object). The index requires no conventions, no laws, for there to be meaning. The index shows itself, its singular self, independently of interpretation. Finally, the body is a genuine index as it 'not only indicates its object, but provides information about it too'.[44] The individual unique body indexes its own being, its own presence in the world. As it is present to its presence it is a self-reflexive index.[45]

The body is an index of itself.

The same reflexive relationship of the body is traced by Martin Kayman in his consideration of Bentham's 'auto-icon'. The terminology comes from Bentham, but the 'auto-icon' appears to be similar to the self-reflexive index. 'The Auto-Icon represents the real of the body in the most direct manner possible, by being constituted by it.'[46] The meaning of the auto-icon, or self-reflexive index, does not depend on cultural norms, rather the auto-icon 'abolishes writing by being

42 Atkin (n 39) 165.

43 Goudge (n 35) 54.

44 'A degenerate index, on the other hand, simply indicates without conveying extra information' Atkin (n 39) 181.

45 Merleau-Ponty writes 'The enigma is that my body both simultaneously sees and is seen. That which looks at all things can also look at itself and recognise, in what it sees, the "other side" of its power of looking. It sees itself seeing; it touches itself touching.' Merleau-Ponty (n 9) 162.

46 Martin A. Kayman, 'Bodies of Law and Sculptural Bodies: Writing, Art and the Real' (2010) 24(5), *Textual Practice* 791, 798.

transparent to what it represents'.[47] The living body is not so much a re-presentation as a presentation. Bentham's auto-icon is a posthumous monument, 'that which would contribute to the happiness of the living'.[48] It seems to me that the living, self-reflexive index may make an even better contribution.

What is this contribution? What does this body tell us? 'The very presence of this embodied truth denounces other discourses or images as fictions…'[49] The truth of the living body is that it can become an auto-icon in Bentham's sense; it will die. The living body shows, exposes, the conditions necessary for the living body. Tautologous as this is, it is nevertheless informative. No 'interpretation' is necessary to see that a body deprived of water dies; that a body that is not given sufficient food cannot live; that a body without air to breathe will expire; that a body not allowed to sleep will perish. If we defamiliarise the body, if we put aside our cultural modes of interpretation, and simply look at it; stare at it for weeks, stare at another for month, these commonalities become clear.[50] We need to look at the body, any body, every body, as though for the first time.

The frame for human rights is the human body. The body is our zero institution, that without which nothing has meaning. But far from being an empty signifier, the body shows us something. The body is an index, an index that can see itself, a self-reflexive index. Looking at the body, paying attention to what it shows, makes clear that people need food to eat, air to breathe, water to drink. The body, at rest, in a position, is asleep. The body also needs rest, it needs to sleep. This is what the body shows us.

There is more to say about the human frame of the body. Each body is singular, every body is unique, but all these bodies exist together in the world. To invent human rights with the frame of the body has consequences not only for what human rights we should have but also for how bodies should live together. I consider what this community of bodies might look like and how the relationship with the Other below. For the moment, I want to make clear the connection between the body as index and human rights. This shows that treating the body as index radically reconfigures what human rights should be.

Is and Ought

If we treat the body as index, with all that this entails, still another move is required to connect it to human rights. Specifically, the fact/value distinction needs to be confronted as I want to argue that seeing the body as index, as what it is, suggests

47 Kayman (n 46) 799.

48 Jeremy Bentham (nd), *Auto-Icon; or, Farther Uses of the Dead to the Living. A Fragment*. From the Mss. of Jeremy Bentham (not published), 1832 http://www.preservedproject.co.uk/jeremy-bentham-auto-icon/ [accessed 16 January 2013]

49 Kayman (n 46) 805.

50 One might think of this as a kind of 'existential ethnography'.

that human rights ought to be something other than what they currently are. I have already argued that it is permissible to invent a new meaning for human rights as they were always an invention. But this of itself does not answer Hume's prohibition on moving from an 'is' to an 'ought'.

There are at least two ways of dealing with the fact value distinction. The first involves arguing that the fact/value distinction is one without a difference. Drawing on the pragmatism of Dewey, Putnam makes the point. Putnam argues that values are inherent in the concept and constitution of 'fact'. What counts as a fact is determined by the particular values that one chooses to prioritise. He argues that a fact cannot exist without a value; to choose something as a fact is already to attribute value in some way. Putnam writes:

> In short (and here I find it convenient to use the term *valuings* as a general term for value judgments of every sort), my position isn't simply that 'valuings are not descriptions'; my position is that *some* valuings, in fact, some ethical valuings, *are* descriptions (though not of anything 'nonnatural'), and *some* valuings are not descriptions. Valuings do not contrast *simply* with descriptions; there is an overlap, in my view, between the class of descriptions and the class of valuings.[51]

Moreover, because of our embodied state, all facts are necessarily contextualised by our human frame.

The second way of overcoming the apparent prohibition on moving from an is to an ought is simply to show that there is no absolute prohibition. This requires looking closely at Hume's original formulation. When passing references are made to this argument, Hume is often read as arguing that one cannot move from an 'is' to an 'ought'.[52] However, in his *Treatise of Human Nature* Hume writes:

> In every system of morality, which I have hitherto met with, I have always remark'd, that the author proceeds for some time in the ordinary ways of reasoning, and establishes the being of a God, or makes observations concerning human affairs; when all of a sudden I am surpriz'd to find, that instead of the usual copulations of propositions, *is*, and *is not*, I meet with no proposition that is not connected with an *ought*, or an *ought not*. This change is imperceptible; but is however, of the last consequence. For as this *ought*, or *ought not*, expresses some new relation or affirmation, 'tis necessary that it shou'd be observ'd and explain'd; and at the same time that a reason should be given; for what seems

---

51 Hilary Putnam, *Ethics Without Ontology* (Harvard University Press 2004) 74.

52 I do not consider the vast philosophical consideration of this passage as it has generated a great deal of discussion. See, for example, Geoffrey Hunter, 'Hume on Is and Ought' (1962) 37(140), *Philosophy* 148–52 and A.C. MacIntyre, '"Is" and "Ought"' (1959) 68(4), *The Philosophical Review* 451.

> altogether inconceivable, how this new relation can be a deduction from others, which are entirely different from it.[53]

While his words are sometimes taken to mean that one can *never* move from an is to an ought, his point is rather different. Hume wonders 'how this new relation can be a *deduction* from others'. As with Hume's well known problem of induction, it seems to me that his target is the application of logic in a particular way; this is a specific, though of course, important argument. *Logically*, one cannot move from an is to an ought. Hume writes that the move from 'is' to 'ought' 'shou'd be observ'd and explain'd; and at the same time that a reason should be given'. While the rules of logic alone do not allow such a shift, if the shift is observed, explained, defended and argued for, if a reason is given, the fact/value distinction ceases to be problematic. Hume's prohibition is an analysis of the limits of logic. In this sense, Hume simply asks that the values and beliefs in moving from 'is' to 'ought' be made explicit.

Hume asks for a reason to be supplied when a move is made from an 'is' to an 'ought' and it is reasonable to supply one. The 'is' from which I begin is the embodied state of people. The body is the human frame, it is our means of existence, our base in the world. Seeing the body as index, looking at what the body is, shows us that bodies need food, water, air and sleep. I therefore want to suggest that human rights should be invented in such a way that these needs are acknowledged. The argument for this move is as follows: If there is no 'ought' if there are no human rights of the kind suggested here, there will be no 'is', that is, there will be no humans. The 'human rights' we ought to have are not the same as the human rights we have at the moment. The human rights we need are those that attend to the body, each body, all bodies.

Taking the body as a universal frame for human rights means that 'human rights' itself is radically reconfigured. As already touched upon, real human rights, 'bare' human rights, are directed towards the survival of the human. Thus, there are two moves that are made here. The first is simply to point out what the body as index directs our attention to; bodies need certain substances to survive. The second move is to stipulate these substances as human rights. This is an invention, or rather a re-invention, but it is necessary. This is not about tussling over the signified, it is about the referent. Without acknowledging basic human needs, 'human' may well become akin to the signifier 'unicorn', that is, a sign without a referent. Indeed, it would be even less than this, as there would be nothing to think or even say 'human'. In short, the argument for moving from the 'is' of the body to an 'ought' of human rights is the continued existence of people.

Putting the corporeality of humans at the heart of human rights takes human embodiment seriously. My argument is that the universal ground for human rights is the human body, that all bodies need food, air, water and sleep to survive. Without these things, there can be no such thing as 'human', individually or

53 David Hume, *A Treatise of Human Nature* (John Noon 1739) 469.

collectively. This is clear at an individual level, especially if the body is treated as an index. But the body has a context, an environment. Before a body can be fed, before water can be drunk, these things need to be available. Understanding human reliance on the environment is fundamental. It makes clear that to fully understand the individual body the environment needs to be considered. Human rights are environmental rights.

Bodies in the World: Climate Theory

It is obvious that bodies need food and water. However, this simple observation has consequences. The need for food and water means that their production and distribution need to be considered. Even before this, however, the possibility of production needs be ensured. Bodies may die because of operation of global food markets but people might also cease to exist if the planet is not capable of sustaining life. While systems that allow suffering need to be addressed, at the most fundamental level environmental rights are human rights. I will discuss natural resources and other issues related to environmental rights in the next chapter. For now, I simply want to make clear that the 'natural' world is not as natural as one might like to think. The distinction between 'human' and 'natural' is a difficult one to maintain.

In 'The Climate of History', the historian Dipesh Chakrabarty argues that we have entered a new historical phase, one in which human action must be understood as having an effect on the planet. Human history and natural history can no longer be considered separately.[54] Chakrabarty documents two important shifts. First, human action has been of such intensity, kind and magnitude to outrun the ability of the environment to renew itself. Natural time frames and human time frames have come to be out of step, with the natural environment not able to keep up with the effects of human activity. 'Humans now wield a geological force.'[55] Fortunately, second, human action in the field of scientific research has brought this to human attention. We now know that human action is not simply marking, bending or scarring the earth; it is changing its behaviour in fundamental and unpredictable ways.[56]

---

54 Dipesh Chakrabarty, 'The Climate of History: Four Theses' (2009) 35(2), *Critical Enquiry* 197, 201.

55 Chakrabarty (n 54) 206.

56 While we think that this knowledge is recent, this is not entirely the case. McIntosh notes:

The idea that the Earth is kept warm by a 'greenhouse' effect is nothing new. It was first put forward in 1824 by the French physicist Joseph Fourier. The possibility that burning carbon-based fuels like coal and oil could ramp this up into global warming was first advanced by the Nobel Prize-winning Swedish chemist Svante Arrhenius. He made some surprisingly accurate calculations as far back as 1896.

The body as index brings the importance of the natural world into focus. The body as index is perfectly suited to considering the threats facing people and the natural world. The body *shows* its dependence on the natural world. While the body is our base, the body needs the things provided by the world. In a similar vein, Chakrabarty suggests considering 'human' in a more biological frame even though 'The idea of species, it is feared, ... may introduce a powerful degree of essentialism in our understanding of humans'.[57] But if the body is seen as what it is, an index, each singular and each unique, essentialism is avoided while nevertheless providing a way of looking at the human appropriate to the 'crisis of climate change'.[58]

Situating the body in the natural world does potentially introduce some difficulties, specifically, how to view other species. The relationship, for example, between humans and other animals needs to be considered[59] because 'humans as a species, [is] a species dependent on other species for its own existence, a part of the general history of life'.[60] It seems to me that all that is required is full recognition of this dependence. The reliance of people on other species and on the natural environment more generally is, at this point in time, a fact. Whether we protect animals by giving them rights or simply out of self-interest is less important than the continuing functioning of the environment on which we all depend.[61] We are all united in our vulnerability.[62] The body as index allows for protection of the environment without having to convince sceptics that animals have rights or trees have standing.

Cripps argues, 'To some extent, given the interconnection of humans and the natural world, the two projects – justice for humans and justice for nonhumans broadly understood – should complement each other.'[63] If by justice we understand protection, and ongoing survival, it cannot be otherwise. Certainly it is no longer

---

Alastair McIntosh, *Hell and High Water: Climate Change, Hope and the Human Condition* (Birlinn 2008) 3.

57 Chakrabarty (n 54) 214.

58 Chakrabarty (n 54) 215.

59 Karen Bakker, 'The 'Common's versus the "Commodity": Alter-globalization, Anti-privatization and the Human Right to Water in the Global South' (2007) 39(3), *Antipode* 430, 448.

60 Chakrabarty (n 54) 219.

61 It is worth noting that the dependence generally operates in only one direction. Animals, insects and other creatures do not need humans; but humans need them.

62 'Vulnerability, as an ontic matter, unites human beings, not only with each other in a way that invites critique of substantive inequalities and their related structural impediments to adequate protection, but unites us, as a species, with all other carbon-based life-forms and the eco-systems of which we are a part.' Anna Grear, *Redirecting Human Rights: Facing the Challenge of Corporate Legal Humanity* (Palgrave 2010) 128.

63 Elizabeth Cripps, 'Saving the Polar Bear, Saving the World: Can the Capabilities Approach do Justice to Humans, Animals and Ecosystems?' (2010) 16, *Res Publica* 1, 8.

possible to protect the environment by leaving it alone.[64] As humans now wield a geological force, non-intervention is no longer possible; humans have already changed the environment. Unfortunately, the changes we have made threaten our future existence. We may have created a world in which we will be unable to live. The creation of this world is connected not only to our physical actions but also to the political models we have chosen. The nation state and the specific construction of the rights-bearing individual both allow, if not encourage, activities that damage the world on which we rely and the people living in it.

In Chapters 6 and 7 I will argue that as a supplement to the body as frame some other frames are required. One of these is the frame of the global. This is implicit in any consideration of the environment as while local ecosystems can be identified, ultimately, natural systems are profoundly interconnected. Taking account of the workings of the natural world makes clear that national boundaries are simply human constructs. Moreover, the natural world challenges the primacy of the nation state. Because human rights are connected to the natural world, by way of the body, it is important to show how they disrupt the nation state not just in terms of geographical boundaries, but at the very moment of their formation.

The connection between political models and the effect of people on the planet has not gone unnoticed. Chakrabarty discusses the shift in terms of 'freedom'. He observes:

> In no discussion of freedom in the period since the Enlightenment was there ever any awareness of the geological agency that human beings were acquiring at the same time as and through processes closely linked to their acquisition of freedom. Philosophers of freedom were mainly, and understandably, concerned with how humans would escape the injustice, oppression, inequality, or even uniformity foisted on them by other humans or human-made systems.[65]

It is this understanding of freedom that led to the human rights we have now. Citizenship rights, rights to political participation and procedural rights were required to stop particular kinds of injustice and oppression. The security of personal property was also seen as central to security and hence to justice.[66] In short, the human rights system we have now is predicated on a particular understanding of freedom; one that is political and bestowed on the citizen.

Foundational for this political freedom is the social contract that makes a distinction between 'private life and political existence'.[67] The social contract is concerned with political existence, with the construction and recognition of the

64 Cripps (n 63) 19.

65 Chakrabarty (n 54) 208.

66 Anna Grear, 'Challenging Corporate "Humanity": Legal Disembodiment and Human Rights' (2007) 7, *H.R.L. Rev.* 511, 534.

67 Giorgio Agamben, *Homo Sacer, Sovereign Power and Bare Life, Daniel Heller-Roazen* (trans) (Stanford University Press 1998) 187.

citizen and with his protection. The contract, both the social contract and the contract of capitalist exchange, is closely linked with conceptions of freedom. As Grear argues, 'the foundations of modern legal rights and the genesis of legal positivism … cannot easily be separated from the distinctive ideological journey of early liberal capitalism'.[68] The contract also allows no space for the body as index. The contract, however, cannot cope with the new climate.

Homo Sacer

According to Agamben, the founding of the state involves an original violence that is linked to the contract. The sovereign ban works to exclude bare life from the political order. Bare life, *homo sacer*, has a function but it is one that involves violence. It 'preserves the memory of the originary exclusion through which the political dimension was first constituted'.[69] *Homo sacer* marks out the domain of the 'us' by excluding the other. It is the founding moment of politics and of the nation state. While the state needs bare life to constitute itself, it does not recognise it as life; it recognises only 'citizens'. The consequences of this exclusion mean that only some bodies matter and even then, they do not matter as bodies. The founding moment of politics puts bare life outside of signification and turns it into a cipher; it can neither be sacrificed nor murdered. 'Corporeal vulnerability is the threat around which the political body is incorporated.'[70] *Homo sacer* is the political zero institution, but it must be excluded for the state to come into existence. This goes a long way in explaining our treatment of the natural world. A political order that does recognise bodies as such cannot be expected to recognise the ground on which they depend.

Seeing the body as index, however, means that corporeal vulnerability is not so much a threat as a fact. In contrast, our current political order would turn vulnerability into a threat, withholding protection from those bodies that do not belong. To be corporeally vulnerable is, in a sense politically impossible. The citizen is not a body and so cannot be vulnerable. Bare life is vulnerable but it is not recognised by the state. This is the threat. In the exclusion of bare life from politics, political life itself becomes profoundly biopolitical as the political order sets out how and what the body can mean. This is especially clear at times of national crisis, during war. Then 'the human body opens itself and allows "the nation" to be registered there in the wound'.[71] Vulnerability thus becomes something invisible, something that must not be seen. The utterly vulnerable, bare life, has no place in

---

68 Grear, *Redirecting Human Rights* (n 62) 77.

69 Agamben, *Homo Sacer* (n 67) 83.

70 Shiloh Y. Whitney, 'Dependency Relations: Corporeal Vulnerability and the Norms of Personhood in Hobbes and Kittay' (2011) 26(3), *Hypatia* 554, 557.

71 Scarry (n 31) 112.

the political order. The body as index has no place in this political order. The body as index is *homo sacer*.

As already noted in Chapter 1, existing regimes of human rights depend exactly on politics, on the nation state, on constructing people in a particular way. Because of this, every human right recognised by the state, every right protected simply gives the state more power.[72] The precondition for claiming a right is, in this system, being recognised, being signified as a citizen. The split that this involves has been well documented. Agamben notes:

> The separation between humanitarianism and politics that we are experiencing today is the extreme phase of separation of the rights of man from the rights of the citizen. In the final analysis, however, humanitarian organizations – which today are more and more supported by international commissions – can only grasp human life in the figure of bare or sacred life, and therefore, despite themselves, maintain a secret solidarity with the very powers they ought to fight.[73]

If, however, the frame for human rights is not the citizen but bare life, things may shift. To call it a shift is to underestimate the change involved; it is a radical revisioning of the world and of the body. It requires recognising that we are all bare life; we are all in the camps. This has profound consequences.

> There is no return from the camps to classical politics. In the camps, city and house became indistinguishable, and the possibility of differentiating between our biological body and our political body--between what is incommunicable and mute and what is communicable and sayable – was taken from us forever. And we are not only, in Foucault's words, animals whose life as living beings is at issue in their politics, but also – inversely – citizens whose very politics is at issue in their natural body.[74]

Agamben insists that there can be no return to classical politics. This, then, requires a break with the sovereign ban, a tearing up of the social contract, and recognition that we are all bare life.

I will provide an alternative to the social contract, to classical politics, in the next chapter. For now, it is enough to say that this new political order will have the body as index, bare life, at its heart. We know that the body needs things; this is what seeing the body as index shows. But in a political order there is more than

---

72 Agamben, *Homo Sacer* (n 67) 121, following Foucault.

73 Agamben, *Homo Sacer* (n 67) 133. See also Michael Agier, *On the Margins of the World: The Refugee Experience Today*, David Fernbach (trans) (Polity, 2008); Paul Farmer, *Pathologies of Power: Health, Human Rights, and the New War on the Poor* (University of California Press, 2005); Slavoj Žižek, 'Against Human Rights' (2005) 34, *New Left Review* 115.

74 Agamben, *Homo Sacer* (n 67) 187–8.

one body and the relationship between them needs to be considered. Just as the body and the soul touch each other[75] people touch each other. More needs to be said about how to treat others and how to look at them.

In one sense, all bodies are the same. All bodies need food, water, air and sleep. But there is more to the human than this. There is another sense in which all bodies, all people, are the same; each is singular. In the following, I want to dwell on the singular nature of every person and the absolute unknowability of the other. Because every person, every body, is absolutely unique, it is not appropriate to group people according to conventional identity markers. Every person must be seen, apprehended and approached not as an instance of 'woman' or 'child' or 'man' but as an individual. While the formation of the political state turns all bodies that matter into citizens, the new political order has to find a way of countering any similar move. To do this, we need to consider the body as index in community with other bodies.

In *The Coming Community*, Agamben is concerned precisely with singularity, with the individual uniqueness of every person. In order to articulate this, he proposes the figure of 'whatever being'. 'Whatever being' insists on attention being given to singularity 'not in its indifference with respect to a common property ... but only in its being *such as it is*'.[76] As it is 'whatever' it does not even indicate space (wherever), speaker (whoever) but rather it sits at the limit of the signification of any particular thing. The relationship between the general and the specific is thus collapsed, or abandoned, at least it has no place in consideration of whatever. 'Whatever is the thing *with all its properties*, none of which, however, constitute difference';[77] whatever is itself and it is incomparable. Like Nancy's corpus, whatever resists categorisation absolutely, is neither 'an essence or an existence, but a *manner of rising forth*'.[78]

For Agamben, 'whatever' is crucial for the entry into a new political community that, because of the way in which the state will, and must, confer an identity, must instead be a community that is 'non-State'. This is simply because of 'an insurmountable disjunction between whatever singularity and the State organization'.[79] It is a singularity that the State cannot tolerate.[80] Thus, whatever can be understood as a development of *homo sacer*, but rather than being exiled it forms the basis of a new political order. Whatever is more than bare life, but what more it is cannot be completely specified. Whatever is itself, whatever that may be.

In Chapter 7 I argue that it is possible to say something more about the person, about whatever being, by paying attention to linguistic universals. This provides a

---

75 Nancy (n 8) 141.

76 Giorgio Agamben, *The Coming Community*, Michael Hardt (trans) (University of Minnesota Press 1993) 1–2.

77 Agamben, *The Coming Community* (n 76) 19.

78 Agamben, *The Coming Community* (n 76) 28.

79 Agamben, *The Coming Community* (n 76) 85.

80 Agamben, *The Coming Community* (n 76) 86.

way of articulating human rights over and above those required for the sustenance of bare life. I defer that discussion, however, as it is important to consider the relationship between whatever beings. Given the singularity of whatever, what the other is cannot be set out in advance. The other does have to be responded to, however. For whatever beings to exist together there needs to be a mode of communication. And while language and signification have been used to read bodies in a way that puts bare life out of view, if we are to interact with the other, if we are to respond to her, something is needed. In what follows, I consider Levinas's concept of the face, connecting it to the body as index and to whatever being. It is then possible to find a place for language not as a signifying system, but as a way of being with, being in touch with, the other.

The Other

In 'Signification and Sense', Levinas starts by setting out the argument that it is impossible to get outside of signification, outside of language. 'In the this as that, neither the *this* nor the *that* is given forthwith, outside of discourse.'[81] But then comes the face. 'The face is in the trace of the absolutely completed, absolutely past Absent … .'[82] The face has meaning, but it cannot be signified. 'The face presents itself in its nakedness.'[83] It presents itself.[84] 'To listen to [531] an other is to take up this ideality that "oozes 'at the edge of words'".'[85] The other is found in the face. It is that which cannot be totalised, cannot be known, and must be responded to. It should not be seized or grasped, but rather looked at, spoken to, considered and caressed.

> A face is not like a plastic form, which is always already deserted, betrayed, by the being it reveals, such as marble from which the gods it manifests already absent themselves. It differs from an animal's head in which a being, in its brutish dumbness, is not yet in touch with itself. In a face the expressed *attends* its expression, expresses its very expression, always remains master of the meaning it delivers. A 'pure act' in its own way, it resists identification, does not

81 Emmanuel Levinas, 'Signification and Sense' in *Humanism of the Other*, Nidra Poller (trans) (University of Illinois Press, 2003) 13.

82 Levinas, 'Signification and Sense' (n 81) 40.

83 Levinas, 'Signification and Sense' (n 81) 39.

84 In Merleau-Ponty's terms we are dealing with 'ideality' which 'as essence belongs to both language and flesh'. Fielding (n 4) 530.

85 Fielding (n 4) 530–31 citing Maurice Merleau-Ponty, *Husserl at the Limits of Phenomenology*, Len Lawlor (ed.), (Northwestern University Press 2002) 24.

> enter into the already known, brings aid to itself, as Plato puts it, speaks. The epiphany of the face is wholly language.[86]

The face sounds very much like the index in that it exposes itself. The face requires a body, as the body is our base. But Levinas's face is not a corporeal face. It is 'a *manner of rising forth*'. The face is itself, it is not a meaning inscribed on the body, it is exscription. The Other is the Stranger, she whom we must welcome. The Other is also a body; the body is other. '*An other is a body* because only *a body is an other*.'[87]

Even though unknowable, ungraspable, Levinas insists that we are responsible for the Other, that we must respond to her. This is the ethical relationship. The temptation when meeting the Other is to think that she is like the self. But as all persons are absolutely singular, there should be no comparison, no incorporation, of the Other with the self. Levinas argues that we should not seek to understand the Other, to totalise her, as this would not be a response to the Other but rather an imposition of the self. We have to look at and respond to the face, without grasping, without seeking to own or comprehend. The responsibility to the Other is the response; this is why the epiphany of the face is wholly language. Language provides the way to respond to the Other, to be responsible to the Other. But just as it takes a particular kind of looking to see the face about which Levinas writes; language needs to be used in a particular way to respond to the Other.

Language allows us to respond to the Other. Note that this is not an address, it is a response; we are responsible for the Other. We are already in debt.[88]

> Language in its expressive function is addressed to and invokes the other ... [the other] places [the same] under an obligation, makes it responsible, that is, makes it speak ... In speech we are not only thinking of the interlocutor, but speaking to him; the very concept we can have of him as a 'interlocutor in general' is something we say to him.[89]

Language at its most basic reveals our indebtedness to, our reliance on the Other. Even to say, to respond to the Other, to say 'I' means there must be a 'you'; this is 'wholly language'. I am not prior to the Other; I depend on her. The use of language, the epiphany of the Other, is not about signification but about the response. While language is generally conceived of in terms of signification, it has other functions. Responding to the Other is to interact with her. And the language of interaction does not so much signify as touch.

The first task is the greeting; or rather, to respond to the greeting.

---

86 Emmanuel Levinas, *Collected Philosophical Papers*, Alphonso Lingis (trans) (Duquesne University Press Pitts 1998) 55.

87 Nancy (n 8) 31.

88 Agamben, *The Coming Community* (n 76) 44.

89 Emmanuel Levinas, *Collected Philosophical Papers* (n 86) 41.

> EL: *Le dire* is a way of greeting an other person, but to greet him is already to respond to him. Of course we speak of some *thing*, of the rain or the fine day, it doesn't matter, but to speak is already to reply.
>
> PN: … Yes, in some cases. But in others, on the contrary, the encounter with another is in the mode of violence, hatred, or disdain.
>
> EL: Sure. But [this analysis of the face] comes first. It's the presupposition of all human relations. … It's that original 'after you, sir', that I've tried to describe.[90]

The face comes first; its epiphany is 'wholly language', not language as a system of signification, not language as a particular view of the world, but language as touch. This is the phatic function of language, when words are used simply to build relations, to construct and maintain a relationship with the Other.[91] We must experience just this: 'the very fact that one speaks'.[92] The phatic is the spoken touch that should not be discussed in terms of communication or signification, but rather in terms of contact. It is the completely open hospitality, not the 'who are you?' that would ask the Other to identify herself in terms that could be grasped and comprehended, but rather 'how are you?'. It is the absolutely open first encounter, where not even the name is asked for.[93]

It seems to me that it is the phatic Levinas alludes to in the distinction he makes between the Saying and the Said. The Said is 'just giving our words in the face of the other'. Saying, in contrast, consists in 'uncovering itself … denuding itself of its skin'.[94] Saying, then, does not consist of the routine phatic interaction, performed out of duty or because of a cultural norm. It is an authentic response, the absolute openness of unconditional hospitality, a way of using language that suggests and acknowledges the singularity of the Other. Saying 'is a passivity

---

90 Emmanuel Levinas, *Éthique et infini: Dialogues, avec Philippe Nemo* (Livre de Poche, 1982) cited in Desmond Manderson, *Proximity, Levinas, and the Soul of Law* (McGill-Queen's University Press 2006) 56; Manderson's translation.

91 Roman Jakobson, 'Closing Statements: Linguistics and Poetics' in *Style in Language Thomas A Sebeok* (ed.) (MIT Press 1960) 355.

92 Agamben, *The Coming Community* (n 76) 83.

93 'Telemachus saw her long before any one else did. He was sitting moodily among the suitors thinking about his brave father, and how he would send them flying out of the house, if he were to come to his own again and be honoured as in days gone by. Thus brooding as he sat among them, he caught sight of Minerva and went straight to the gate, for he was vexed that a stranger should be kept waiting for admittance. He took her right hand in his own, and bade her give him her spear. "Welcome", said he, "to our house, and when you have partaken of food you shall tell us what you have come for."' http://classics.mit.edu/Homer/odyssey.mb.txt. See also Jacques Derrida and Anne Dufourmantelle, *Of Hospitality* Rachel Bowlby (trans) (Stanford University Press 2000).

94 Emmanuel Levinas, *Otherwise than Being or Being Beyond Essence* (Kluwer 1991) 15.

more passive than all passivity';[95] the state in which all foundations are taken away. It 'is the proximity of one to the other, the commitment of an approach, the one for the other, the very signifyingness of signification'.[96]

The proximity of the Other and the responsibility for the Other, can be described not just in terms of the saying and the said, but also in other modes. Consideration of the tactile and the visual show the same kind of relationship and both are well suited to the corporeal human frame. I turn to the visual in a moment. First, I want to consider the touch as it reveals not only the vulnerability of people but also our potential violence in an immediate and visceral way. The body is vulnerable to touch, in potentially positive and negative ways. This is not to make any claims about human nature; rather, it is simply to focus on the nature of being human. We are vulnerable to violence of others, as well as to the violence of natural forces.

Consider the body. It invites touch. It is a touchable body. It is already touched and touching, a self-reflexive relationship. Experience of our own body, touching itself and the touches of others, make our bodies. Traces are left. But the touch that soothes is exactly the same and yet exactly not the same as the touch that strikes. The difference is contextual, interactional and radically unpredictable before the contact. Touch is as ambiguous as it is potent. The ethical touch, the human touch, is one that understands this ambiguity and does not seek to understand the body it seeks to touch. The responsible touch, one that responds to the Other, is not so much of a statement as a question.

The same holds true in relation to the visual. While the body can be touched, it can also be seen. It is the body we need to look at. And while the face is not of this body, it is somehow connected to it. Levinas's face is not so much corporeal or abstract, but rather a way of looking, a certain kind of approach that is a response. It is a particular kind of staring.

> Staring bespeaks involvement, and being stared at demands a response. A staring encounter is a dynamic struggle – starers inquire, stares lock eyes or flee, and starers advance or [4] retreat; one moves forward and the other moves back. A staring interchange can tickle or alienate, persist or evolve.[97]

Garland-Thomson observes that 'being stared at demands a response'. What if the response, the responsibility Levinas identifies, could be done through a kind of looking, a kind of staring? The staring encounter involves contact, a kind of touch; the stare can be gentle, even loving, or it can be violent and threatening. There is

95 Levinas, Otherwise (n 94) 15.

96 This is the realm of language rather than language defined as system, as the Said subordinates the Saying 'to the linguistic system and to ontology, [it] is the price that manifestation demands'. Levinas, *Otherwise* (n 94) 5, 6.

97 Rosemarie Garland-Thomson, *Staring: How We Look* (Oxford University Press 2009) 3–4. See also 102.

good staring and bad looking as the look can dominate and oppress.[98] Staring can be a violent act, where the violence inheres in wanting the Other to obey, to be seen in a way the looker can comprehend. Staring may try and grasp the Other, to engage the Other in a battle. But there is another kind of staring, where the Other is not grasped but caressed, where the staring is a response rather than a threat. Good staring sees the Other as whatever being, in her ungraspable singularity.

> Seeing something simply in its being-thus – irreparable, but not for that reason necessary; thus, but not for that reason contingent – is love.
>
> At the point you perceive the irreparability of the world, at that point it is transcendent.
>
> How this world is – this is outside the world.[99]

There is a kind of vertigo in looking, in staring. Moreover, the stare may be used to open up a questioning space. What do we stare at? We stare at those we love and those we hate, we stare when in deep concentration, exhaustion or a meditative state. We stare at things we don't fully understand, we stare when we are unable to understand because our emotions overwhelm us or because our physical bodies or mental capacities fail us. This is what staring invites us to consider; we do not understand. We cannot grasp the world in its totality, we do not understand why we love the one we stare at, we think we know all there is to know about the one we stare at in hatred and anger. We do not.

All we can know is that the Other is (in) a body. The body has needs, things without which it would not now be living, things without which continuing life will be impossible. Realising that we know no more than this may move us towards a 'newness' that changes everything including how we look at the Other.[100] 'We can become ethical starers by being conscious in the presence of something that compels our intense attention.'[101] This is about being conscious, not conscious of, but just in a particular frame of mind, to look at the human frame aware of our own human frame. We can be conscious of the Other, not in order to recognise her, in the sense of knowing and comprehending the Other, but simply by seeing her singular existence: 'To be recognized, one needs literally to be seen.'[102] Looking at, staring at, the Other reminds us that that 'each one' is suffering.[103]

98 Garland-Thomson (n 97) 43.

99 Agamben, *The Coming Community* (n 76) 104.

100 Garland-Thomson (n 97) 188.

101 Garland-Thomson (n 97) 188.

102 Following Elaine Scarry, Garland-Thomson notes that the 'compact between starer and staree is not static but collaborative', Garland-Thomson (n 97) 194, 187.

103 Nancy (n 8) 93.

Singular whatever beings have in common the fact of their bodies. Bodies are dependent on each other and on the continued existence of the natural world.[104] We might say we need the Other; but this suggests a primacy of the self, when Levinas tells us that this is not so. The Other cannot be known; nevertheless the Other must be responded to. We must respond to the Other; we are responsible for the Other. We are already in debt. The encounter with the Other begins with a radical inequality. This has consequences for the coming community, for the being together of all embodied whatever beings. This community cannot be founded on a contract, as the contract is predicated on equality.[105]

> Either way, as vulnerability and as opportunity, language begins, like all trust, with inequality. It is not an agreement to be secured but a fine risk to be run, with no promise of a return.[106]

Language begins, like all trust, with inequality.[107] What is required, and what would be a turn away from classical politics, is trust; a human trust.

104 Murphy argues that both currents can be found in Cavarero and Butler even though they stop short of producing a normative set of human rights. Ann V. Murphy (2011), 'Corporeal Vulnerability and the New Humanism' (2011) 26(3), *Hypatia* 575.

105 In terms of the social contract, that is to say, all citizens are equal. Non-citizens are not simply unequal, they are not factored into the contract.

106 Desmond Manderson, *Proximity, Levinas, and the Soul of Law* (McGilll-Queen's University Press 2006) 48.

107 'Language, as the manifestation of a reason, awakens in me and in the other what we have in common. But it assumes, in its expressive intention, our alterity and duality. It is practiced between beings, between substances who do not enter into their words, but who proffer them.' Emmanuel Levinas, 'The/ and The Totality' in *Entre Nous*, Michael B. Smith and Barbara Harshaw (trans) (Continuum 2006) 22.

Chapter 5
The Living Body

In the previous chapter, I argued that treating the human body as a frame for human rights requires that it be seen as an index. Treating the body as an index shows what the body presupposes, that is, what the body needs to survive. To live, humans need potable water, clean air, shelter, food and sleep. These are basic human needs, even of the being exiled from the political order – *homo sacer* – and as such are absolutely fundamental. However, for these human rights to be meaningful, more needs to be done. For example, to speak sensibly of a human right to water requires that water exists and is available. This means that protection of the environment is ultimately a human right. Because people need water and because water comes from the physical environment, the most fundamental human rights are in fact what would more usually be called environmental rights. But this presents a problem, as environmental protection doesn't fit easily into existing human rights frameworks. The first issue is that while human rights are generally held by individuals, environmental rights seem to be 'held' by the environment. It is certainly possible to argue that trees should have standing;[1] this is an attractive argument, as it takes seriously the importance of the natural world. There is a risk, however, that such a position will be interpreted as holding that trees are more important than people. It seems to me that it is not a question of 'ranking' the rights of trees relative to humans, rather, it is the dependence of people on the natural environment that needs to be made clear.[2] The reliance of humans on the

1 '... there will be resistance to giving the thing "rights" until it can be seen and valued for itself; yet, it is hard to see it and value it for itself until we can bring ourselves to give it "rights" – which is almost inevitably going to sound inconceivable to a large group of people.' Christopher D. Stone, *Should Trees Have Standing? Law, Morality and the Environment*, 3rd ed. (OUP 2010) 3.

2 It would also be possible to put the protection of the environment in another frame and argue for the crime of ecocide. See Anja Guager at al. 'Ecocide is the Missing 5th Crime Against the Peace', 2012 http://www.sas.ac.uk/sites/default/files/files/hrc/Events%20Documents/Ecocide%20is%20the%20missing%205th%20Crime%20Against%20Peace.pdf. Accessed 21 January 2013; Polly Higgins (2010) *Eradicating Ecocide: Laws and Governance to Stop the Destruction of the Planet* (Shepheard-Walwyn 2010); Polly Higgins, *Earth is Our Business: Changing the Rules of the Game* (Shepheard-Walwyn 2012); Ling-Yee Huang, 'Not Just another Drop in the Human Rights Bucket: The Legal Significance of a Codified Human Right to Water' (2008) 20 *Fla. J. Int'l L.* 353, 363, 366; Kirti Singh Chauhan and Surender Sing Chauhan, 'Ecological Destruction vis-à-vis Environmental Jurisprudence in India: A Survey' (2009) 27(3), *Journal of Human Ecology*, 207.

environment underpins this chapter as I suggest that it is possible to protect the environment in a 'human centred' way.

The second problem with attempting to protect the environment in terms of existing human rights frameworks is that the environment does not respect national borders. Pollution, desertification and subterranean water courses are not containable according to political borders. Thus, the environment presents a challenge to an international human rights system that relies on the importance of the nation state.[3] As the previous chapter suggested, a global perspective is required. Finally, the protection of the environment is not something that can sensibly be dealt with at an individual level or even national level. While we can all seek to conserve and protect natural resources, full protection of the environment can only occur if proper account is taken of the interdependence of people and human reliance on the natural world. The environment is not a thing; it is a series of interrelated systems on which humans depend.

Water, water everywhere and none of it is infinite. Water is a fixed commodity.[4]

To develop a model for the protection of the environment in human terms, this chapter takes the case of water. To have a meaningful human right to water requires that the fundamental human need for water be acknowledged and that water be understood and dealt with in a way that takes account of this need. Currently, the importance of water to human survival is not always acknowledged. While water is certainly understood to be valuable its value is generally realised in economic terms. Water has become property in the full legal and economic sense,[5] treated as a tradable good and even subject to WTO regulation.[6] The trade in bottled water is no doubt that with which most consumers are familiar.[7] Within the last few decades, bottled drinking water has exploded as a market, with a proliferation of brands targeting a range of consumers.[8] Seeking 'pure' refreshment, consumers often ignore the environmental impact of the processes involved in its extraction, treatment, packaging and shipping. This has served to both obscure and exacerbate

---

3 Conor Gearty, (2010) 'Do Human Rights Help or Hinder Environmental Protection?' (2010) 1(1), *JHRE* 7, 9.

4 Rose George, *The Big Necessity: Adventures in the World of Human Waste* (Portobello 2009) 257.

5 David Shaw, 'The Specter of Water Piracy: The World Trade Organization Threatening Water Security in Developing Nations' (2008) 19 *Colo. J. Int'l Envtl. L.& Pol'y* 129, 130.

6 Surya Deva, 'Human Rights Realization in an Era of Globalization: The Indian Experience' (2006) 12 *Buff.Hum.Rts.L.Rev.* 93, 129. See also Giovanna Ricoveri, *Nature for Sale: The Commons versus Commodities* (Pluto 2013) 76; Raghav Sharma, 'Green Courts in India: Strengthening Environmental Governance?' (2008) 4(1), *Law, Environment and Development Journal* 52.

7 Douglas A. Kysar, 'Sustainable Development and Private Global Governance' (2005) 83 *Tex. L .Rev.* 2109, 2166; Shaw (n 5) 137.

8 BBC/Open University, *The Foods that Make Billions: Episode 1 – Liquid Gold*, first broadcast 23 November 2010.

the nature of water as a fundamental human need. Water is valuable because it is a finite resource. It is also valuable because people need it.

Water provides a way of thinking about environmental rights as human rights, taking account not only of the interconnectedness of the natural world but also the fact that people rely on it. In order to identify the relevant issues around natural resources, and in order to suggest a way of thinking that would protect them, I consider the case of Plachimada India, where a multinational company and a village fought a legal battle over who had a right to local groundwater. The case law around Plachimada demonstrates that it has become routine to treat water as property and to treat corporations as people. The issue in Plachimada is essentially one of ownership, with the courts having to decide who owns the water. Paying attention to the details of the case, I argue that treating water as property and treating corporations as people is not always conducive to the well-being of real people. I propose that some things, like water, need to be taken out of the property frame. I also suggest that the contractual relationships that facilitate regimes of private property do not capture the relationships that people actually have with each other or with the environment. I argue instead that environmental goods be treated as a 'human trust'. The 'human trust' is developed by drawing on strands of the Plachimada case law as well as on Roman law. The 'human trust' allows for environmental goods to be treated not as property ('goods') but rather in a way that takes account of what is good for people. Treating water as a human trust serves as a model for how the environment more generally should be treated.

To further protect the human trust, I draw on an existing remedy in tort law, the *quia timet* injunction, to propose a new action: 'anticipatory negligence'. This action seeks to recognise the relationships of people with each other – resulting in a generalised duty of care – as well as acknowledging the fundamental importance of protecting the natural environment. And while discussion of injunctions may suggest that I am prioritising legal protection, I simply want to show that the human trust is potentially compatible with existing legal structures as well as to highlight the creative potential of law. Given the facts of the Plachimada case, this is important because neither developing environmental law in India nor the recognition that the Constitutional right to life includes a right to water were enough to protect the local environment in Plachimada. Finally, the human trust suggests an alternative to the social contract, a political order founded on the body as index.

Water as a Human Right

Water is so basic, so essential that it is surprising that it is not already a well-established human right. Part of the reason for this absence may be to do with the current human rights system and the rights it protects, that is, the classic liberal rights of autonomy, liberty and ownership of property. As such, a human right to water and environmental rights more generally fall outside the normal frame of human rights.[9] That is not to say that a human right to water has not been recognised to some extent. There is already a great deal of argument and advocacy for the recognition of water as a human right[10] especially as a protest against its privatisation and commodification.[11] While not consistently recognised as a human right (though see the Constitution of South Africa),[12] it is arguably implied by other well established rights.[13] Hughes, for example, observes its recognition in The Convention on the Rights of the Child[14] and Zaylia argues for its implicit presence in CEDAW (Convention on the Elimination of Discrimination Against Women).[15] There is some official acknowledgment of the right in UN Resolution 64/292 adopted by the General Assembly in 2010. This recognises 'the right to safe and clean drinking water and sanitation as a human right that is essential for the full enjoyment of life and all human rights'.[16] Sometime before this, in 2002, the United Nations Committee on Economic, Social and Cultural Rights, having recognised the right to water previously, noted 'The human right to water is indispensable for leading a life in human dignity. It is a prerequisite for the realization of other human rights.'[17] The Committee provide a textual basis for

9 'The link between human and environmental rights was first made in 1972 at the Stockholm conference on the Human Environment.' Gearty (n 3) 12. This relationship continues in, for example, the *Journal of Environmental and Human Rights*. Attention is not paid to environmental law here, except in relation to specific issues around water and the Plachimada case.

10 Taposik Banerjee, 'Right to Water: Some Theoretical Issues' (2010) 6(1), *Contemporary Issues and Ideas in Social Sciences*. http://journal.ciiss.net/index.php/ciiss/article/view/79/76 Accessed 31 July 2012; Amanda Cahill, '"The Human Right to Water – A Right of Unique Status": The Legal Status and Normative Content of the Right to Water' (2005) 9(3), *Intl J Hum Rts* 389; Huang (n 2); PLoS Medicine Editors, 'Clean Water Should be Recognised as a Human Right' (2009) (6) *PLoS Medicine* 1 www.plosmedicine.org.

11 Karen Bakker, 'The "Common's" versus the "Commodity": Alter-globalization, Anti-privatization and the Human Right to Water in the Global South' (2007) 39(3), *Antipode* 430, 437.

12 Anna Grear, *Redirecting Human Rights: Facing the Challenge of Corporate Legal Humanity* (Palgrave 2010) 194; Kysar (n 7) 2129.

13 Bakker (n 11) 437; Richard P. Hiskes 'Environmental Human Rights and Intergenerational Justice' (2006) April–June, *Human Rights Rev.* 81, 82; Huang (n 2) 356.

14 Richard A. Hughes, 'Pro-Justice Ethics, Water Scarcity, Human Rights' (2009–10) 25 *J.L. & Religion* 521, 532.

15 Jessica Leigh Zaylia, 'Questioning the Coke Side of Life: Groundwater Appropriation, Absolute Property Rights, the Public Trust Doctrine and Gender Inequality in India' (2009) 6(2), *Manchester Journal of International Economic Law* 159, 175.

16 United Nations, 'The Human Right to Water and Sanitation' General Assembly Resolution 64/292 (2010) 28 July http://www.un.org/ga/search/view_doc.asp?symbol=A/RES/64/292 accessed 16 October 2013.

17 Committee on Economic, Social and Cultural Rights, 'The Right to Water' General Comment no 15, 2002 Article 1.1 http://www.unhchr.ch/tbs/doc.nsf/0/a5458d1d1bbd713fc1256cc400389e94/$FILE/G0340229.pdf. Accessed 4 June 2013.

the right, arguing it is included in Article 11 of the Covenant, CEDAW and The Convention on the Rights of the Child. It is a right involving both 'freedom and entitlements', one that requires active protection by governments.[18] Attention is also given to environmental concerns, for example, 'The manner of the realization of the right to water must also be sustainable, ensuring that the right can be realized for present and future generations.'[19]

While the Committee on Economic, Social and Cultural rights is clear about the textual basis, nature and extent of the right to water, this does not always translate into local human rights systems.[20] As Bakker concludes, 'Human rights are individualistic, anthropocentric, state-centric, and compatible with private sector provision of water supply.'[21] Thus, recognition of water as a human right within existing paradigms may ultimately work against the provision of water to thirsty people as it may simply confirm the idea that the natural world can be owned.[22] The problems with treating water as property are discussed below. In relation to the specific case considered here, it is worth noting at the outset that India does recognise, at least to some extent, a right to water, as part of a 'right to life' enshrined in the Constitution. However, as the Plachimada case shows, this was not enough to protect the environment on which the villagers depend. Even though the right to water may result in the government providing basic supplies, brought to villages by trucks,[23] this does not solve the root problem. This water has to come from somewhere. In the following, I pay close attention to the Plachimada case in order to develop a different way of thinking about water, and by extension, the natural environment more generally.

Plachimada: People and Property

The story of Plachimada is now well documented due to the action of NGOs and the extensive media coverage of the on-going legal battles.[24] Plachimada is in the

18 Article 7.

19 Article 11.

20 Despite the clear articulation of the right, the UN system lacks 'any real bite to back up the plethora of treaties that it has so enthusiastically endorsed'. Gearty (n 3) 9.

21 Bakker (n 11) 447. See also Gearty (n 3).

22 Gearty notes, 'The idea of the world outside the human as being inherently capable of belonging to the individual … is one that is very deeply entrenched … .' Gearty (n 3) 8.

23 Zaylia (n 15) 163.

24 Ananthakrishnan Aiyer, 'The Allure of the Transnational: Notes on Some Aspects of the Political Economy of Water in India' (2007) 22(4), *Cultural Anthropology* 640; Philippe Cullet, 'Water Sector Reforms and Courts in India: Lessons from the Evolving Case Law' (2011) 19(3), *RECIEL* 19(3) 328; S.R. Jitha, 'Bureaucracy and Sustainable Development' (2011) Oct–Dec, *PRAGATI Quarterly Research Journal* 23; Sujith Koonan, 'Legal Implications of Plachimada: A Case Study' (2007) *IELRC Working Paper* 2007-05 www.ielrc.org/content/w0705.pdf. Accessed 31 July 2012; Kysar (n 7); P. Madhu, 'Business

village of Moolathara in the state of Kerala in India, a semi-arid region though one with a great deal of groundwater. In 2000, Coca-Cola[25] set up a bottling plant there, having been granted a licence to do so by the local Panchayat[26] the year before. This licence permitted establishment of the factory, including use of electricity and ground water but on the understanding that the factory would provide employment and deal appropriately with waste.[27] Raman reports that the company was invited to invest by the left liberal state government in the interests of 'neoliberal development' but arguably in violation of the Kerala Land Utilisation Act 1967.[28] In 2003, the Panchayat, giving in to NGO pressure,[29] refused to renew the licence on the grounds of 'ecological problems' and 'exploitation of excess ground water' that led to a lack of drinking water for the local population.[30] The refusal was ultimately referred up to the Director of the Local Self Government Department that led to the Panchayat being overruled on the grounds of lack of proper scientific evidence.[31] This decision was challenged in the courts.[32] This case concerns not just the use of ground water, but also pollution by waste water and a sludge by-product of the production process, that Coca-Cola allegedly encouraged

---

Ethics: Should it Remain an Oxymoron?' (2010) 1(1), *MES Journal of Technology and Management* 83; Jeremiah McWilliams, 'Coca-Cola Will Face Claims in India' (2011), *The Atlanta Journal – Construction*, 26 Feb. p 12A from http://www.lexisnexis.com/uk/nexis/; Mark Thomas, *Belching Out the Devil: Global Adventures with Coca-Cola* (Ebury Press 2008); James L. Westcoat, Jnr., 'Submerged Landscapes: The Public Trust in Urban Environmental Design, from Chicago to Karachi and Back Again' (2009) 10, *Vermont Journal of Environmental Law* 435; Zaylia (n 15).

25 It should be noted that Coca-Cola has a franchise structure. Hence, the legal actor in these cases is actually Hindustan Coca Cola but will be referred to as 'Coca-Cola' here. Nevertheless, 'the Hindustan Coca-Cola Beverage Pvt Ltd is owned by The Coca Cola Company.' Thomas (n 24) 309.

26 The local council.

27 Ravi K. Raman, 'Transverse Solidarity: Water, Power, and Resistance' (2010) 42(2), *Review of Radical Political Economics* 251, 254.

28 Raman (n 27) 253; see also Jitha (n 24) 26.

29 Raman (n 27) 256.

30 *Hindustan Coca-Cola Beverages v Perumatty Grama Panchayat*, 2005 (2) KLT 554 p. 13.

31 Jitha (n 24) 29; Madhu (n 24) 90.

Invocation of the precautionary principle may have been appropriate here; see James Cameron and Juli Abouchar, 'The Precautionary Principle: A Fundamental Principle of Law and Policy for the Protection of the Global Environment' (1991) 14(1) *B. C. Int'l & Comp. L. Rev.* 1. http://lawdigitalcommons.bc.edu/iclr/vol14/iss1/2. Accessed 2 August 2012.

32 It should be noted that the case involved a number of agencies and legislative regimes, including the State Pollution Control Board, the Local Self Government Department, Kerala Ground Water Act, Water (Prevention and Control of Pollution) Act, 1974, Environment (Protection) Act 1986. Raman (n 27) 258; Jitha (n 24) 27.

local farmers to use as fertiliser.[33] The sludge apparently contained high levels of heavy metals that entered the food chain and had a negative effect on agriculture more generally.

There did seem to be some 'resolution' of the case with the passing of the Plachimada Bill by the Keralan state in 2011 (26 February).[34] This provides for a Tribunal to award damages to those harmed by Coca-Cola's actions. The 'High Power Committee' tasked with measuring 'the scale and nature of the damages' provided for US 48 million (Rs 2162.6 million) in compensation from the company according to the polluter pays principle.[35] The Preamble of the Bill accepts that the corporation has had a deleterious effect on the local environment and people.[36] However, because of the various allegations of bribery, manipulation of scientific data and general politicking it is perhaps unsurprising that as of February 2014, the Bill has still not been given the necessary Presidential assent to bring the Tribunal into existence.[37] While it is not practically possible for the company to re-start production at the plant[38] because of licence conditions and continuing local resistance, Dwivedi argues that 'legally' production could begin at any time.[39] In the meantime, the local water continues to be undrinkable and unsuitable for domestic purposes. The land is still contaminated and agriculture, on which the majority of locals depend, continues to be affected.[40]

---

33 Raman (n 27) 254. Oddly, use of Coca-Cola as a pesticide in India is not uncommon. Mike Adams, 'Coke, Pepsi Used as Agricultural Pesticides by India Farmers', 2008 *Natural News* http://www.naturalnews.com/News_000590_Coke_Pepsi_pesticides.html. Accessed 31 July 2012.

34 The Bill itself presents a number of problems not addressed here. The Plachimada Coca-Cola Victims Relief and Compensation Claims Special Tribunal Bill 2011 http://www.niyamasabha.org/bills/12kla/plachimada%20victims.pdf. Accessed 27 July 2012.

35 Raman (n 27) 265; see also Tineke Lambooy. 'Corporate Social Responsibility: sustainable water use' (2011) 19, *Journal of Cleaner Production* 852, 855.

36 This may be why the preceding investigations have been questioned by Cola-Cola. McWilliams (n 24).

37 *Times of India*, 'UN petitioned for early nod to Plachimada bill' (2014) 19 February www.timesofindia.indiatimes.com. Accessed 9 May 2014.This is not the only Bill to suffer delays. Pratul Sharma, 'Bills fall Victim to rocky Centre-state relationship' (2013) May 12th *Sunday Standard* newsindiaexpress.com Accessed 5th June 2013. See also *The Hindu*, 'Calls for presidential asset to Plachimada Bill', (2012) 5 June www.thehindu.com. Accessed 25 July 2012. Jitha (n 24) 28; Madhu (n 24); Raman (n 27) 255. There were also reports that the government was 'entertain[ing] legal opinion prepared on behalf of' Coca Cola on the Bill. New Indian Express, 'Chidambaram urged to forward Plachimada Bill' (2011) 24 September from http://www.lexisnexis.com/uk/nexis/.

38 Jitha (n 24) 29.

39 Gaurav Dwivedi, *Revisiting Important Water Conflicts in Kerala* (Forum for Policy Dialogue on Water Conflicts in India 2011) 57 http://www.conflicts.indiawaterportal.org/sites/conflicts.indiawaterportal.org/files/Kerala%20Water%20Conflicts%20Report%20Final.pdf. Accessed 2 July 2013.

40 Dwivedi (n 39) 59–60.

What is striking about this case is that the discourse of property rights appears to be inescapable. Even though at first instance it was held that the company did not have absolute rights to groundwater, this conclusion was nevertheless framed in terms of property rights.

> In other words the groundwater under the land of second respondent (the company) does not belong to him.[41]

The discourse of property is so firmly entrenched that even when arguing that water should be protected, it is done in terms of property. Thus, the judge at first instance uses the language of ownership in relation to water; 'it can be safely concluded that the underground water belongs to the public'.[42] Indeed, it is difficult to imagine a way of dealing with the issue without relying on the language of property. This makes clear the hegemonic status of private property. The discourse is even starker in the Appeal court decision.

> *We have to assume that a person* has the right to extract water from his property, unless it is prohibited by a statute. Extraction thereof cannot be illegal. We do not find justification for upholding the finding of the learned Judge that extraction of ground water is illegal. It is definitely not something like digging out a treasure-trove. We cannot endorse the finding that the company has no legal right to extract this 'wealth'. If such restriction is to apply to a legal person, it may have to apply to a natural person as well. *Abstract principles cannot be the basis for the Court to deny basic rights*, unless they are curbed by valid legislation. Even reference to mandatory function, referred to in the third schedule of the Panchayat Raj Act, namely 'Maintenance of traditional drinking water sources' *could not have been envisaged* as preventing an owner of a well from extracting water therefrom, as he wishes. The Panchayat had no ownership about such private water source, in effect denying the proprietary rights of the occupier and the proposition of law laid down by the learned Judge is too wide, for unqualified acceptance.[43]

Property rights are sacred. To limit them, the court requires a most explicit legislative act. Such a prohibition would have to be very explicit indeed, given that even legislative protection of 'traditional drinking water sources' is not enough to qualify the property rights of a (legal) person, even though it may be enough to compel the State to do something (that is, provide drinking water). In short, that someone (or something) has property rights over the ground water is not in

41 *Perumatty Grama Panchayat v State of Kerala*, 2004 (1) KLT 731 p. 13 http://www.ielrc.org/content/e0328.pdf. Accessed 30 July 2012.

42 (n 41) p. 34.

43 *Hindustan Coca-Cola Beverages v Perumatty Grama Panchayat*, 2005 (2) KLT 554 p. 35; my emphasis.

dispute in either decision.[44] For the Appeal court, the equivalence of legal persons is also not in dispute. This is suggested by the use of 'person' in lines just quoted and confirmed when the Appeal court anthropomorphises the company: 'A water based industry, with a huge investment has to receive water, to quench its thirst without inconveniencing others.'[45] Whether that individual is a natural or legal person, the underlying trope is that of individual liberty of action.

If the court is correct in its legal reasoning, if this is the state of Indian law, the judgment cannot be faulted for impropriety. However, it has been argued that the Division bench decision is out of line with existing Indian Constitutional jurisprudence. While Cullet describes the outcome of this case as evidencing 'the limited evolution of the case law' in the area of environmental protection,[46] Koonan is more critical.[47] He notes the scant attention to the Article 21 right to life and a lack of understanding of water systems, evident when water is treated as 'private property'.[48] Koonan reprises a number of points made by the court of first instance. This is necessary, as crucial parts of the first judgment were given little attention by the Appeal Court. Thus, while at first instance it was held that water is a public trust, the Appeal Court simply asserted the property rights of the company making no explicit reference to the 'public trust'.[49] Likewise, it only alluded to the case law on Article 21, stating 'The reliance placed by the learned Judge in Kamal Nath's case (*M.C. Mehta v Kamal Nath* (1997) 1 SCC 388)[50] is not sufficient to dislodge the claim [to water under one's property].'[51] This is surprising, as while it is written in the traditional language of the right to life, Article 21 has been given a broad interpretation.

> 21. No person shall be deprived of his life or personal liberty except according to procedure established by law.

---

44 It should be noted that the legal status of groundwater is not completely resolved in India. Videh Upadhyay, 'Water Rights and the "New" Water Laws in India: Emerging Issues and Concerns in a Rights Based Perspective' in *India Infrastructure Report 2011: Water: Policy and Performance for Sustainable Development Infrastructure* (OUP 2011) 56–66. http://www.idfc.com/pdf/report/IIR-2011.pdf. Accessed 1 August 2012.

45 (n 43) 40. While 'human rights' are not named here, granting the same rights to both legal and natural persons is reminiscent of Grear's argument about corporations claiming human rights. For discussion of water rights and environmental rights as human rights see Cahill (n 10); Joseph L Sax, 'The Search for Environmental Rights' (1990) 6 *J. Land Use & Envtl. L.* 95.

46 Cullet (n 24) 333.

47 Koonan (n 24).

48 Koonan (n 24) 12.

49 'The observation in paragraph 13 that the ground water under the land of the respondent does not belong to it may not be a correct proposition in law' (n 43) 43.

50 This case recognises the public trust doctrine in India particularly in relation to environmental protection.

51 (n 43) 43.

As Sharma details, the Indian Supreme Court 'has adopted an expanded view of "life" under Article 21 and enriched it to include environmental rights by reading it along' with other parts of the Constitution.[52] The court at first instance appears to follow this approach, holding that the Constitution has changed and limited the application of received English law in relation to ownership of water.[53] K. Balakrishnan Nair, J. concludes

> ... that the underground water belongs to the public. The State and its instrumentalities should act as trustees of this great wealth. The State has got a duty to protect ground water against excessive exploitation and the inaction of the State in this regard will tantamount to infringement of the right to life of the people guaranteed under Art.21 of the Constitution of India.[54]

As noted, this interpretation of Article 21 was not followed by the Division court.

Considering that Article 21 was raised, the Division bench equation of legal and natural persons is particularly troubling. That said, it should be noted that the single bench also appeared to treat the company as a quasi-person, granting it the same rights to water as a 'real' local person. The company was permitted to draw as much water as would be needed for agriculture on its 34 acres.[55] Thus, both decisions identify 'property' and 'person' as key categories, as the question both courts decide, albeit differently, is who owns the water. Because of this, in the following I want to consider three things. The first relates to the category of 'person' and whether treating corporations in the same way as natural persons is problematic. The second involves an examination of the consequences of corporations owning water. Finally, I consider whether it is appropriate to consider water as property.

Thirsty Corporations

The Division Bench in the Plachimada case is clearly unperturbed about treating corporations in the same way as natural people. The failure to mention Article 21 or 'life' further suggests that real people are not a high priority. There is a tension in the judgment, however, that becomes apparent in the anthropomorphising of the company as something that can be 'thirsty'. This thirst can only be a figurative one even though corporations are (in one sense) composed of people. While the morphology and etymology of 'corporation' suggests a body, or a collection of bodies, as Grear argues, there is no 'simple continuity between the corporation and its human sub-stratum for the purposes of attributing the individual human rights

52 Sharma (n 6) 53; see also Zaylia (n 15) 166.
53 (n 41) 24.
54 (n 41) 34.
55 (n 41) 15.

of human beings to the corporate form'.[56] The issue here is not that legal persons are problematic in every sense, but rather that it is not clear they should be treated in the same way as natural persons in all cases.[57]

When the Division bench in Plachimada asserts, 'We have to assume that a person has the right to extract water from his property, unless it is prohibited by a statute' they appear to take as unproblematic the equivalence of all legal persons. However, as Naffine argues, there are at least three kinds of legal person (P1, P2 and P3).[58] While some of these persons require a human form (P2 and P3) even the disembodied legal person (P1) has property rights. Indeed, there seems to be a close connection between the disembodied legal subject and 'an exclusory private property construct'.[59] As long as water is treated as property, it is difficult to argue that its ownership should be restricted to certain kinds of legal persons. Even if this could be accomplished, it is not clear that this would assist in meeting human needs. As there are real people in this case suffering a real lack of water, the equivalence of all legal persons is particularly problematic. This only becomes an issue, however, because of the treatment of water as property. Before the human right to water can have any hope of being protected, water – and the environment more generally – needs to be removed from the property frame. How natural goods should be framed will be discussed below. First, I want to explore the models that underpin and encourage the treatment of water as property.

Money and Sense

The environment and its natural resources are often framed in terms of finance, markets and economics. Given the general dominance of these discourses, such

56 Anna Grear, 'Challenging Corporate "Humanity": Legal disembodiment, embodiment and human rights' (2007) 7 *H. R. L.Rev.* 511, 517.

57 In fact, they are already treated differently in at least one respect as 'A corporation holds its rights as a unitary entity, rather than a collective.' Grear, 'Challenging Corporate Humanity' (n 56) 518.

58 P1 is the most abstract, legal person, including corporations and other non-human legal entities. The numerical progression signals the addition of certain requirements, thus increasingly excluding members of P1 from P2 and P3. In short 'P1 does not (formally) depend on the physical human form of the entity (as does P2) or the mental attributes of the entity (as does P3).' Ngaire Naffine, 'Who are Law's Persons – From Cheshire Cats to Responsible Subjects' (2003) 66, *MLR* 346, 366.

59 Grear, 'Challenging Corporate Humanity' (n 56) 523. Grear argues that the paradigm legal subject is more like a corporation than a person. 'At the structural level, the artificiality of law better suits corporations than concrete human beings. At the ideological level, the construction of the archetypal liberal legal actor, law's privileged insider, the acquisitive, rational, narcissistic, will-driver, self-interested possessive quasi-disembodied individual is an almost precise match for the corporation as the acquisitive persona of capital' (524).

framing is perhaps unsurprising. Indeed, some of these strategies are appealing: setting out the relative costs of prevention versus cure for environmental damage, for example, can be persuasive. To be sure, cost benefit models exist that are able to capture a wide range of effects. However, there are at least three problems with this approach. First, it may be very difficult to tell the difference between competing CBA (cost benefit analysis) models. Without very close attention and relevant expertise, it is hard to know whether all 'costs' have been appropriately allocated. Moreover, some costs may be so difficult to quantify that they are simply left off the balance sheet.[60] I am not suggesting that economically-based arguments have no place; they may well persuade precisely the individuals who would resist other strategies, but they need to be carefully considered. The second problem is that use of these arguments may suggest that economic costs are the most suitable way of determining value and action. The choice of economic and market value over other values not only obscures alternative framings, it has further consequences. The third problem relates to these consequences in that once an economic frame is chosen, property rights become foundational. Wolcher argues:

> Given CBA's [Cost Benefit Analysis] uncritical attitude about questions of distributive justice, the legitimacy of its policy or welfare recommendations necessarily depends on the unquestioned legitimacy of the particular property rights that underlie the relevant supply and [150] demand functions, and that co-determine the 'psychological reference point' for people's subjective beliefs about ownership.[61]

CBA depends on a concept of property. Undertaking a CBA necessarily involves the use of property, money and related constructs. At least two things follow from this. First, conceiving of environmental issues in monetary terms suggests that money is all that is required to restore ecosystems. One does not need to be an environmental scientist or a hydrologist to know once ancient aquifers are depleted, glaciers melted and water cycles broken, money alone is not enough to fix the problem. We simply do not yet have the technology to repair a broken environment. Second, and more importantly, any such costing also trades off real human lives. In this paradigm, where all losses need to be 'costed', loss of human life is simply another cost to be factored in. This may be assessed in terms of human economic productivity. But given the most vulnerable (and generally speaking the least culpable) may be costed very modestly (as such people don't contribute to an economy in 'acceptable' ways), large numbers of individuals can be sacrificed with very little impact on the 'bottom line'. As Radin concludes 'the rhetoric of commodification has led us into an unreflective use of market characterizations and comparisons for almost everything people may value, and hence into an inferior

60 Kysar (n 7) 2126.

61 Louis E. Wolcher, 'Senseless Kindness: The Politics of Cost-Benefit Analysis' (2007) 25, *Law and Inequality: A Journal of Theory and Practice* 147, 149–50.

conception of personhood'.[62] There is a further indirect costing of human lives. If a living person is not considered to be 'worth' the cost of their maintenance, their life is easily disposed of. In short, treating natural resources like water as property, as commodities that can be costed, prioritises the nominal form of 'good' rather than the adjectival form. The issue of water rights boils down exactly to the difference between 'good' as chattel and 'good' as human value.

The ease with which the noun and adjective can be conflated should not be underestimated. Here I take as an example a recent book authored by the economist Paul Collier. His argument that 'environmentalists and economists need each other ... because they are on the same side in a war that is being lost' suggests that he values the sustainable use of natural resources.[63] However, it is not clear that economics as a discipline (without more) values the environment as an adjectival rather than a nominal good. Indeed, Collier goes on to state that 'natural assets are being depleted and natural liabilities accumulated in a manner that both environmentalists and economists would judge to be unethical'.[64] The use of 'natural assets' and 'natural liabilities' may well be ironically metaphorical.[65] However, that the terms are used at all is the first sign that economists may not actually be on the same side as environmentalists. Collier does acknowledge the difference between the 'natural' and the human made world when he makes a distinction between 'private assets' and 'natural assets'. Thus, while 'wild fish' are natural assets, farmed fish are private assets.[66] This appears straightforward, especially if temporal and spatial context is confined.[67] But the distinction collapses as Collier argues that the interests of future generations are best protected through regimes of private property: 'In the absence of private property rights all natural assets are liable to be plundered unless defended by local social conventions, and such conventions do not usually survive rapid social change'.[68] This turns 'natural assets' into property for which a specific entity is responsible.

---

62 Margaret Jane Radin, 'Market Inalienability' (1987) 100(8), *Harv. L. Rev.* 1849, 1936.

63 Paul Collier, *The Plundered Planet: How to Reconcile Prosperity with Nature* (Allen Lane 2010) 9.

64 Collier (n 63) 9.

65 However, when Collier writes 'some recent work on climate change within the Utilitarian framework has argued that without action climate change will be so severe that the future will be poorer than we are' (n 63) 200. I am compelled to point out that, 'without action climate change will be so severe that there will be no human future'. No doubt I am somewhat apocalyptic in my general assessment of the situation.

66 Collier (n 63) 160.

67 Nevertheless, there is, for example, no consideration in this distinction of how farming fish may have effect on wild fish or the broader environment.

68 Collier (n 63) 161.

Collier's position is essentially a reprise of the 'tragedy of the commons' argument,[69] such that the only responsible kind of ownership is private ownership.[70] Suggesting that the 'most reasonable place to lodge the rights to natural assets is with governments'[71] Collier confirms that 'natural assets' should be treated as property, that somewhat undoes his distinction between natural and private assets. He also implicitly relies on governments acting in the interests of current and future generations. However, as Collier himself goes on to demonstrate, governments do not always act in their own best long-term interests.[72] In short, by Collier's own account, it is not clear that private ownership really does protect resources. Moreover, in the case of water, Hughes points out that this approach, that led to the privatisation of water services, 'ha[s] neither conserved water nor protected its sources'.[73] Nor have such models delivered water to the poor.[74]

Collier uses the tragedy of the commons argument to suggest that environmental protection and intergenerational justice depend on seeing the environment as property. And while the 'tragedy of the commons' narrative does have a certain persuasive power, it relies on foregrounding some historical examples at the expense of others.[75] It also appears to ignore the market forces that often catalyse such a 'tragedy' as well as the socio-economic position of the protagonists. That is, it is possible to understand the tragedy of the commons as precipitated by the pressures of an external market, as exploiting the commons only really makes sense if there is market to sell produce to. More often than not, the tragedies are blamed on 'irresponsible' individuals and communities, followed by recommendations that the community engage even more deeply with exactly the economic models and markets that first precipitated the tragedy.

Doubtless the clear delineation of property, protection of ownership and rights, has benefits, among them, the ability of owners to trade their goods. 'Trade in turn yields information about who *wants* what and how much, permitting individuals

69 Gareth Hardin, 'The Tragedy of the Commons' (1968) 162, *Science* 1243 http://dieoff.org/page95.htm. Accessed 2 August 2012.

70 For a summary – though not endorsement of this position – see Bakker (n 11) 430.

71 Collier (n 63) 162.

72 Collier (n 63) Chapter 6, 'Selling the Family Silver'.

73 Hughes (n 14) 535.

74 Hughes (n 14) 535.

75 See Avital Margalit, 'Commons and Legality', in Gregory S. Alexander and Eduardo M. Peñalver (eds), *Property and Community* (OUP 2010) 141; Carole M. Rose, 'Expanding the Choices for the Global Commons: Comparing Newfangled Tradable Allowance Schemes to Old-Fashioned Common Property Regimes' (1999), *Faculty of Scholarship Series*, paper 1803 http://digitalcommons.law.yale.edu/fss_papers/1803. Accessed 17 May 2011; (1999) 10 (1) *DELPF* 45-72 ; Carol M. Rose 2002. 'Common Property, Regulatory Property and Environmental Protection' in Elinor Ostrom et al (eds) *The Drama of the Commons* (National Academies Press 2002) 233, 251–3.

to specialize their labor on the things that others desire.'[76] For many products, this may be a synergistic relationship; beneficial for both consumer and labourer. However, in the case of water, something is left out. Trade, and the commodification that precedes it, provides information about desire. Eventually, it also provides information about willingness and ability to pay for the satisfaction of this desire. Need, however, is not at issue.[77] Nor is vulnerability or any difference in power between individuals, even though such disadvantage may be produced by the very same economic systems that encourage the acquisition of property.[78] As Collins-Chobanian notes, 'The market economy is fuelled by environmental resources, and does not always meet needs, while destroying the ability of many to meet their own needs from such methods as biodiverse, traditional agriculture.'[79] The needs of the market are put before needs of people; goods that are property are more important than what is good for people. As noted, the central term here is 'good', both adjective and noun. The question that emerges is thus, is it always good to see something as a good? The presence of two meanings in the same form suggests a sleight of hand but also the possibility for re-invention.[80]

Before natural goods can be properly protected, they need to be properly characterised. That is, if they remain with a property frame, it will be very difficult to challenge their owners' rights (whatever type of legal person this may be) to do with them as they wish. This is the problem in Plachimada. Further, any model used to protect natural goods for the human good needs to acknowledge people, the environment and their interdependence. To return to the Plachimada judgments, the decision at first instance suggests such a model in its reliance on the public trust. As it stands, the public trust does not completely escape the problem of

76 Carol M. Rose, 'The Several Futures of Property: Of Cyberspace and Folk Tales, Emission Trades and Ecosystems' (1998), *Faculty Scholarship Series* paper 1804 http://digitalcommons.law.yale.edu/fss_papers/1804 (1998-1999) 83 *Minn. L. Rev.* 129, 131, emphasis in original.

77 Even the hybrid property that Rose discusses cannot escape this dynamic (Rose (n 76) 164). That is not to say that the hybrid approach is not the most promising, especially when communities are legitimate owners (Rose (n 76) 177). It is, however, a second step.

78 Martha Albertson Fineman, 'The Vulnerable Subject: Anchoring Equality in the Human Condition' (2008) 20(1) *Yale J. L. & Feminism* 1.

79 Shari Collins-Chobanian, 'Beyond Sax and Welfare Interests: A Case for Environmental Rights' (2000) 22(2) *Environmental Ethics* 133, 141.

80 Looking back, we find a similar shift in the case of 'right'. As Lametti notes, following Finis, 'there is a watershed moment in the meaning of the word ius between the time of Thomas Aquinas and Francisco Suarez. When Aquinas wrote in the twelfth century, ius was primarily an objective term meaning "what was right" or "what was just". By the time Suarez wrote three centuries later, the meaning of ius had shifted to being a claim right against other persons or groups.' David Lametti, 'The Objects of Virtue' In Gregory S. Alexander and Eduardo M. Peñalver (eds), *Property and Community* (OUP 2010) 1, 23; see also Costas Douzinas, *The End of Human Rights* (Hart 2000) 53; Grear *Redirecting Human Rights* (n 12) 70.

property. But work on the public trust, particularly on its origins, does suggest scaffolding that could support a different imagining of water as a human right.

The Public Trust

Relying on previous decisions and jurisprudence related to Article 21 of the Indian Constitution, K. Balakrishnan Nair, J. asserts 'it can be safely concluded that the underground water belongs to the public'.[81] Protecting the interests of the villagers, his decision was based on a determination that water is a public trust for which the state is responsible. The public trust, however, does not take water out of a property frame; it 'belongs' to the public. Koonan notes that 'The basis of the [public trust] doctrine emanates from the property relationship',[82] but the connection between public trust and property is not universally endorsed. In relation to India, Cullet states that 'in the context of water, [the public trust] provides a basis for considering water without starting from the perspective of property rights'.[83] But as the Division bench decision demonstrates, neither a public trust of water nor Article 21 rights are firmly enough entrenched in Indian law to withstand private property arguments. The Plachimada case is thus better explained by Koonan's position on the nature of the public trust. However, as long as the public trust has a property element it may well be vulnerable to other property claims.

The public trust also puts the state in a powerful position. Sax's classic account of the public trust acknowledges both the central role of the state and the centrality of property. As well as being responsible for a public trust in terms of its management, the state is also the original 'owner':

> The most common theory advanced in support of a special trust obligation is a property notion: historically, it is said, certain resources were granted by the government to the general public in the same sense that a tract of public land may be granted to a specific individual.[84]

This responsibility of the state for public trusts is made clear at first instance by K. Balakrishnan Nair, J: 'The Panchayat and the State are bound to prevent [Coca-Cola's extraction of water].'[85] However, the public trust does not provide a great deal of room for individuals; indeed, the status of individuals in relation to the public trust generally is not settled. Sax points out that while certain uses 'such as navigation and fishing' were 'preserved for the benefit of the public' it

81 (n 41) 13.
82 Koonan (n 24) 8.
83 Cullet (n 24) 332.
84 Joseph L. Sax, 'The Public Trust Doctrine in Natural Resource Law: Effective Judicial Intervention' (1970) 68(3), *Mich.L. Rev.* 471, 478.
85 (n 41) 13.

was not clear whether individuals could enforce their rights 'against a recalcitrant government'.[86] There are some restrictions on the state, however, and if we pay attention to these it is possible to argue for a very different kind of trust.

Sax notes three restrictions on government activity with respect to trust property. If we focus on the details of these, it may be possible to ground the public trust in something other than property.

> … first, the property subject to the trust must not be only used for a public purpose, but it must be held available for use by the general public; second, the property may not be sold, even for a fair cash equivalent; and third, the property must be maintained for particular types of uses.[87]

The requirement that the trust be generally available invites a conception of the trust outside the property frame. The restriction on selling continues the alienation of the public trust from the world of property. It could be argued that these two restrictions move the public trust from the domain of property to the domain of 'thing'. However, it is Sax's description of the third restriction that is most promising, especially as it relates to water.

> Either it is urged that the resource must be held available for certain *traditional uses*, such as navigation, recreation or fishery, or it is said that the uses which are made of the property must be in some sense related to the *natural uses peculiar to that resource.*[88]

While the use of 'resource' may suggest a discourse and practice of property and ownership (and thus easily appropriated into that domain), 'traditional use' and 'natural use' work against this. The plain meaning of 'tradition' as well as the examples given, point to customary usage of an area. While recognition of such customary activity is important, especially for establishing claims to land,[89] 'uses peculiar to that resource' suggests a less time-bound approach, pointing to a particular quality of the entity that other substances do not have. In these terms, one of the 'peculiar' and natural uses of fresh water is the sustenance of human life.[90]

86 Sax, 'The Public Trust Doctrine' (n 84) 475.

87 Sax, 'The Public Trust Doctrine' (n 84) 477.

88 Sax, 'The Public Trust Doctrine' (n 84) 477; my emphasis.

89 For a historical perspective, see Andrea Loux Jarman, 'Urban Commons: From Customary Use to Community Right on Scotland's Bleaching Greens', in A. Lewis et al (eds), *Law in the City* (Four Courts Press 2007); Andrea Loux Jarman, 'Customary Rights in Scots Law: Test Cases on Access to Land in the Nineteenth Century' (2007) 28(2), *The Journal of Legal History* 207.

90 In Plachimada, the Division bench were curiously blind to this. Commenting on the Single bench decision, they note 'No reason is however given as to why agriculture has a priority than an industrial activity' (n 43) 36.

This view is also compatible with Sax's account of the conceptual support for the public trust. 'The approach with the greatest historical support holds that certain interests are so intrinsically important to every citizen that their free availability tends to mark the *society* as one of *citizens* rather than serfs.'[91] The move from 'serf' to 'citizen' suggests a possible parallel move for water, from being seen as property to being understood as something else.[92] Sax continues, 'An allied principle holds that certain interests are so particularly the gifts of nature's bounty that they ought to be reserved for the whole populace.'[93] This is not a regime of property rights, rather, it is about relationships and interdependence. This is particularly clear in relation to water.

> Finally, there is often a recognition, albeit one that has been irregularly perceived in legal doctrine, that certain uses have a peculiarly public nature that makes their adaptation to private use inappropriate. The best known example is found in the rule of water law that one does not own a property right in water in the same way he owns his watch or his shoes, but that he owns only an usufruct – an interest that incorporates the needs of others. It is thus thought to be incumbent upon the government to regulate water uses for the general benefit of the community and to take account thereby of the public nature and the interdependency which the physical quality of the resource implies.[94]

This offers some hope. If we rather focus on seeing water as a 'gift', something in which people have an 'interest', an interest that is not based on conceptions of property, we find a more appropriate ground. Making this clear requires that attention be paid to the 'peculiar' nature of water, and the natural environment more generally, coupled with the interests of the embodied person.[95] Regimes of property need to be limited by the human frame, by the needs of the body. Takacs argues:

> … human laws must reflect some ecologically ordained restraints. To survive as a civilization, or as a species, means to heed the limits a mechanical natural world imposes on us. We are biological creatures who pretend we transcend biology. 'Private property' advocates sometimes argue that they are best stewards of the land, but it would take several more papers to document how reality often fails to reflect this. In the name of capitalism – a social and economic system that largely ignores the ecological basis of our existence – private property owners

91 Sax, 'The Public Trust Doctrine' (n 84) 484; my emphasis.

92 See n. 80.

93 Sax, 'The Public Trust Doctrine' (n 84) 484.

94 Sax, 'The Public Trust Doctrine' (n 84) 485.

95 Bakker does this by suggesting that 'The more appropriate, but less widely used, antonym of water as a "commodity" would more properly be a water "commons".' Bakker (n 11) 436.

> exploit resources we increasingly recognize we need for the public good, or even for human survival.[96]

The public trust suggests that water might not be property; but the move away from the property frame needs to be more emphatic. It is possible to develop a model from other currents of trust law to better protect the interests Takacs identifies. This will rely on paying attention to what is good for people. To do this, I trace the public trust back to its source, Roman law, in order to find yet another peculiarity that allows 'good' to be understood not as a commodity but in relation to human beings.

Roman Law

As K. Balakrishnan Nair, J. notes, the public trust can be traced back to Roman law.[97] While called 'common property', some forms are less like property than others.[98] *Res communes* (open to all by their nature – air and oceans), *res publicae* (things belonging to the public and open to them because of law) and *res universitatie* (belonging to a public group in corporate capacity) are all in one way or another open to more than one individual, while *res nullius* (things belonging to no-one as not yet appropriated) have the potential to be owned through appropriation. There is a further category: *res divini juris*.

> The things classed under this rubric in Roman law – temples, tombs, religious statuary – were considered to belong to no one because they were [109] dedicated to the service of the gods, or because an offence to them was considered to be offensive to the gods. Such things were in a class of *res nullius* because although they are physically capable of appropriation, they are still unowned; the impediment to propertisation is not natural but divine.[99]

This definition suggests a valuable model for environmental goods as while the physical possibility of appropriation is acknowledged *res divini juris* have nevertheless been taken outside the frame of property. For this category to be useful in relation to water, some framing in terms of the human (rather than the divine) needs to be undertaken. While *res divini juris* was recognised so as not to offend the gods, the environment needs protection so as to not let people suffer

96 David Takacs, 'The Public Trust Doctrine, Environmental Human Rights and the Future of Private Property' (2008) 16 *N. Y. U. Envtl. L. J.* 711 http://ielrc.org/content/a0804.pdf. Accessed 1 August 2012, 711, 742.

97 (n 41) 13.

98 Carol M. Rose, 'Romans, Roads and Romantic Creators: Traditions of Public Property in the Information Age' (2003) 66(1/2), *LCP* 89, 91.

99 Rose 'Romans, Roads and Romantic Creators' (n 98) 108–9.

and die. The living person, the human who needs food, water and air, is that which should not be offended when it comes to considering how to frame the environment in terms of a trust. Thus, rather than the divine being at the centre, the vulnerable, embodied human is placed at the heart of the model proposed here.

Modelled directly on *res divini juris*, I propose the 'human trust'. Constructing a Latin version may help pin down exactly which aspects of the human are to be highlighted here, hence *res mortalis naturae*. The mortal human (*mortalis*) takes the place of the immortal god (*divini*) while law (*juris*) is replaced with nature (*naturae*). The following definition is guided by Rose's description of *res divini juris*. Thus, *res mortalis naturae* are 'dedicated' in the sense of being necessary, to the existence of people. Offending such things, by destroying or polluting them, is offensive to all human kind because of the interconnection between geographically diverse and even apparently unconnected natural resources. *Res mortalis naturae* are capable of appropriation in a sense, but the impediment to this is both natural and ethical in so far as the consequences of appropriation ultimately lead to putting a price on human life. Protecting these things is good for people; not doing so is bad for people. Because people rely on the human trust, *res mortalis naturae* would also include *res communes*.

Proposing a new phrase, in a dead language may seem otiose. Clearly new phrases are not always useful. They can, however, focus attention and shift frames of reference. The relative opacity of a concept framed in a dead language demands our further attention. It also bears traces of its provenance and thus may make it more likely to be taken up by judicial regimes. Ultimately, the proposed category seeks to do two things. First, it acknowledges that natural resources do have property-like elements. It is important to remember this, as it reminds us of the temptation to treat them simply as self-contained objects. Second, paradoxically, it helps us to see that natural systems are also very unlike property because of the interrelationship of ecological systems, the dependence of humans on these systems and the interdependence of people. Natural systems are unlike property in the same way that we have come to understand that people are not property. The move from serf to citizen that Sax describes involved recognising that people are not property. (I will return to the problem that 'citizen' presents.) The argument here is that to treat water as property is tantamount to treating people as property; the link between the two needs to be recognised. Granting a legal person absolute rights over natural goods ultimately grants them power over human life. The human trust seeks to remind us of this and to remind us that natural persons have very different needs to disembodied legal entities. By taking the natural world outside the frame of property relations, the human trust can also act to prevent the dominance of property rights that we see in Plachimada. The result of the human trust is that no one 'owns' the water. In short, the human trust effects a transition from water as a good to recognising that water is good for people.

Anticipatory Negligence

The human trust seeks simply to provide a focal point for the fact that people depend on each other and on the environment. It seeks to take the environment out of property relations and prioritise the human body, paying attention to the literally thirsty body of the person rather than the metaphorical thirst of the corporation. But the human trust is only one part of what would have assisted the people of Plachimada. Fortunately, recognition of the human trust has other consequences. Specifically, the very nature of the human trust entails responsibilities and obligations; it reveals a duty of care. This duty has political consequences, but it could also underpin a legal action that I call 'anticipatory negligence'. Obviously such an action falls into the field of tort law. This is an appropriate legal domain as tort law resonates with the concerns of the human trust. While contract law is generally concerned with property, tort law is concerned with relationships.[100] Exploring the nature of this proposed action provides a way of starting to think through the political consequences of the human trust and the duty of care.

The relevant relationship in tort law is that which gives rise to the duty of care. In the case of Plachimada, a rather literal interpretation of the 'neighbour' principle would be appropriate. Coca-Cola were the physical neighbours of those seeking redress. But there is more to the principle than this.

> Who, then, in law is my neighbour? The answer seems to be – persons who are so closely and directly affected by my act that I ought reasonably to have them in contemplation as being so affected when I am directing my mind to the acts or omissions which are called in question.[101]

Because of the interwoven nature of the environment, all persons may be 'closely and directly affected' by damage to it. The duty of care that arises from the human trust is one that exists between all people. It is a result of the fact that when it comes to the environment, we are all neighbours. This too aligns with the broader concerns of negligence law that

> reflects not some artificial limitation on our imagined natural freedom, but our initial indebtedness to 'a neighbour'. It is in fact a profound statement of the human necessity of what has come to be known, broadly, as the 'duty of care'.[102]

This duty also has political consequences, to which I return below.

Protection of the human trust may not seem well suited to negligence law, as it is not usually possible to ask for redress before the damaging act. But there

---

100 Desmond Manderson, 'Levinas and the Philosophy of Negligence' (2006) 14, *Tort L. Rev* 1, 6.

101 *Donoghue (or McAlister) v Stevenson* [1932] AC 562, 580 (Lord Atkin).

102 Manderson (n 100) 9.

are some exceptions to this. Indeed, anticipatory negligence simply develops an existing remedy available in tort law, an anticipatory injunction. 'A *quia timet* injunction may be issued to restrain a tort which has not yet been committed, but commission of which is threatened, so long as substantial damage appears imminent.'[103] Even though such injunctions are normally only available to protect property, Murphy argues that bodily integrity should be taken at least as seriously.[104] He also takes issue with any strict requirement for 'imminence' of danger focusing instead on potential harm to a person. Murphy argues that injunctions should be available 'where a claimant can show intentional or reckless conduct on the part of the defendant such that the claimant finds himself in a position of unjustifiable risk' taking into account the probability of harm and 'the particular kind of harm threatened'.[105] The argument is that such injunctions should be given, especially in cases where the damage cannot be undone. Indeed, 'there are certain kinds of risk that no level of precautions can ever justify, and which no amount of social utility can ever outweigh'.[106] This is an argument that puts the potential victim at the heart and takes the duty of care seriously: 'the effect of the injunction is to force the defendant to do the very thing that will actually protect the claimant'.[107] The 'claimant' would be any embodied person. That is, the 'risk' should be considered in relation to an embodied person rather an abstract construct.

Anticipatory negligence shows that the law can provide models for thinking and innovation even from areas that are not obviously relevant to human rights. The idea that it should be possible to stop environmental damage before it occurs is justifiable when the possible harms are considered. Because of the existing *quia timet* injunction in the common law, it does not seem impossible that something similar could be argued in cases of threats to the environment. The principle way anticipatory negligence differs from the usual tort of negligence is that it does not require actual damage. Murphy provides a justification for allowing this in terms of the severity and probability of the future damage. However, it is also worth noting that even a classic claim of negligence requires some construction of 'future' events in so far as damage must be 'foreseeable'. That is, the apparent difference in this respect between negligence and anticipatory negligence is one of degree rather than kind as the tort of negligence relies on making judgments about what was known before the damaging event. Foreseeability is one of the defining features of negligence, as such it already relies on real or constructed

103 John Murphy, *Street on Torts*. 12th ed. (OUP 2007) 646.

104 John Murphy, 'Rethinking Injunctions in Tort Law' (2007) 27(3), *OJLS* 509, 518.

105 Murphy, 'Rethinking Injunctions in Tort Law' (n 104) 510.

106 Murphy, 'Rethinking Injunctions in Tort Law' (n 104) 523.

107 Murphy, 'Rethinking Injunctions in Tort Law' (n 104) 535. 'If the hesitancy in granting mandatory injunctions is in large part associated with respect for the autonomy of the defendant who has not yet committed an actionable tort, surely it also makes sense to afford equal respect to the autonomy of the claimant whose bodily integrity is jeopardized' (533).

fore-knowledge, at least in so far as the model of 'the reasonable person' would allow. In short, negligence actions require that we imagine a parallel world, one in which the bad event did not occur. Both anticipatory negligence and negligence ask us to imagine other worlds; anticipatory negligence simply asks that action is taken before damage is done.

Anticipatory negligence would be particularly useful against large corporations and multinationals exactly because the effects they may have on the environment can be extreme, and hence present an unjustifiable risk in Murphy's terms. In assessing the 'probability' of this risk, I propose that attention be paid not only to the situation at hand[108] but also to the past behaviour of the entity in question. That is, a distinction could be made between corporations with a history of causing environmental hazards and those without such a track record. While this may seem to offend the rule of law, there is analogous precedent in tort law that simply requires a shift of perspective. Prohibitory injunctions are available against those who have already committed a tort in order to stop them repeating it.[109] While this would normally apply to commission of the same tort in the same place (repeated trespass on a piece of land, for example) in terms of the environment it is appropriate for 'place' to be globally conceived. Natural systems are not discrete. Pollution does not respect national boundaries and water flows where it will. It makes sense to conceive of the human trust as a global entity. The site of an offence against a human trust is the planet itself. Thus, if an entity has damaged the environment before, it seems reasonable that they be treated in the same way as a habitual trespasser.

Anticipatory negligence is a necessary complement to the human trust; it is a shield protecting the environment on which real people rely. The harm that it proposes to avert is not only grave, it is also irreparable. It may be that technological and scientific innovation will be able to restore ecosystems to their *ex ante* state; unless and until this is possible, such damage needs to be averted out of consideration to people, their lives and their bodies.

Trust and the Political Order

Proposing anticipatory negligence as a way of thinking about protecting the human trust and the development of the concept of the human trust itself is not ultimately about specific legal mechanisms. Rather, the human trust is a way of thinking about human relationships – with the world and with each other – outside of property and contract relations. As seen in the previous chapter, there is no return to classical politics.

108 Such consideration would include application of a strong form of the precautionary principle.

109 Murphy, *Street on Torts* (n 103) 645.

> In the camps, city and house became indistinguishable, and the possibility of differentiating between our biological body and our political body – between what is incommunicable and mute and what is communicable and sayable – was taken from us forever. And we are not only, in Foucault's words, animals whose life as living beings is at issue in their politics, but also – inversely – citizens whose very politics is at issue in their natural body.[110]

Classical politics is the sovereign ban, the social contract that creates and excludes bare life. The human trust is the antithesis of this. While the contractual person is a citizen subject, the human trust person is bare life, any embodied person. The human trust puts bare life at the centre and conceives of human relationships not as contractual but as based on trust and interdependence. While the body as index provides a way of looking, the human trust takes seriously the consequences of this index as it seeks to acknowledge the vulnerable body on which it relies. As the human trust is ultimately concerned with sustenance of life, it suggests a new political order, one in which the thirsty person rather than the citizen is the primary entity.

Above, the move from 'serf' to 'citizen' noted by Sax in relation to the public trust was mentioned. The 'human' of the human trust is a further development. While the serf is essentially owned, the citizen is subject to the nation. The human is responsible not to an owner, nor to a nation, but to other humans. The human must respond to the Other as the existence of any person depends on the existence of other people. A person cannot actually come to exist in the absence of other people. For the continued existence of humans, there needs to be more than one person. The human trust is predicated on the existence of more than one person, on the continuing existence of people.

The human trust also makes clear that the existence of other people, the reliance of each person on other people, involves a duty. Just as there is a duty to the natural world, there is also a duty to the Other. In a sense this is no more than a duty to self, fully conceived. If we consider this relationship in the context of the human trust, we are left with infinite responsibility for the Other in the absence of any claim to property (hers or ours). Rather, we are all bound together in the human trust. We are all then non-owners, of the environment and of each other, and yet nevertheless infinitely responsible for natural resources because of the responsibility we have to the Other. This is the logical consequence of the body as index, the interdependence of people and our necessary connection to the natural world.

It is difficult to say more about what this political order would look like as it cannot be structured in the same way as existing states and nations. In a sense, the structure is beside the point. What matters is attention to both the individual and the corpus of bodies that inhabit the globe. What needs to happen is for the

---

110 Giorgio Agamben, *Homo Sacer Sovereign Power and Bare Life*, Daniel Heller-Roazen (trans) (Stanford University Press 1998) 187–8.

citizen to become a person. We cannot change the human condition, but it can be acknowledged. The issue then becomes not one of political theory so much as empirical questions. How can water resources be managed in the interests of all bare life? What needs to happen to global food production and distribution to ensure that it reaches hungry bodies? These are political issues, but their answers depend on accessing the best information we have about how environmental systems work while acknowledging our fallabalism in this, and all other, matters. It is a paradigm shift, one that focuses on the bare life of whatever being all the while knowing that the suffering of each and every one can never be completely removed. This does not mean that we should not try. We need to learn to see the world, and each other, differently.

A Coda

We are water.

By weight, over half the human body is water. We are fluidly connected to the world and to each other through this substance. Water, however, is endlessly variable. While essential to life, it can also spell death; whether because of invisible contamination, mass movements of it in the form of tidal waves, rain and tsunamis, or the simple truth that humans cannot breathe under water. The body will die of thirst before it dies of hunger and yet in English we lack a verb to ask for the watery equivalent of food. While a person can say 'feed me', there is no equivalent for water. That it is so fundamental may, paradoxically, explain why this need is often forgotten in the West. In the UK, some doctors have found it necessary to 'prescribe' water for patients as their thirst is not being quenched.[111] We only think about water when it may be taken away. But for there to be life, there must be water. The body as index presupposes water, but this does not guarantee its continued existence or availability.

The needs of the body have to come from somewhere and this somewhere, the natural environment, needs to be protected if bodies are to continue to exist. The human trust proposed here does not require leaving the natural world to itself. It is too late for this. Rather, actions that stop the environment sustaining itself must cease. It seems to me that we need a way of conceiving of the global commons humans inhabit. This conception needs to be something that is itself human; if not, we will neither be able to comprehend it nor act on it in any meaningful way. In the next chapter, I consider this by paying attention to a uniquely human attribute: language.

111 Jeremy Laurance, 'Hospital patients "left so thirsty doctors had to prescribe water"', *The Independent* 26 May 2011 www.independent.co.uk. Accessed 5 June 2013.

Chapter 6
The Embodied Mind

So far I have argued that environmental rights and the basic needs of the body as index are human rights. The body as index, as zero institution, shows us that bodies need food, air, water, shelter and sleep. These are necessary for the body to live. The body also shows us that it depends on other bodies; indeed, the existence of a body presupposes the existence of other people. The previous chapter argued that seeing the environment in terms of a human trust is necessary as it takes natural goods outside of the property frame. Because of the effects of property regimes on natural resources, this reframing is necessary. Indeed, environmental rights are the most important human rights, as without a functioning environment not even bare life can be sustained. But seeing the environment as something humans all depend on needs a frame. The 'environment' is a somewhat of an abstract idea even though it is directly related to our physical existence. Moreover, as Chakrabarty's work makes plain, the environment is now also a human construction in so far as humans now wield a geological force.

In this chapter, I argue that as well as seeing the human body as a frame for human rights another frame is required. That is, in order to be able to conceive of the world as a human trust, a global commons, a global frame is needed. This frame is ultimately a way of seeing that all humans share something, that we all depend on the human trust that is the natural environment. In order to arrive at this global frame, I start with something else that all people share, that is, language. Language is closely linked to the body; it is corporeal in a variety of ways. For speech a body is required while writing also presupposes a body. This chapter shows that the relationship between language and the body is more complex than this.

As language is a distinctly human ability, it is perhaps surprising that the study of language has not played a larger part in the discussion of human rights foundations or the substance of human rights. Part of the reason for this may be that generally language is seen as a problem in the context of human rights, especially when it comes to law. As discussed in earlier chapters, language is associated with the violence of categorisation and the proliferation of unsatisfiable rights.[1]

1 Colin Perrin, 'Breath from Nowhere: The Silent "Foundation" of Human Rights' (2004) 13(1), *Social and Legal Studies* 133, 134; James R. Dawes, 'Language, Violence and Human rights Law' (1999) 11, *Yale Journal of Law & the Humanities* 215. Douzinas argues that language is a problem in relation to rights: 'In semiotic terms, the right to work cannot be distinguished easily from the right to party. If something can be put into language, it may acquire rights and can certainly become the object of rights.' Further, 'Rights are linguistic

Language either writes the body by discursively constituting it, or cuts the body off from itself. Language, especially the language of law, is not an appropriate way of representing the body and its experiences. Conklin observes:

> The expert's language cannot recognize the pain and suffering which any one individual or group has previously experienced without *re*-presenting the pain through signifiers which experts alone can 'know'.[2]

Language and the human, language and the body are necessary and yet apparently ill-suited companions. For example, while Eagleton takes for granted that people are 'made up of both a body and a language' he argues this is not a good fit.[3] The body will 'never be entirely at home in language' and will 'instead be scarred and fissured by it'.[4] While language means 'our bodies can transcend themselves' it also means that we can never resolve the gap between the body and language or between the local and the universal.[5]

Work in linguistics, however, is rather less bleak. In this chapter, research from cognitive linguistics is considered as it shows the close link between the body and language.[6] This suggests that the problem is not language as such but the way it

---

fictions that work and recognitions of a desire that never ends.' Costas Douzinas, *The End of Human Rights* (Hart 2000) 255, 261.

2 William E. Conklin, 'Human Rights, Language and Law: A Survey of Semiotics and Phenomenology' (1995) 27(1), *Ottawa Law Review* 129, 137.

3 Terry Eagleton, 'Local and Global', in Obrad Savić (ed.), *The Politics of Human Rights* (Verso 1999) 258.

4 Eagleton (n 3) 258.

5 Eagleton (n 3) 258.

6 There is also important work in linguistics and human rights that can't be properly covered here. This research argues for language as a human right. This goal of this research is to protect endangered languages with the discourse of human rights. Likening the death of languages to genocide (hence 'linguicide'), the persuasive power of two key discourses is used: human rights and ecological diversity. Skutnabb-Kangas points out that ecological and linguistic diversity often coincide geographically. This connection foregrounds the environment and also makes it possible to defend language diversity with arguments usually used to argue for ecological diversity. Just as environmental biodiversity can be defended in terms of its pragmatic benefits (in terms of resources for science and medicine) linguistic diversity can be argued for in a similar way especially as languages bring with them knowledge of the natural world. Tove Skutnabb-Kangas and Robert Phillipson, 'A Human Rights Perspective on Language Ecology' (2008) 9, *Encyclopedia of language and education* 3. Tove Skutnabb-Kangas, 'Language Ecology', in Jan-Ola Östman and Jef Verschueren (eds), *Pragmatics in Practice* (John Benjamins 2011) 177. Tove Skutnabb-Kangas, *Linguistic Genocide in Education – Or Worldwide Diversity and Human Rights?* (Orient Longman 2008). See also Turner who includes a right to language as the 'fundamental cultural right'; 'Without a recognized language, [people] are second-class citizens within somebody else's language community.' Bryan S Turner, *Vulnerability and Human Rights* (Penn State University Press 2006) 49, 50.

has been understood and used in relation to the body. Work in cognitive linguistics confirms three things. First, the body/mind and language are intimately connected; the mind is embodied. Second, this is a universal connection with some generic level similarities. Third, it confirms what work in human rights tells us; there is cultural variation that needs to be taken into account. Even so, there are some conceptual structures that appear to be common across cultures. It is important that these be treated carefully, however, because, as scholars working in the field argue, just because something is shared does not mean it is beneficial. Care also needs to be taken in moving from conceptual universals to what would be human rights. This is clear when considering claims that morality is somehow innate. Such arguments often rely on a particular view of evolution but as cognitive linguistics shows, the values and metaphors we live can be interrogated, questioned and changed.

The frame I propose as a supplement to the human body as frame draws on insights from cognitive linguistics and the nature of the physical environment. Taking these two together allows the invention of a new frame for thinking about our relationship with the world, a frame that is compatible with shared conceptual structures. I begin by examining Lakoff and Johnson's account of the embodied mind that includes attention to their model of metaphor as conceptual. How this model works, that there seem to be generic conceptual universals and culturally specific metaphors, will be explained by looking at metaphors of time, thought and emotion. This model of metaphor also draws attention to the importance of interaction with the world. Moreover, the interaction between people and the world allows a critical space for the re-evaluation of metaphors and values that appear to be natural. I then deal briefly with the argument that morality is somehow innate, a result of evolution. Finally, I suggest that we need a different frame; we need to look at ourselves from outside.

The Body and the Mind

As Chapter 3 argued, there is a close connection between knowledge, self and embodiment; our experience of the world is necessarily mediated by our corporeal state. Language also depends on embodiment in so far as we need bodies to speak and to hear others' voices. But the connection between body and language is more intimate than this. Perhaps the best known study of the connection between mind and body is Lakoff and Johnson's *Philosophy in the Flesh*. In this work, Lakoff and Johnson argue that embodiment has a profound effect on both thought and language.

> There is no severing, separation from, or bleaching out of the bodily dimensions of meaning. Mind is embodied, meaning is embodied, and thought is embodied in this most profound sense. This is the substance of *embodied* realism.

> Embodied realism, as we understand it, is the view that the locus of experience, meaning, and thought is the ongoing series of embodied organism-environment interactions that constitute our understanding of the world. According to such a view, there is no ultimate separation of mind and body, and we are always 'in touch' with our world through our embodied acts and experiences.[7]

The consequences of the connection between mind, language and body are far reaching, as taking embodiment seriously requires a reconfiguration of what we understand by 'truth'. '*What we take to be true in a situation depends on our embodied understanding of the situation* ... Truth for us, any truth that we can have access to, depends on such embodied understanding.'[8] It may be that there is a truth, a reality, that exceeds human perceptual capacity, but as embodied beings we will never have access to it.[9] For better or worse, we orient to the world through our bodies.[10] This is, because of our embodied nature, unavoidable. More importantly, the way humans think and speak cannot be separated from corporeal, embodied existence.[11]

> The problem with classical disembodied scientific realism is that it takes two intertwined and inseparable dimensions of all experience – the awareness of the experiencing organism and the stable entities and structures it encounters – and erects them as separate and distinct entities called subjects and objects. What

---

7 Mark Johnson and George Lakoff, 'Why Cognitive Linguistics Requires Embodied Realism' (2002) 13(3), *Cognitive Linguistics* 245, 249.

8 George Lakoff and Mark Johnson, *Philosophy in the Flesh* (Basic Books 1999) 102; emphasis in original.

Rohrer points out that 'embodiment' is a contested term in cognitive linguistics. He outlines ten meanings of the concept as relevant to cognition. Tim Rohrer 'Pragmatism, Ideology and Embodiment: William James and the Philosophical Foundations of Cognitive Linguistics' in René Dirven, Bruce Hawkins, Esra Sandikcioglu (eds), *Language and Ideology: Volume I: Theoretical Cognitive Approaches* (John Benjamins 2000) 49.

9 As Putnam puts it, 'We need not entertain the idea that something could be a good solution although human beings are in principle unable to recognize that it is. That sort of rampant Platonism is incoherent.' Hilary Putnam, 'Are Values Made or Discovered' in *The Collapse of the Fact/Value Dichotomy: and other essays including the Rosenthal Lectures* (Harvard UP 2002) 109.

10 Lakoff and Johnson, *Philosophy in the Flesh* (n 8) 34.

11 Lakoff and Johnson identify two kinds of embodiment, or rather, two facets of the connection between mind and body. The first, 'phenomenological embodiment' is related to how 'we schematize our own bodies and things we interact with daily', the second, 'neural embodiment' is connected to neural mechanisms which develop in an interactive way with physical senses (n 8) 36. Thus, their work connects with and informs a number of fields of enquiry including neurobiology, linguistics and psychology. It is the interaction between the neural and the physical that matters and the constraints and affordances that this sets up. That is, the connection between mind and body is not a deterministic one.

> disembodied realism (what is sometimes called 'metaphysical' or 'external' realism) misses is that, as embodied, imaginative creatures, we never were separated or divorced from reality in the first place. What has always made science possible is our embodiment, not our transcendence of it, and our imagination, not our avoidance of it.[12]

The distinction between self and the world, between body and mind, are human inventions. They are categories that people have invented. That is not to say that there is anything wrong with categories as such.

> Living systems must categorise. Since we are neural beings, our categories are formed though our embodiment … the categories we form are part of our experience! … We cannot, as some meditative traditions suggest, 'get beyond' our categories and have a purely uncategorized and unconceptualized experience.[13]

And while the imperative to categorise may suggest that specific categories are inevitable, this is not the case. Categories are required but what they are can be chosen. For this to be done, it is important to understand what these categories look like and how they are formed. Work in the field of cognitive linguistics reveals that many of these categories are informed by our experience as embodied beings: 'The resources of our bodily experience are appropriated for abstract thinking.'[14] Interaction with the world, and with other beings, leads to our categories and our metaphors.[15] How this works will be detailed presently in relation to time and space and emotion. First, Lakoff and Johnson's understanding of metaphor needs to be outlined, as this is how bodily experience and language come together.

Metaphor

Metaphor is fundamental in Lakoff and Johnson's work, however their model should not be confused with the meaning that 'metaphor' has in literary contexts.

---

12 Lakoff and Johnson, *Philosophy in the Flesh* (n 8) 93.

13 Lakoff and Johnson, *Philosophy in the Flesh* (n 8) 19.

14 Mark Johnson, *The Meaning of the Body: Aesthetics of Human Understanding* (Chicago University Press 2007).

15 'In the emergence of meaning, that is, in the process of something becoming meaningful, the human body plays a distinguished role [refs omitted]. It is especially what is known as image schemas that are crucial in this regard. Image schemas are based on our most basic physical experiences and are inevitable in making sense of the world around us.' Zoltán Kövecses, 'Conceptual Metaphor Theory: Some Criticisms and Alternative Proposals' (2008) 6, *Annual Review of Cognitive Linguistics* 168, 177.

> … from a cognitive perspective metaphors are much more than occasional ornamental figures of speech occurring primarily in literary contexts; rather, they are all-pervasive components of everyday language and reflections of how we cognitively structure our world.[16]

In the Lakoff and Johnson model, metaphor is a conceptual structure.[17] The linguistic evidence for these metaphors is found in metaphorical expressions or realisations. For example, the expression 'We came to a parting of the ways' is evidence for (and a realisation of) the RELATIONSHIP IS A JOURNEY metaphor[18] that underpins a number of other linguistic expressions. Lakoff and Johnson argue that these metaphors have an effect on how we apprehend and process the world, that we really do behave (including at a cognitive level) as though these metaphors are true. We conduct arguments as though they are wars (ARGUMENT IS WAR) we behave, speak and think as though time really is tangibly valuable (TIME IS MONEY).[19] At the same time, to say that metaphors are conceptual structures is not to suggest that specific metaphors are hardwired into the brain; even metaphors that are widespread can be subject to change and to local variation. They can also be challenged. For example, the previous chapter suggests the conceptual metaphor NATURAL RESOURCES ARE COMMODITIES is both powerful and widespread; but it is neither innate nor inevitable. Moreover, it is entirely possible to critique these metaphors. Indeed, an important part of Lakoff and Johnson's documentation of metaphors is to allow scrutiny of the values and actions these conceptual metaphors suggest.

Nevertheless, their account of existing metaphors is sometimes understood as an endorsement of them or as a claim to their universality. Nedelsky, for example, describes Lakoff and Johnson's account of THE BODY IS A CONTAINER

16 Solveig Granath and Michael Wherrity, 'Thinking in Space: The Lexis of Thinking from a Cognitive Perspective' (2008) 24(1), *English Today* 41.

17 Though see Rakova's critique which, among other things, argues that metaphor is not obviously required in their model of embodiment. Marina Rakova, 'The Philosophy of Embodied Realism: A High Price to Pay?' (2002) 13(3), *Cognitive Linguistics* 215.

18 Conventionally, the conceptual metaphor is written in small caps.

19 Lakoff and Johnson write: 'But metaphor is not merely a matter of language. It is a matter of conceptual structure. And conceptual structure is not merely a matter of the intellect—it involves all the natural dimensions of our experience, including aspects of our sense experiences: color, shape, texture, sound, etc.' Further, 'It is important to see that we don't just talk about arguments in terms of war. We can actually win or lose arguments. We see the person we are arguing with as an opponent. We attack his positions and we defend our own. We gain and lose ground. We plan and use strategies. If we find a position indefensible, we can abandon it and take a new line of attack. Many of the things we do in arguing are partially structured by the concept of war. Though there is no physical battle, there is a verbal battle, and the structure of an argument—attack, defense, counterattack, etc.—reflects this. It is in this sense that the ARGUMENT IS WAR metaphor is one that we live by in this culture; it structures the actions we perform in arguing.' George Lakoff and Mark Johnson, *Metaphors We Live By* (University of Chicago Press 1980) 235, 4.

metaphor as a 'mistake'.[20] She reads Lakoff and Johnson as endorsing the idea that we 'are physical beings, bounded and set off from the rest of the world by the surface of our skins, and we experience the rest of the world as outside us'.[21] But it is also possible to read Lakoff and Johnson as simply providing an account of a culturally 'natural' metaphor.[22] As Nedelsky's own work shows, the body as something with boundaries is a pervasive idea, so ingrained that it is treated as self-evident. This metaphor is widespread. Whether it is 'true' or whether it has positive consequences for people is a separate question. Charting these common metaphors to demonstrate their metaphorical structure is important, but that is not the end of Lakoff and Johnson's work. They make clear that no metaphor is a 'true' or 'real' account of the subject or entity, rather, because of our corporeal state we are destined to conceive of the world and ourselves through metaphorical structures.[23] What these metaphors *should* be is another question. It is an important question and I return to it below. For the moment, I consider how metaphors make clear the importance of embodiment to both language and thinking, linking the body and cognition. I pay particular attention to metaphors connected to thinking, space and time in order to show that there is at least some measure of convergence across languages.

Thought, Feeling and Space

While English tends to deal with thinking in terms of sight, eating and journey metaphors, 'there are other possibilities. The Ongee of the Andaman Islands in the South Pacific, for instance, order their lives by smells [refs omitted] and the Tzotzil

---

20 'For example, Lakoff and Johnson make a startling "mistake" in their discussion of the body as a source of imagery and metaphor. Despite their recognition of cultural diversity, of the way in which some metaphors "are so natural and so pervasive in our thought that they are usually taken as self-evident, direct descriptions of mental phenomena," they treat the experience of the body as a "container" to be exactly such a self-evident, direct description of "our" experience of the body. They assert that "we are physical beings, bounded and set off from the rest of the world by the surface of our skins."' Jennifer Nedelsky (1990) Law, Boundaries, and the Bounded Self, (1990) 30 *Representations* 162, 178.

21 Lakoff and Johnson, *Metaphors We Live By* (n 19) 29.

22 See Rita Carter, (2006) 'The Limits of Imagination' in Robin Headlam Wells and Johnjoe McFadden (eds) *Human Nature: Fact and Fiction*, (Continuum 2006) 133.

23 Concluding a chapter on Descartes, they remark 'Eventually it may be possible to revise or replace this folk theory, but we will only be able to replace it with still other metaphors. Like time, events, and causation, the mind can only be comprehended metaphorically.' Lakoff and Johnson, *Philosophy in the Flesh* (n 8) 414.

of Mexico consider heat (hence, touch) to be the basic force of the cosmos.'[24] Other languages use 'hearing' for thinking, knowing and other cognitive processes.[25]

> ... different peoples may be attuned to different aspects of their bodily functioning in relation to a target domain, or that they can ignore or downplay certain aspects of their bodily functioning as regards the metaphorical conceptualization of a particular target domain.[26]

The variation between cultures (and within cultures) has led to proposals for more general metaphors that would capture this variation while still retaining a useful perspective. While Núñez and Sweetser suggest KNOWLEDGE IS VISION,[27] they point out that broad metaphors 'coexist with very local models. No language reflects only one construal of the world.'[28] Given that not all languages prioritise sight, Ibarretxe-Antuñano recommends UNDERSTANDING IS PERCEPTION rather than understanding is vision.[29] In similar vein, Lakoff and Johnson argue for THINKING IS PERCEIVING.[30] Because of our embodiment and the different models with which we apprehend the world, conceiving of thinking as seeing, touching, hearing or perhaps even tasting are all captured by these more general metaphorical structures. Sweetser makes it even more generic arguing that the

24 Iraide Ibarretxe-Antuñano, 'Vision Metaphors for the Intellect: Are they Really Cross-linguistic?' (2008) 30(1), *Atlantis: Journal of the Spanish Association for Anglo-American Studies* 15, 25. There are other ways of accounting for, or at least tracing, the connection between thinking and perception, not least through a more 'mundane' kind of metaphor through language change. Solveig and Wherrity examine etymology in relation to various terms for thinking. By doing this, they draw attention to connections of thinking with space, food and balance. 'It is obvious that very much of our thinking was originally conceived of in terms of visual perception' (44). While etymologically grounded in these areas, the connection is 'opaque'. Granath and Wherrity (n 16) 44, 45.

25 Nick Evans and David Wilkins, 'In the Mind's Ear: The Semantic Extensions of Perception Verbs in Australian Languages' (2000) 76(3), *Language* 546, 576, cited in Ibarretxe-Antuñano, 'Vision Metaphors for the Intellect' (n 24) 24–5.

26 Zoltan Kövecses, *Metaphor in Culture. Universality and Variation* (Cambridge University Press, 2005) 246 cited in Ibarretxe-Antuñano, 'Vision Metaphors for the Intellect' (n 24) 28.

27 They argue that 'that all sighted humans have a basic and central correlation between vision and knowledge ..... Visual intake is a constant source of new information.' Rafael E. Núñez and Eve Sweetser, 'With the Future Behind Them: Convergent Evidence from Aymara Language and Gesture in the Crosslinguistic Comparison of Spatial Construals of Time' (2006) 30, *Cognitive Science* 401, 438.

28 Núñez and Sweetser (n 27) 440.

29 Ibarretxe-Antuñano, 'Vision Metaphors for the Intellect' (n 24) 29.

30 Lakoff and Johnson, *Philosophy in the Flesh* (n 8) 238. Johnson and Lakoff, 'Why Cognitive Linguistics Requires Embodied Realism' (n 7) 254.

appropriate formulation is THE MIND IS A BODY.[31] That there are differences that can nevertheless be captured by a conceptual metaphor like THE MIND IS A BODY indicates that embodiment provides affordances but also constraints. The same kind of variation is found in the field of emotion, where the body also plays an important role.

While emotion is often thought to be universal, and scholars have sought to identify which emotion terms are shared across languages (as well as identify facial expressions of these emotions), 'emotion' itself is not universal.[32] That is, in so far as emotion is distinguished both from reason and from other feelings, it is an Anglo-Western concept. In some languages, the closest equivalent to emotion is rather more corporeal with the same word covering all feelings. For example, Okazaki notes that the Fante Language has no word for the English term 'emotion'. Rather, 'Participants in [her] focus group frequently used the word *atsinka*, which covers both emotional experiences (such as happy and sad) and psychological states (such as hunger and thirst).'[33] If the focus is on feelings, rather than on emotion, the body clearly emerges as a common figure, even though the parts of the body associated with feeling vary. But while in Anglo culture emotions are prototypically experienced in the heart, for Fante speakers, the eye and the skin or self perform this function.[34] In a more specific investigation, Yu documents the connection between courage and the gallbladder in Chinese.[35] It is not the case, however, that all emotions find their seat in this organ. 'In Chinese culture, it is the heart that might be considered a container since it is regarded as the location of both thinking and the emotions. The heart radical *xin* appears in the character for "mind".'[36]

The connection between the body and feelings, as with other abstract entities, varies when it comes to the details of metaphorical mappings. Hence, Kövecses, surveying work on anger, concludes, 'it seems that different languages and cultures base their anger-concepts on different components and levels of embodiment,

31 Eve Sweetser, *From Etymology to Pragmatics. Metaphoric and Cultural Aspects of Semantic Structure* (Cambridge University Press 1990). 'MIND-AS-BODY is a conceptual metaphor whereby the mind is conceptualised in bodily terms. That is to say, the mind is understood as a separate person, with its own bodily functions and necessities. One of these bodily functions is perception – a biological process wherein the brain derives descriptions of objects and events in the world, using the information gathered by the senses.' Iraide Ibarretxe-Antuñano (2002), 'Mind-as-body as a Cross-linguistic Conceptual Metaphor' (2002) 25, *Miscelánea. A Journal of English and American Studies* 93, 113.

32 Anna Wierzbicka, *Semantics, Culture, and Cognition: Universal Human Concepts in Culture-Specific Configurations* (Oxford University Press 1992) 178–9.

33 Sumie Okazaki, 'Happiness in the Eye and the Heart: Somatic Referencing in West African Emotion Lexica' (2006) 32(2), *The Journal of Black Psychology* 117, 127.

34 Okazaki (n 33) 131.

35 Ning Yu, 'Metaphor, Body and Culture: The Chinese Understanding of Gallbladder and Courage' (2003) 18(1), *Metaphor and Symbol* 13.

36 Granath and Wherrity (n 16) 48 n 3.

thereby creating partly universal, partly culture-specific concepts'.[37] This variation nevertheless supports Lakoff and Johnson's central point; that the long-standing bifurcations between mind and body, between the rational and the irrational, are simply not representative of human experience. Rather, we need to understand the central role that embodiment plays. And while '… we cannot … claim that there is a global conceptual metaphor behind, or underlying, each and every metaphorical expression' this does not rule out a foundational role for the body and the embodied mind.[38] This role is perhaps clearest when considering the way time is conceptualised.

'Most of our understanding of time is a metaphorical version of our understanding of motion in space.'[39] Construing time in terms of space appears to be very close to constant across cultures. Núñez and Sweetser note that 'a few basic metaphor mappings from the spatial domain to the temporal one recur in language after language'.[40] The variation found is a result of mapping time to space in different ways. For example, while for some languages the future is in front of us (in front of the body) for others it is behind the body.[41] Both metaphors can be understood in terms of different aspects of embodiment. When life is considered a journey, the future will be in front of the body, as this is how people generally walk. However, if the connection between seeing and knowing is a more dominant metaphor, the past will be behind the body because like that which is behind us, it cannot be seen or known.

As we orient to the world through and with our bodies, it makes sense that the body is used as a source domain for understanding the spaces of the world. 'English, Chinese, and Mixtec all use body-part concepts, both to understand spatial relations and as a basis for metaphorical structuring of abstract concepts. They use body-part concepts because of the crucial role of sensorimotor structures in our very ability to experience meaning.'[42]

Even though this might suggest a universal set of associations[43] linked to the commonality of human embodied experience, there is discussion about the precise role of the body and its place in the context of metaphorical mappings. Levinson, for example, argues that the source domain for metaphors of space and spatial

37 Kövecses 'Conceptual Metaphor Theory' (n 15) 178.

38 Kövecses 'Conceptual Metaphor Theory' (n 15) 171.

39 Lakoff and Johnson, *Philosophy in the Flesh* (n 8) 139.

40 Núñez and Sweetser (n 27) 401.

41 Núñez and Sweetser (n 27).

42 Johnson and Lakoff 'Why Cognitive Linguistics Requires Embodied Realism' (n 7) 252.

43 'According to the standard view of metaphor in this [cognitive linguistics] framework … the conceptual associations between source and target domains are usually considered universal, since they are grounded on an experiential bodily basis, i.e. embodied human experience.' Ibarretxe-Antuñano, 'Vision Metaphors for the Intellect' (n 24)15.

orientation is not always the body.[44] He contends that in Tzeltal, it is not so much metaphor at work but something more algorithmic, a process that does not depend on the body as source domain, even though it depends on vision and visual fields.[45] Because of the importance of the visual here, however, it seems the body still has a place.

> ... all human beings use the senses for gathering and processing information, but ... the sense they choose in order to access that knowledge depends on the culture they are embedded in.[46]

What is Universal?

The connection between mind, language and embodiment suggests that humans have something in common over and above the corporeal state. What this is, and what it might mean for human rights is not straightforward. While Lakoff and Johnson argue for the universality of the embodied mind and for the general operation of metaphor at a cognitive level, they have also been understood to be arguing for substantive universals (see above). Kövecses also notes that some of the examples Lakoff and Johnson give suggest 'that the universality of embodiment mechanically produces universal meanings'.[47] As with the case discussed above, it is possible to see how this reading is arrived it, even though it is hard to reconcile with other aspects of their model. Nevertheless, Kövecses argues that we can overcome the tension between universalism and relativism as long as we don't see embodiment 'as a homogenous, monolithic factor'.[48] Kövecses explains:

---

44 Thus, he argues against the 'strong directionality constraint', that the body is always the source domain. 'Though the directionality constraint is in fact one important component of the embodiment hypothesis, Lakoff and Johnson have repeatedly emphasised the interactional and pragmatic character of embodiment. The body does not exist by itself, in isolation from the world, but instead develops in contact and through experimentation with it.' Rohrer (n 8) 58.

45 Stephen C. Levinson, 'Vision, Shape, and Linguistic Description: Tzeltal Body-part Terminology and Object Description' (1994) 32, *Linguistics* 791.

46 Ibarretxe-Antuñano, 'Vision Metaphors for the Intellect' (n 24) 16. 'The five senses give us information about the world in which we live, but the way this information is received, processed and understood by human beings is different' (19). This is seen in the connection between gesture and language, and in turn the evidence these provide for embodiment, summarised by Núñez and Sweetser (n 27) 419–20. 'Embodiment and situatedness are inseparable in gesture', Eve Sweetser, 'Regular Metaphoricity in Gesture: Bodily Based Models of Speech Interaction', in (1998) *Actes du 16e Congrès International des Linguistes* (CD-ROM), Elsevier 2. <http://linguistics.berkeley.edu/~sweetser/sweetser.cil.98.pdf>. Accessed 10 August 2011, 2.

47 Kövecses 'Conceptual Metaphor Theory' (n 15) 177.

48 Kövecses 'Conceptual Metaphor Theory' (n 15) 177. Rakova (n 17).

> This is made possible by the idea that embodiment ... consists of several components and that any of these can be singled out and emphasized by different cultures (or, as a matter of fact, individuals within [178] cultures).[49]

Kövecses calls this 'differential experiential focus'.[50] He suggests that 'we think of metaphorical conceptualization as a process in which speakers are under two competing pressures: the pressure of universal embodiment and that of local context'.[51]

Embodiment is universal as is the use of conceptual metaphor, which is itself linked to the body. But just as people can accomplish the same task in a variety of ways, so too can the universal of embodiment have different consequences when it comes to the construction of conceptual metaphors. This is clear in the case of thinking, time and emotion discussed above. Differences in the more specific realisations of metaphors are linked to culture and cultural values. As seen above, as metaphors related to understanding draw on the senses, understanding may be conceptualised in terms of the visual, auditory of even tactile.[52] Nevertheless, there do seem to be some universal conceptual metaphors, even though these are at a generic level. These include HAPPY IS UP[53] THE BODY IS A CONTAINER[54] and THE MIND IS A BODY.[55] Of course, this is not to say that these metaphors have positive effects, as Nedelsky argues in the case of the body as container. Further, universally accepted 'values' may not be positive; such values need to be tested against the human being. A value or metaphor may be universal, but that does not mean it is beneficial for people. All values, all metaphors, have to be measured against that upon which they rely: the human body.

The evaluation of the consequences of metaphors and the values they bring with them can be seen clearly in Lakoff and Johnson's discussion of the 'moral order' metaphor. The 'moral order' is the great chain of being, that places god above men, who are placed above women and so on.

> The consequences of the metaphor of Moral Order are sweeping, momentous, and, we believe, morally repugnant. The metaphor legitimizes a certain class of existing power relations as being natural and therefore moral.[56]

---

49 Kövecses 'Conceptual Metaphor Theory' (n 15) 177–8.

50 Kövecses 'Conceptual Metaphor Theory' (n 15) 178.

51 Kövecses 'Conceptual Metaphor Theory' (n 15) 182.

52 Ibarretxe-Antuñano 'Mind-as-body' (n 31).

53 Zoltán Kövecses 'Universality and Variation in the Use of Metaphor' in N.-L. Johannesson and D.C. Minugh (eds), *Selected Papers from the 2006 and 2007 Stockholm Metaphor Festivals* (Department of English, Stockholm University 2008) 55.

54 There is also an apparently near universal THE ANGRY PERSON IS A PRESSURIZED CONTAINER. Kövecses 'Universality and Variation' (n 53) 56.

55 Ibarretxe-Antuñano 'Mind-as-body' (n 31).

56 While the second sentence suggests that the metaphor itself is to blame, it is rather the use of the metaphor which is the problem as the association with power suggests.

Universal prevalence of a metaphor does not make it beneficial. However, the common conflation of 'universality' and 'naturalness' may foreclose any discussion about the merits of such 'natural' values. Whether a metaphor has positive benefits can be established. This should first be done in relation to the body, our zero institution.

Given that metaphors depend on our embodiment, this makes sense. If a metaphor threatens that on which it depends, it is a metaphor with a limited life span. While Lakoff and Johnson title one of their books *Metaphors We Live By*, some metaphors can be so dangerous that they are perhaps better conceived of *Metaphors We Die By*. Seeing the environment only as a commodity is exactly such a metaphor. The consequence of this metaphor is that while some people profit, others die and the natural world is destroyed. Similarly, seeing the body as a container makes it difficult to conceptualise the interdependence of bodies on each other and the world; it also tends to reduce the body to an inert thing.

Attention to metaphor and the embodied mind may seem not have offered much in the way of development of human rights. If metaphors, like the moral order, need to be measured against the human body, it may appear that we have not moved very far. This work, however, does provide some valuable information. It confirms the importance of the body and it suggests that language may have more to tell us about both human life and human rights. (I return to language in the next chapter.) It also makes clear that we cannot do without metaphor as the way we make sense of the world is always in metaphorical terms. This foregrounds both human creativity and human fallibility. What has not yet been discussed is the importance of the interaction between people and the world, especially as it relates to the formation of metaphor.

Universally Interacting

Embodiment and metaphor are universal and both are related to being in the world. That is, metaphors are influenced by our experience of the world, both individually and culturally.[57] As suggested by the metaphors above, this interaction is at least partly corporeal. Because of the effect of the body on both the generation and the substance of these metaphors, the relationship between mind and body, between body and the world, is interactive and recursive. I now briefly consider this interaction in more general terms, exploring what it tells us about the relationship between the body and the mind.

In arguing for a connection between embodiment and linguistic meaning, Gibbs proposes that we adopt the 'embodiment premise':

> People's subjective, felt experiences of their bodies in action provide part of the fundamental grounding for language and thought. Cognition is what occurs

---

Johnson and Lakoff 'Why Cognitive Linguistics Requires Embodied Realism' (n 7) 304.

57 Kövecses 'Universality and Variation' (n 53) 66.

> when the body engages the physical, cultural world and must be studied in terms of the dynamical interactions between people and the environment. Human language and thought emerge from recurring patterns of embodied activity that constrain ongoing intelligent behavior. We must not assume cognition to be purely internal, symbolic, computational, and disembodied, but seek out the gross and detailed ways that language and thought are inextricably shaped by embodied action.[58]

Subjective though these experiences may be, they ground existence, language and thought. Because we think in the world and because we are embodied, both the world and our corporeal state must have an effect on thinking.[59] As they are linked, however, determining what comes first is problematic. The temptation is to frame this discussion in terms of what is 'innate' and what is 'cultural'. However, discussing anything in terms of innateness is problematic as it can lead to determinism. Fortunately, Johnson and Lakoff's work provides a way of striking a careful balance between what is universal/innate and what is cultural/learnt. Their research suggests 'the existence of both built-in and learned cognitive mechanisms'.[60] They stress that it is interaction between the two that matters; 'Meaning comes, not just from "internal" structures of the organism (the "subject"), nor solely from "external" inputs (the "objects"), but rather from recurring patterns of engagement between organism and environment.'[61] Thus focusing on interaction makes the distinction between innate and learnt less acute, though it does not entirely disappear. Moreover, a focus on interaction provides a way of dealing with human fallibility. As long as conceptual structures are revisited and critiqued in the light of this interaction they can be modified. This interaction between organism and environment is important, especially in the light

58 Raymond W. Gibbs, Jr., 'Embodied Experience and Linguistic Meaning' (2003) 84, *Brain and Language* 1, 2.

59 As Granath and Wherrity explain 'In cognitive theory, language is not regarded as a representation of objective reality, but rather, as the product of our interaction with the world as entities in three dimensional space. The metaphors we use to structure experience conceptually are grounded in this interaction' (n 16) 41.

60 Johnson and Lakoff, 'Why Cognitive Linguistics Requires Embodied Realism' (n 7) 248.

61 Johnson and Lakoff, 'Why Cognitive Linguistics Requires Embodied Realism' (n 7) 248. For consideration of the interaction between culture and the body, see Dirk Geeraerts and Juana I. Marín-Arrese, 'Dirk Geeraerts: Cognitive Sociolinguistics and the Sociology of Cognitive Linguistics', Interview (2007) 5, *Annual Review of Cognitive Linguistics* 289, 293 and Arthur S. Parsons, 'The Conventions of the Senses: The Linguistics and Phenomenological Contributions to a Theory of Culture' (1998) 11(1), *Human Studies* 3, 4. The problem here is the same issue identified in chapter 3. While the body is undoubtedly culturally constructed, too much emphasis on this hides the brute corporeality of the body as index.

of arguments that seek to root morality in biology.[62] Despite the wealth of work in this field, it will only be discussed briefly. However, it is important to discuss if only show that grounding human rights in the body as index is not the same as arguments for the innateness of morality.

Bad Biology

As noted, there has not been a great deal of research linking linguistics to human rights in terms of dealing with foundations or origins of these rights.[63] But there is one strand of work worth considering. The connection is not between linguistics as such, but by way of Chomsky's Universal Grammar. The argument is that in the same way humans have an innate capacity for language, we also have an innate moral grammar, known as Universal Moral Grammar (UMG).[64] This extensive body of work will not be dealt with in detail here, suffice to say that there is much debate about both the evidence and what it means.[65] Here I want to focus on the troubling nature of the turn to evolution, and evolutionary psychology, when making claims about universal morals and thus recommendations about social structures.[66] While I have argued that the body needs to be the fundamental frame

---

62 Lakoff and Johnson have also argued for a moral system. See George Lakoff, 'The Metaphor System for Morality' in Adele D. Goldberg (ed.), *Conceptual Structure, Discourse and Language* (CSLI Publications, Centre for the Study of Language and Information, 1996); Lakoff and Johnson, *Philosophy in the Flesh* (n 8) 300; Roberta Pires de Olivera (2000) 'Language and Ideology: An interview with George Lakoff', in René Dirven, Bruce Hawkins, Sandikcioglu (eds), *Language and Ideology: Volume I: Theoretical Cognitive Approaches* (John Benjamins 2000) 23. I do not discuss this in detail here. This system is more descriptive than prescriptive, which is line with their general theory of metaphor. For example, responding to the criticism that he was claiming certain values are innate, Lakoff insists: 'When I said that, all things being equal, one is better off if one is rich rather than poor, I was not referring necessarily to monetary wealth, but to whatever forms of wealth are valued in a given culture, whether beads, cows, chickens, land or yams. To say that this IS true, is NOT to say that it [34] SHOULD BE true' (Pires de Oliveira 33–4).

63 However, see Lakoff and Johnson's work on morality (n 62).

64 In particular, see Marc D. Hauser, *Moral Minds: The Nature of Right and Wrong* (Harper Perennial 2007).

65 See Michael F. Brown, 'Cultural Relativism 2.0' (2008) 49(3), *Current Anthropology* 49(3): 363; Hauser (n 64); John Mikhail, 'Moral Grammar and Human Rights: Some Reflections on Cognitive Science and Enlightenment rationalism', in Ryan Goodman, Derek Jinks, Andrew Woods (eds), *Understanding Social Action, Promoting Human Rights* (OUP 2012) 160; H. Rose and S. Rose, 'Darwin and After' (2010) 63, *New Left Review* 91; M.R. Waldmann, J. Nagel and A. Wiegmann, 'Moral judgment' in K.J. Holyoak and R.G. Morrison (eds), *The Oxford Handbook of Thinking and Reasoning* (Oxford University Press 2012) 364.

66 For a critique of evolutionary psychology see Deborah Cameron, 'Language: Sociolinguistics and Sociobiology' (1997) 39(4), *Critical Quarterly* 81; Deborah Cameron,

for human rights, it is important that the body is understood in a way that protects it and the environment on which it depends.

Arguments relying on evolution tend to see evolution as teleological. This is problematic. They also tend to see the mind as 'driven by goal states that served biological fitness in ancestral environments, such as food, sex, safety, parenthood, friendship, status and knowledge'.[67] Whether this is true is one question; whether this approach is useful is another. The short answer to this second question, and the problem with turning to evolution more generally, has two parts. First, we have created a world in which human survival may be under threat. That is, the environment in which we live is no longer 'natural', it has been fundamentally altered by human action.[68] Second, even if evolution has shaped our minds, humans are not condemned to live and behave simply on an instinctual basis. We have changed our environments and we can also change our minds. As work in cognitive linguistics shows, even though the metaphors we live by are influenced by our corporeal nature it is possible to change them (especially if the consequences of these metaphors threaten the continuation of human life).

Such change is clearly possible and it is not the result of evolution. Changes to metaphors and their associated values occur because of cultural shifts. As Malik points out, 'Only in the last 200 years have we begun to view [slavery] with revulsion' because of 'political ideas', the 'changing economic needs of capitalism' and 'the social struggles of the enslaved and the oppressed'.[69] While we now see slavery as inhuman, it is 'a belief we have arrived at historically, not naturally'.[70] If the essence of being human were determined by biology or evolution, it is not clear what would be used to challenge ideas, or to 'rebel' against our 'nature'.[71] Fortunately, humans are not so fixed. While embodiment provides constraints and

---

'Sex/Gender, Language and the New Biologism' (2009) 31(2), *Applied Linguistics* 173. For discussion of the link between biology and the law see Anna Grear, *Redirecting Human Rights: Facing the Challenge of Corporate Legal Humanity* (Palgrave 2010) 124–5.

67 Steven Pinker, 'The Biology of Fiction', in Robin Headlam Wells and Johnjoe McFadden (eds), *Human Nature: Fact and Fiction* (Continuum 2006) 27, 30.

68 Dipesh Chakrabarty, 'The Climate of History: Four Theses' (2009) 35(2), *Critical Enquiry* 197.

69 Kenan Malik, 'What Science Can and Cannot Tell us about human nature' in Robin Headlam Wells and Johnjoe McFadden (eds), *Human Nature: Fact and Fiction*, Continuum (London 2006) 164, 174. See also Kwok Leung and Kwok-Kit Tong, 'Justice across cultures: A Three-stage Model for Intercultural Negotiation' in Michele J. Gelfand and Jeanne M. Bredd (eds), *The Handbook of Negotiation and Culture* (Stanford Business Books, 2004) 313.

70 Malik (n 69) 174.

71 'Human values, presumably, do not float down from the sky, but emerge out of human thought and behaviour. How then do they originate if not through "natural selection and neurophysiology" that contemporary naturalists hold to be the basis of all other behaviours?' Malik (n 69) 177.

affordances for language and culture, language and culture can also be used to protect the body.

> … the acquisition of language introduces difference into the continuity of the world, and thereby bars us irreversibly from any purely organic, instinctual existence. By these means, culture alters those who internalize it, defining what seems obvious, constraining what appears possible. Children, most people agree, have to *learn* to interact, to love, to think clearly and make sound choices. These processes of socialization and education help us to realize our capabilities, but they also change us.[72]

There is no question that we are biological beings. This is what the body as index seeks to highlight. But this is a starting point rather than a destination; the body needs to be acknowledged but the mind, while clearly influenced by the embodied state, is not determined by biology.[73] There is also no question that we live in a 'natural' environment in so far as we depend on the functioning of the natural world. But we have changed this too, not simply through the cumulative action that has led to this new epoch but also in terms of how we think about it. Because of human action and our ways of life, there are at least two 'environments' that need to be considered. The first is the natural environment.

In the previous chapter, I argued that we need to radically reconfigure our understanding of our relationship with the natural environment if we are to physically survive. Our cultural norms and ways of life have so estranged us from natural processes that we deal with the environment at arm's length; it is seen through a lens of property ownership, commodification and money. This lens is the second environment we need to consider and as it is culturally natural it is often unquestioned. This view of the world is also sometimes endorsed in discourses that while purporting to take a neutral stance are nevertheless profoundly influenced by cultural norms. As Belsey points out, arguments about evolution and culture often hold up Western society as evidence of progressive and productive change.

> [A]s luck would have it, human nature, left to its own devices, is widely held in popular science to issue in the way of life the West currently holds most dear …

72 Catherine Belsey, 'Biology and Imagination: The Role of Culture' in Robin Headlam Wells and Johnjoe McFadden (eds), *Human Nature: Fact and Fiction* (Continuum 2006) 111, 122. See also Jackendoff who points out children acquire morals in the same way. Ray Jackendoff, 'The Natural Logic of Morals and of Laws' (2009) 75(2), *Brook. L. Rev.* 379.

73 '[H]umans, unlike non-human animals, can also forge universal values and behaviours through social interaction and historical progress. In this sense the human essence – what we consider to be the common properties of our humanity – is as much a product of our historical and cultural development as it is of our biological heritage.' Malik (n 69) 170.

> The coincidence between the lessons of natural selection and the aspirations of the stockbroker belt might just give us pause for thought. Human nature, as science and suburbia both interpret it, appears just a little – well – *unimaginative*. Surely our intellectual capabilities can visualize at least the possibility of something more challenging for us than this?[74]

This shows how important the second lens, our cultural environment, is to our conception of the world. Indeed, it is worth remembering that choices are rational if they cohere with the world in which we live. A great many of us live in a particular political and economic environment; neo-liberal capitalism. In this context, granting a licence in Coca-Cola in Plachimada was rational. In this context, aspiring to a life in the 'stockbroker belt' is absolutely sane. Following the logic of (social) Darwinism, it makes total sense to exploit the environment, to disregard other people and to simply acquire as much money as possible. To survive in the contemporary world, it is more rational to pursue ruthless self-interest than to pay any attention to other people. But, as we have seen, this way of life is a direct threat to our more fundamental frame. Neo-liberal capitalism is hospitable to the disembodied legal subject, not the corporeal human person. In short, if contemporary social and political structures are the outcome of evolution and biology, we are a species with a death wish. We are creating a world in which it will be impossible to live. Fortunately, humans are thinking animals and there is – at the very least – a possibility that our death can be averted.

Step Outside

Cognitive linguistics confirms the position of the body and shows its connection to language. Humans are embodied beings and this has consequences not just for the way we live, and what we need to survive, but also for how we think and for language. Lakoff and Johnson's work makes at least two things clear. We are embodied and we rely on metaphors to understand the world. Lakoff and Johnson argue that 'our common embodiment allows for common, stable truths'.[75] But we need to be careful about what we identify as true and the language we use to do it. This also applies to how we use language as evidence in such arguments. Rohrer maintains that 'Neither the arcane depths of neuroscience nor the heights of cultural analysis are any more real or any less necessary to explaining language.'[76] He suggests a focus on 'the shared facets of our bodies, brains, development and cultures'.[77] Breaking down the distinction between mind and body, the rational and the irrational, means understanding the mind as physical but it also requires

---

74 Belsey (n 72) 114.

75 Lakoff and Johnson, *Philosophy in the Flesh* (n 8) 6.

76 Rohrer (n 8) 76.

77 Rohrer (n 8) 76.

that we see the body as more than biological. It asks us to imagine a kind of 'extended embodiment', a body without its normal boundaries.

> This 'extended embodiment' does not exist in a vacuum: it is not, as it were, a property of the objects 'in themselves'. Rather, it is constituted and exemplified by the participation of the objects in an entire matrix of cultural practices, some of which are linguistic (or discursive) practices, and some of which are nonlinguistic. [78]

This suggests that a broad view of the relationship between body and mind needs to be found, while still respecting the fact that we are embodied, that without corporeal sustenance people would not exist.

Looking Differently

As the concepts with which we think are a result of our embodiment and our experience interacting with the world and with others, it is possible to create new conceptual metaphors. This happens all the time; THE MIND IS A MACHINE cannot predate the concept of machines,[79] while new variations like THE MIND IS A COMPUTER (with hardware and software) are very recent.[80] What I suggest is in some sense analogous to Rorty's sentimental education or Hunt's argument about the transformative power of the novel.[81] I am suggesting a cognitive intervention, the promotion of a concept that would serve people well, protecting the environment and our bodies. To so this, I draw on one of the widespread metaphors discussed above: thinking is perceiving. As a high level conceptual metaphor, that relates cognition to embodiment, it does not appear to be 'contaminated' by any values that may be contentious or damaging to the body. The thought I suggest needs perceiving is that outlined in the previous chapter, that people depend on the natural world and on each other. Concepts like the human trust require some kind of objective correlative, something that communicates the interdependence that this construct tries to describe.

---

78 Chris Sinha and Kristine Jensen de Lopez (2000), 'Language, Culture and the Embodiment of Spatial Cognition' (2000) 11(1/2), *Cognitive Linguistics* 17, 36. Love's account of the 'distributed mind' is also useful here. Nigel Love, 'Cognition and the Language Myth' (2004) 26, *Language Sciences* 525, 528.

79 Lakoff and Johnson, *Metaphors We Live By* (n 19) 27.

80 'The mind is a neural computer, fitted by natural selection with combinatorial algorithms for causal and probabilistic reasoning about plants, animals, objects, and people.' Pinker (n 67) 30.

81 Lynne Hunt, *Inventing Human Rights: A History* (Norton 2007). Richard Rorty (1999) 'Human Rights, Rationality and Sentimentality' in Obrad Savić (ed.), *The Politics of Human Rights* (Verso 1999) 67–83.

Thinking is perceiving suggests that an image may be appropriate.[82] This image is a supplement, or companion, to the zero institution of the body as index; it cannot displace the body. The image also needs to be a zero point, a frame re-invented for the purposes of human rights. As conceptual metaphors may be the result of cultural history,[83] the frame proposed should be stripped of as much existing cultural meaning as possible in order to found a common starting point. The image I propose is connected to arguments I have made about the environment, specifically, that it is not possible to deal with environmental concerns at just a local level. As the previous chapter showed, the environment is global. And while economic globalisation is understood as being a threat to the natural environment, globalisation of another sort could work to protect it.

Globalisation is a phenomenon, a field of study, an orientation and certainly an entirely new vocabulary. It can be defined in economic, political and cultural ways, and is often linked to discussions of global finance and trade. It is seen as both a challenge and opportunity for human rights.[84] But globalisation can also provide a new perspective. If thinking is perceiving and understanding is perception what people understand by 'globalisation' may provide a new vista.[85]

Trying to establish what 'globalisation' means, Garrett, Evans and Williams surveyed people in the US, Australia, the UK and New Zealand to gather their understandings of 'globalisation'.[86] With an open question, they simply asked respondents to write down the first five things they thought of when considering the

---

82 While appreciating that not all cultures prioritise the visual in this metaphor, images are much easier to distribute than sounds, smells and surfaces.

83 'One of my students, Niki Köves (2002), showed in a small-scale study that Hungarians primarily use the LIFE IS WAR and LIFE IS A COMPROMISE metaphors for comprehending the concept of life in general, whereas Americans predominantly employ the LIFE IS A PRECIOUS POSSESSION and LIFE IS A GAME metaphors. Why do Hungarians use the metaphors they do for life, and why do Americans use different ones? The issue obviously has to do with the peculiarities of Hungarian and American history. Hungarians have been in wars throughout their more than one thousand-year- old history as a nation and [67] state and had to struggle for their survival, as they are wedged between powerful German-speaking and Slavic nations. Given this history, it is not surprising that for many Hungarians life is struggle – and less of a game. To point this out is, of course, trivial as far as history is concerned, but it is not trivial as far as the study of the emergence of a particular metaphorical conceptual system is concerned.' Kövecses, 'Universality and Variation' (n 53) 66–7.

84 Michael Goodhart, 'Origins and Universality in the Human Rights Debate: Cultural Essentialism and the Challenge of Globalisation' (2003) 25(4), *HRQ* 935; Micheline Ishay (2004), 'What are Human Rights? Six Historical Controversies' (2004) 3(3), *Journal of Human Rights* 359.

85 Ibarretxe-Antuñano, 'Vision Metaphors for the Intellect' (n 24) 29.

86 Peter Garrett, Betsy Evans and Angie Williams, 'What does the word "globalisation" mean to you?: Comparative Perceptions and Evaluations in Australia, New Zealand, the USA and the UK' (2006) 27(5), *Journal of Multilingual and Multicultural Development* 392.

word 'globalisation'. Analysis of the 1,673 keywords produced categories relating to business, trade, economy, communication, anti-globalisation, war and peace, ecology and health. A category labelled 'Culture, unity, co-operation and diversity' had a number of sub-categories (including 'unity' and 'co-operation'). But, 'the most obvious and largest grouping in this category as regards associations with 'globalisation' concerns keywords such as "global", "world" etc'.[87] This included words such as 'the globe' and 'the world'. While this might simply be a response to the form of the word 'globalisation' it also suggests something else; it suggests a view of the earth from outside. While this could only have been an imaginary vision in the not too distant past, since the advent of space travel photographs can make it more tangible.

'Occasionally, we need a remote satellite in order to get the best view of our own earth.'[88]

The Earthrise photographs taken from the moon in 1968 provide this view.[89]

> The image of the earth as a single spaceship traveling through the fathomless void of the cosmos neatly encapsulated two key elements of the environmentalist message: first, the interdependence of all life on earth, and, second, the finite nature of the resources on which that life depends.[90]

For the first time, we were able to see our world from outside.[91] Borman, an astronaut on Apollo 8 remarked 'the most indelible image that remains in my mind's eye is the wonderful view of Earth ... National boundaries and artificial barriers that separate countries were invisible.'[92] The experience of seeing the world from outside has had a significant effect on many of the people fortunate to have had access to this view. White calls it the 'Overview Effect' and argues it is a change in consciousness not 'limited to space travelers alone'.[93] It describes the 'different philosophical point of view' that comes about 'as a result of having

---

87 Garrett, Evans and Williams (n 86) 403.

88 Douzinas (n 1) 45. Apparently the human eye can see things from space that were not thought possible. Thus, Cooper, an astronaut on Mercury could see, from orbit 'trucks, trains and smoke from buildings'. Robert Poole, *Earthrise: How Man First Saw the Earth* (Yale University Press 2008) 68.

89 They even led to a novel metaphor, 'spaceship earth'. R.S. Deese, 'The artifact of nature: "Spaceship Earth" and the Dawn of Global Environmentalism' (2009) 33(2), *Endeavour*70Forimageseehttp://www.nasa.gov/multimedia/imagegallery/image_feature_1249.html Accessed 29 April 2014.

90 Deese (n 89) 70.

91 When the astronauts first saw earthrise, it was referred to as a 'picture'. Poole (n 88) 1. See also Benjamin Lazier, 'Earthrise; or, The Globalization of the World Picture' (2011) 116(3), *The American Historical Review* 602.

92 Cited in Poole (n 88) 34.

93 Frank White, *The Overview Effect: Space Exploration and Human Evolution* (Houghton Mifflin 1987) 4.

a different physical perspective'.[94] He argues that while this experience can be difficult to communicate, a broader dissemination of this perspective is possible and desirable as this literally new vista provides a different way of thinking about and framing the world.

In the last chapter, it became clear that in the case of the environment it is true that we are all connected, that we are all part of the same thing. Pollution does not respect national sovereignty, the water cycle is not locally determined. However, given our embodiment and our generally limited vision, it is difficult to conceptualise this interrelatedness. Quite simply, it is difficult to see that we are all connected. It was not always easy to see the earth from outside; even the astronauts on the moon 'had to learn how to look'.[95] The image of the globe from outside provides a way of learning, visually, that we depend on the earth and each other, that national borders are not 'natural' and that all parts of the earth are ultimately connected. While the earthrise images have prompted all manner of metaphors and discourses, including many concerned with environmental awareness and protection,[96] these images have not yet been connected to human rights.[97] But given a focus on the body as index and the importance of the environment, it is an easy connection to make.

The image of the world from outside complements the body as index.[98] While the body is close, singular and immediate the image of the earth from space provides an entirely new perspective, one that is only possible because of human invention and technology. It reminds us that all humans have something in common; it also reminds us that we are not determined by our biology. The Earthrise images ask us to think about human control and progress as well as physical fragility. They provide a frame for thinking about how we are all part of the same thing, and for recognising universal human suffering.

Considering the earth from outside allows attention to be given to the global and the local at the same time. It is not so much a text as an ecstatic position.[99] It provides a frame for seeing and thinking the human. As the earth is where we find ourselves, it makes sense for it to be part of the foundation of human rights. 'The sight of the whole earth gave the world a picture to think with.'[100] It can also provide a vision to think human rights, to understand the world of the body as index, by looking at it from the outside.

---

94 White (n 93) 4.

95 Poole (n 88) 100.

96 Poole (n 88).

97 Although Poole does mention the Universal Declaration of Human Rights. Poole (n 88) 193.

98 Interestingly, like the body the earth was also constructed as female, a helpless woman both commodified and needing to be rescued. Poole (n 88) 168.

99 'What is needed for human rights thinkers to awaken to the real problem of human suffering is a quasi-religious attention to universal human suffering, and a radicalized compassion that manages to let go of obsessive attachment to textual foundations.' Louis Wolcher, 'The Tragic Foundations of Human Rights' (2006) 24, *Wis. Int'l L. J.* 523, 554.

100 Poole (n 88) 198.

Chapter 7

The Linguistic Body

In previous chapters, I have argued that the protection of the environment and the protection of the corporeal human are the most important human rights. They are related in that without a functioning environment it will be impossible to protect human rights to food, water, shelter and sleep. These two rights protect bare life and have been conceived in terms of the human body as index and frame and the globe, viewed from outside, as a way of framing the interconnection of people with each other and with the environment. But there is more to human life than this.

In Chapter 6 the connection between language, mind and body was explored. The human condition is clearly an embodied one. It is also clear that the human condition is a linguistic one. Language requires the body and there is an interaction between the two at least in so far as interaction with the world and with other people has an effect on cognitive and linguistic structure. While I argued that it is well to be cautious about claims to innate human capacities, it appears that the capacity for language is innate. It is not a given, however, and the acquisition of language depends on input, on interaction with other people during the crucial acquisition window.

The capacity for language is a uniquely human capacity. It is surprising, then, that language has not often been linked to a discussion of human rights.[1] As the previous chapter showed, however, languages do seem to share something, albeit at a general level, and linked to human embodiment. However, if there are universals in language, these may be useful in adding to the rights proposed so far. Here, I argue that language is the third frame required for human rights. Language fleshes out what it means to be human, over and above corporeality. It suggests a third right, protection against dehumanisation.

In order to focus on language, here I rely on Wierzbicka's Natural Semantic Metalanguage (NSM). NSM is a mini-language, replete with words and syntax, both common to all languages. The elements of NSM provide a language for thinking about what people are, over and above their embodiment. The aim here is not to reinstate the body/mind split; we have already seen that mind is embodied. Rather, the goal is to provide a list of features that flesh out the concept of human and so of human rights. This project, the search for a universal foundation for human rights, was originally inspired by Anna Wierzbicka's work, that searches for what languages share, while being acutely aware of and sensitive to how they

---

1 As noted in Chapter 6, linguistic human rights is a significant area of research and advocacy.

differ. My own search led me from language to the body. As I have argued, the body is the absolute zero institution, that on which all else depends. But the fact that humans have language tells us that there is more to people than their corporeality.

I begin by describing NSM and addressing some of the concerns that scholars have raised about the model. I then explore how 'human' and 'rights' relate to the NSM primes. While 'human' is not problematic, as 'person' is included in NSM, 'rights' are less straightforward. Fortunately, Wierzbicka's work is of assistance here as she argues that 'right' has a specific meaning, linked to English culture. Specifically, 'right' is connected to concepts of 'good', a term that is an NSM prime. The discussion of 'human' and 'rights' leads to the third right I am proposing, that is, a prohibition against dehumanisation.

After defining and explaining dehumanisation, I consider why it occurs. I argue that the dehumanisation of people is closely linked to the personification of non-human entities, corporations in particular, and to the underlying ideology that allows this to happen. Discussion of an American case on free speech shows how corporations are not only personified, they are more important than real people. Other work demonstrates that rather than being treated as human, people are conceptualised as animals (especially in the case of immigrants) and as brands. The two are linked, as while branding of the self is now a function of the market, this was originally a way of marking livestock. But the contemporary operation of branding shows that the most important figure, the most important 'person', in the modern world is the market. The market has not only been personified, it has been deified. This is a consequence of the hegemonic dominance of capitalism, a dominance that drives the personification of corporations and the dehumanisation of people.

The dominance of the market is connected to the dominance of a particular ideology; it is linked to the systematic operation of capitalist values. As this ideology systematically dehumanises people it can be understood as a root cause of dehumanisation. The last part of this chapter considers these root causes in relation to human rights abuses. This shows that not only can we not do without human rights, we need more of them. This is not a call to identify further particular rights, rather, it is to argue that like the root causes of human rights abuses, human rights also needs to be a root driver of change. A paradigm shift is required such that human rights are recognised in every place, in all interactions, for every person.

Natural Semantic Metalanguage

Natural semantic metalanguage (NSM) provides a metalanguage for semantic analysis that differs from systems that use 'artificial symbols' as these 'have to be explained'.[2] The distinctive feature of this metalanguage is that NSM is a subset of natural language.

> Semantic primes provide a principled 'vocabulary' for semantic-conceptual representation: clear, accessible, minimal, non-circular, non-ethnocentric. Because the vocabulary and syntax of NSM are recruited from ordinary language, it can achieve much greater [20] clarity and accessibility than is possible with more technical and more obscure modes of representation. Because the metalanguage is minimal in size, one can achieve maximum resolution of semantic detail and ward off any possibility of circularity. It is or aspires to be a formal semantic metalanguage based on natural language.[3]

It is worth noting that the search for human universals of this kind is not altogether new, indeed the project of finding the 'alphabet of human thoughts' was initially a philosophical quest and has its roots in Enlightenment ideas.[4] The NSM approach, however, focuses on language while still paying attention to thought.

The 'semantic primes' of NSM are universal; that is, they are found in all languages. That is not to say that they are realised in precisely the same form in each language (see below). Currently, there are around 60 such primes and they have important properties. First, they are undecomposable into simpler components. They are 'primitive' as their meanings are self-evident. They can be understood as the building blocks of the language, as they are 'unanalyzable elements of meaning which underlie a given language's entire semantic system and are the cornerstone of its entire lexicon'.[5] While this may seem to encourage expansion of the list of primes:

> From the very beginning it was demanded that the list of indefinables 'must be as small as possible; it should contain only those elements which are really [172] absolutely essential while being at the same time adequate to explicate **all** utterances' (Wierzbicka 1972: 13, original emphasis). In other words, the inventory of semantic primes cannot be established solely by theoretical

---

2 Anna Wierzbicka, *Semantics, Culture, and Cognition: Universal Human Concepts in Culture-Specific Configurations* (OUP 1992) 17.

3 Anna Wierzbicka, 'Bodies and their Parts: An NSM Approach to Semantic Typology' (2007) 29, *Language Sciences* 14, 19-20.

4 Leibniz, cited in Anna Wierzbicka, *Semantics, Primes and Universals* (OUP 1996), 13.

5 Anna Wierzbicka, 'Mental Lexicon', in Tilman Berger, Kalr Gutschmidt, Sebastian Kempgen and Peter Kosta (eds), *The Slavic Languages: An International Handbook of their History, their Structure and their Investigation*, (Mouton de Gruyter 2009) http://www.griffith.edu.au/__data/assets/pdf_file/0011/347528/wierzbicka-mental-lexicon.pdf. Accessed 17 May 2013, 2.

> considerations concerning the primitiveness of some concepts, but it has to be verified through empirical semantic investigations.[6]

As well as the primes, NSM provides syntactic structures. The universality of both primes and syntax is empirically tested and thus subject to change; though the set is now reasonably stable.[7] The primes together with the syntax constitute a mini, universal, natural language.

> Thus, the theory posits the existence not only of an innate and universal 'lexicon of human thoughts', but also of an innate and universal 'syntax of human thoughts'. Taken together, these two hypotheses amount to positing something that can be called 'a language of thought', or *lingua mentalis* ... [8]

NSM is generally used as a semantic metalanguage; a neutral and natural way of explicating the meaning of concepts, words and expressions. It has been successfully deployed in relation to cross-cultural concepts to both show the non-equivalence of what look like similar lexemes as well as to provide a way of explicating meaning.[9] It has also been useful in explicating 'native' cultural concepts..[10] Nevertheless, the way I use NSM here is far from canonical as my interest in NSM is not related to the semantic analysis or cross-linguistic comparisons, but rather to the irreducibility and universality of the primes. The primes, I want to claim, point to what people share.

---

6 Uwe Durst, 'The Natural Semantic Metalanguage Approach to Linguistic Meaning' (2003) 29 *Theoretical Linguistics* 157, 171-2. This can be seen to parallel arguments that the number of human rights should be small in order to gain maximum agreement; see chapter 1.

7 For example, 'world' was an early prime which was discarded; and the addition of 'body' is relatively recent. 14 primitives were proposed in Wierzbicka's Semantic Primitives (1972). There are now just over 60. Durst (n 6) 171-2.

8 Wierzbicka, *Semantics, Primes and Universals* (n 4) 20.

9 For example, see Wierzbicka, *Semantics, Culture, and Cognition* (n 2); Anna Wierzbicka 'Is "remember" a Universal Human Concept? "Memory" and culture', in Mngistue Amberber (ed) *The Language of Memory in a Crosslinguistic Perspective, Human Cognitive Processing 21* (John Benjamins, 2007) 13. While not discussing NSM directly, there are those who argue that the quest for universals is pointless. See Nicholas Evans and Stephen C. Levinson, 'The Myth of Language Universals: Language diversity and its Importance for Cognitive Science' (2009) 32(5), *Behavioral and Brain Sciences* 429.

10 Anna Wierzbicka, *English: Meaning and Culture* (OUP 2006).

Table 7.1 Semantic primes, natural semantic metalanguage (NSM)

Substantives:
I, YOU, SOMEONE, PEOPLE, SOMETHING/THING, BODY
Determiners:
THIS, THE SAME, OTHER/ELSE
Quantifiers:
ONE, TWO, SOME, MANY/MUCH, LITTLE/FEW, ALL
Evaluators:
GOOD, BAD
Descriptors:
BIG, SMALL
Intensifier/Augmentor:
VERY, MORE
Mental predicates:
THINK, KNOW, WANT, FEEL, SEE, HEAR
Speech:
SAY, WORDS, TRUE
Actions, events, movement, contact:
DO, HAPPEN, MOVE, TOUCH
Location, existence, possession, specification:
BE (SOMEWHERE), THERE IS, HAVE (SOMETHING), BE (SOMEONE/SOMETHING)
Life and death:
LIVE, DIE
Time:
WHEN/TIME, NOW, BEFORE, AFTER, A LONG TIME, A SHORT TIME, FOR SOME TIME, MOMENT
Space:
WHERE/PLACE, HERE, ABOVE, BELOW; FAR, NEAR; SIDE, INSIDE;
Logical concepts:
NOT, MAYBE, CAN, BECAUSE, IF
Relational substantives:
KIND OF, PART OF
Similarity:
LIKE/AS/WAY[11]

I will consider the primes in relation to human rights in detail below. For the moment, given my reliance on their universality, it is worth considering this aspect in more detail. In particular, the claim that there are linguistic universals should not be understood as meaning that all languages are the same. Indeed, the fact that languages are not the same is exactly why NSM is useful in explicating cultural

11 Adapted from Cliff Goddard, 'Semantic Primes, Semantic Molecules, Semantic Templates: Key Concepts in the NSM Approach to Lexical Typology' (2012) 50(3), *Linguistics* 711, 713. For versions in other languages, see Cliff Goddard and Anna Wierzbicka (eds), *Meaning and Universal Grammar: Theory and Empirical Findings* (John Benjamins 2002).

concepts. Wierzbicka notes that while her theory is 'radically universalist' there are two 'provisos'.

> ... first, that I fully accept the Humboldtian view that despite the presence of universals, on the whole the semantic systems embodied in different languages are unique and culture-specific; and second, that the presence of 'embodied' (that is, lexicalized) universals does not mean perfect equivalence in language use.[12]

The approach 'accepts the uniqueness of all language-and-culture systems, but posits a set of shared concepts, in terms of which differences between these systems can be assessed and understood ...'.[13]

It is also important to note the distinction between semantic and lexical universals, as one lexeme may serve for more than one meaning. This has been the cause of much debate, especially in relation to the 'strong lexicalisation hypothesis' that states that 'Every semantically primitive meaning can be expressed through a distinct word, morpheme, or fixed phrase in every language.'[14] However, even those who don't agree with the lexical universality may allow for conceptual universality.[15] As Durst reminds us, 'It has to be emphasized, however, that semantic equivalents in two languages do not have to be formally identical.'[16] Moreover, some words are polysemous, a claim that is neither lightly nor easily made.[17]

> For example, we know that non-compositional polysemies are relatively common between SAY and DO, between SAY and WANT, between THERE IS and BE, and between BE and LIVE, among others.[18]

In addition to polysemy, NSM also takes account of allolexy, that primes may have more than one form, depending on the context of their use.

> If one word (or morpheme) can be associated with two different meanings, one meaning can often have two or more different lexical components. By analogy

12 Wierzbicka, *Semantics, Primes and Universals* (n 4) 15.

13 Wierzbicka, *Semantics, Primes and Universals* (n 4) 16.

14 Goddard 1994: 13-14, cited in Maria Koptjevskaja-Tamm and Inger Ahlgren, 'NSM: Theoretical, Methodological and Applicational Problems' (2003) 29, *Theoretical Linguistics* 247, 252.

15 Jurgen Bohnemeyer, 'NSM without the Strong Lexicalization Hypothesis' (2003) 29, *Theoretical Linguistics* 211.

16 Durst (n 6) 169.

17 Wierzbicka, *Semantics, Culture, and Cognition* (n 2) 13–14.

18 Cliff Goddard, 'Towards a systematic table of semantic elements', in Cliff Goddard (ed.), *Cross-Linguistic Semantics* (John Benjamins 2008) 72; see also Wierzbicka, *Semantics, Primes and Universals* (n 4) 28–9.

> with 'allomorphs' and 'allophones', such different exponents of the same primitive are called in NSM theory 'allolexes'.[19]

For example, 'I' and 'me' are allolexes of the same primitive 'I'. Goddard argues that allolexy is not problematic.

> I would like to suggest an analogy with the human body. The human body is clothed and decorated differently in different cultures and societies around the world. To the naked eye, people's physical forms look different in different parts of the world – so much so that we can often guess where someone comes from by how they look. But beneath the clothing, headgear, jewellery, tattoos, scarification, and other superficial alternations, the essential human body is the same all around the world, and nobody is much troubled by this.[20]

NSM does trouble scholars, however, with some finding the whole approach untenable.[21] There are reservations about the what 'primitive' in relation to primes means,[22] whether some primes are actually primitive or universal, how to decide and account for polysemy, how to construct and the read scripts, and whether the reductive paraphrases that NSM produces really help to explain concepts in an accessible way.[23] It is certainly true that the syntax and style of the NSM takes some getting used to. But this is true of any metalanguage. The fact that NSM is a subset of natural language should make this process easier. There are two particular issues I will deal with here as they are the most relevant to ways in which I use NSM. The first is whether the universality of the primes means that they are innate and the second is whether the primes are in fact primitive.

The list of primitives is, admittedly, 'hypothetical' and has been both expanded and altered over the years in the light of empirical work.[24] However, Wierzbicka argues that the fact people with different languages do manage to communicate

19 Anna Wierzbicka, *Semantics, Primes and Universals* (n 4) 26.

20 Cliff Goddard, 'Natural Semantic Metalanguage: The State of the Art', in Cliff Goddard (ed), *Cross-Linguistic Semantics* (John Benjamins, 2008) 1, 7.

21 Bart Geurts, 'Semantics as Lexicography' (2003) 29, *Theoretical Linguistics*, 223.

22 Koptjevskaja-Tamm and Ahlgren (n 14) 252. In particular, it is argued that it is not clear that the metalanguage is neutral or self-evident in its meaning; that is, Matthewson argues that the primes are actually rather complex, referring to extensive work by formal semanticists. Lisa Matthewson, 'Is the Meta-language really Natural?' (2003) 29, *Theoretical Linguistics* 263.

23 Barker argues that paraphrase is not enough, and that NSM cannot articulate the meaning of important linguistic meanings, such as names or performatives (2003). Chris Barker, 'Paraphrase is not Enough' (2003) 29, *Theoretical Linguistics*, 201–9. Colour terms have also been subject to discussion; Paul Kay, 'NSM and the meaning of color words' (2003) 29, *Theoretical Linguistics* 237.

24 Wierzbicka, *Semantics, Primes and Universals* (n 4) 13.

suggests that something must be shared at a basic level.[25] The primes are at this basic level and are indefinable, indecomposable and, for Wierzbicka, innate.[26]

> Thus, although words like *good* and *bad* in English, *bonus* and *malus* in Latin or *ii* and *warui* in Japanese are indeed human creations, the fact that we find such words – with exactly the same meaning – in all languages suggests that the concepts they express are innate, or to use Rorty's (1989) terms, 'found' rather than 'made'.[27]

This is a reasonable suggestion, but there is perhaps another explanation, albeit one that includes an extra step. In line with arguments made so far, it may well be that what looks to be 'innate' is instead grounded in human embodiment. In terms of the utility and soundness of NSM, it's not clear to me that innateness is crucial. Wierzbicka believes 'that language is not independent of the rest of cognition, and that meaning underlies language, not the other way around' that suggests that it may not be necessary to claim innateness for the words.[28] As Chapter 6 argued, cognition is linked with embodiment and with interaction with the world. Thus, what could be called innate might also be a function of embodiment together with the innate *capacity* for language. While this may seem to be splitting unnecessary hairs, I am wary of claiming the primes are innate for two reasons. First, if empirically shown to be universal whether they are innate is not relevant for the arguments I want to make here. Second, as I have argued previously, claiming that something is innate suggests inevitability, a kind of determinism and as such is potentially dangerous. As the previous chapter showed, concepts and metaphors that are universal may not have positive results for people and they can be challenged and altered on this basis. However, once something is considered innate, arguing for change can be more difficult.

To argue that the primes are innate would be useful in dealing with the criticism that rather than the NSM primes being undecomponsable they are actually complex.[29] Mathewson draws attention to work in formal semantics, and the struggles that scholars in this field have had when dealing with some of the words identified as primes. In the sense that primes cannot be decomposed into other, simpler, elements of natural language, it seems to me that the primes are not complex. Rather, complexity is introduced when they are used, that is, when they are combined with other words. For example, while the prime 'good' seems in isolation to be a non-complex term, irreducible to anything simpler in natural language, when combined with other words what 'good' means is inflected by context. Thus, a 'good knife' is one that is good for cutting or spreading butter or

25 Wierzbicka, *Semantics, Primes and Universals* (n 4) 14.
26 Wierzbicka, *Semantics, Primes and Universals* (n 4) 14.
27 Anna Wierzbicka, *What Did Jesus Mean?* (OUP 2001) 168.
28 Wierzbicka, *Semantics, Primes and Universals* (n 4) 21.
29 Matthewson (n 22).

whatever kind of knife it is. A 'good day' is one that brings feelings of happiness or purpose. There is a positive value judgement in both cases, against certain accepted criteria. While it is important to note that 'words don't have any meaning in isolation, but only in sentences …',[30] if all the contexts of use are considered, a meaning that is common to all uses should emerge. This will not capture the range of meanings, the complexity of the word, but it will reveal a semantic core.

In what follows here, the primes are treated largely in isolation. I do not mean to dismiss the arguments made about complexity, however this issue may not be problematic if the primes are considered separately. Moreover, when compared with some of the other universals proposed in relation to human rights, such as 'autonomy', 'personhood', 'fairness' and 'freedom',[31] it seems reasonable to think that the primes are both more primitive and more widespread. This does not mean that they can or should replace natural languages.

> A genuinely 'culture-free' nuclear vocabulary cannot exceed the set of word meanings which constitute the intersection of the vocabularies of all languages. Although such a minimal (but truly universal) vocabulary is sufficient for the elucidation of culture-specific concepts encoded in 'full' natural languages, as shown by the extensive corpus of NSM semantic studies, it is not sufficient for tasks like negotiating international agreements, conducting business negotiations, safeguarding human rights or coordinating anti-terrorism or disaster-relief operations on a global scale. For such purposes speed is as important as accuracy.
>
> Clearly then, a truly nuclear, culture-free subset of English cannot fulfil such a role: only a much richer, larger subset of English can do that, and such a larger subset cannot be 'culture-free'. In particular, culture-specific concepts like 'negotiations', 'compromise', 'deal', 'agreement', 'efficiency', 'evidence', 'commitment', 'deadline', 'probability', 'performance', 'competition', 'opportunity', 'feasible', 'reasonable' and 'fair' are unlikely to disappear from English-based international communication. On the other hand, NSM English, being culture-free, can play a useful role in the contemporary world as a

30 Wierzbicka, *Semantics, Primes and Universals* (n 4) 241. This quote refers to semantic invariable, that is, instead of meanings being fuzzy or indeterminate, Wierzbicka argues for a semantic invariant, or semantic core. She argues that by paying attention to how a word is used, we can find what is invariant in that meaning; this does not exhaust all possible meanings, but the semantic invariant can be delineated.

31 Finnis argues that there are seven 'basic forms of good': 'life, knowledge, play, aesthetic experience, friendship, practical reasonableness and religion'. John Finnis, *Natural Law and Natural Rights* (Clarendon 1980) 90, see also 85ff.

> universal cultural notation for elucidating meanings, ideas, assumptions, and so on, i.e. as an auxiliary language.[32]

NSM may not, by itself, be enough for the work of international law and politics with respect to human rights. But in challenging the idea that there is nothing shared among people, in resisting the idea that there is only diversity,[33] NSM provides a way of fleshing out the human frame of the body. Providing information about what it means to be a person, it leads to the third human right.

NSM and Human Rights

The primacy of embodiment has already been established and the corporeal is recoverable from the primes themselves (e.g. 'body'). Moreover, as language presupposes the body, these words could not exist without the embodied human. That humans have language, however, suggests that there is more to the human condition than corporeal survival. The primes help bring this into focus. Consideration of the relevance of primes to humans leads me to the third human right: a prohibition against dehumanisation. To understand this prohibition, however, one needs to know what a 'human' is. I first detail what the primes say about being human before considering the status of the concept of 'rights' in the light of Wierzbicka's work. I then discuss dehumanisation.

The list of primes may not immediately seem relevant to human rights. The process of fleshing out the human with NSM is a difficult one to document as I want to suggest that the primes show us, in simple terms, what it means to be a person. My approach to the primes was simply to consider them in relation to the human figure and try and see what they might be showing. This consideration involved something like entailment and presupposition. That is, the presence of a prime entails certain other things. For example, 'say' entails something like language and presupposes a body in an existential sense (rather than a pragmatic or semantic one). While my reading of the primes does not always conform to a strict understanding of either entailment or existential presupposition, this is the process I followed. And while paradoxical, given the primitive nature of primes, the results of this observation need to be framed in terms that are more complex than the primes themselves; otherwise, I would be reduced to simply reproducing the list in Table 7.1.

---

32 Cliff Goddard and Anna Wierzbicka, 'Semantic Primes and Cultural Scripts in Language Learning and Intercultural Communication', in Gary Palmer and Farzad Sharifian (eds), *Applied Cultural Linguistics: Implications for Second Language Learning and Intercultural Communication* (John Benjamins 2007) 105, 119.

33 Wierzbicka, *What Did Jesus Mean?* (n 27) 119.

'Human'

Relating NSM to human rights at first looks problematic as 'human' is not included. However, PERSON is present in so far as it is an allolex of someone.[34] Every person is a SOMEONE rather than a SOMETHING. More can be said about these persons. Persons have a BODY. While NSM is not required for this connection, the presence of BODY as universal term is reassuring (especially as it was not always included in the set of primes).[35] As the body as index shows, people LIVE and DIE; these are primes and universal facts. A person is also in relation with other persons; this is clear from the inclusion of I and YOU. As these are shifters, their referents change depending on who is speaking to whom. A person is both an I and a YOU at various times and in various places.

People are not simply embodied, however, they can also do things. A person can SAY something and other people can HEAR it. This is done with WORDS, and what is said may be TRUE or NOT TRUE. SAY and WORD also point to our relationship with other people. Just as our physical existence presupposes the existence of other people, language indicates the presence of a larger community.[36] Certainly a person may be the last surviving member of a speech community, but there would be no-one for them to say these words to.[37] One can't have a language (in anything but a metaphorical way) all by oneself. I, YOU, SAY, HEAR and WORD seed a world of people with common communicative codes.

The primes TRUE and NOT TRUE suggest two things. First, there is a world that people have access to which can be used as a measure of what is said, of what is the case. It also suggests the ability to say something that is not true; in this sense, it points to the choices that people have with respect to what they say and think. Indeed, THINK, KNOW and WANT also tell us that we have some kind of agency, we can DO things. These primes also tell us that people are capable of monitoring the input of the outside the world, even if only by naming the processing of modes of information – SEE, HEAR, TOUCH.

Our relationship with the world is a mediated one. We SEE the world through parts of our body. As it is a body with many senses it is possible to SEE, HEAR and TOUCH. The world that we sense is populated by people and things, that also DO things, that MOVE and that makes things HAPPEN. We distinguish things that are BIG and things that are SMALL. We can divide things into PARTS, classify them into KINDS and appreciate similarities and differences in that some things are LIKE other things. It is a multidimensional world, that we can reckon from

34 Wierzbicka, *Semantics, Primes and Universals* (n 4) 114 ff.

35 It was added by 2002, see Durst (n 6) 159.

36 Notwithstanding the difficulty of defining 'speech community', see Ben Rampton, 'Speech Community and Beyond' in Nikolas Coupland and Adam Jaworski (eds), *The New Sociolinguistics Reader* (Macmillan 2009) 694.

37 Of course, linguists trained in documenting languages would be able to develop knowledge of the language and would be appropriate interlocutors.

some reference point and realise that HERE is a place with space ABOVE it and BELOW with other places both NEAR and FAR away. There is a temporal aspect here as well, a NOW that is BEFORE what will happen in A SHORT TIME from now, or even A LONG TIME from now. Time, like space, is of different shapes; things can last FOR SOME TIME or just for a MOMENT. It is a world that we can handle, interact with, observe and assess. We know the difference between ONE and SOME between TWO and MANY. All people have these primes, and we have a sense of that very large number too, ALL. We can also HAVE relations to things as have can be used in the context SOMEONE HAS SOMETHING.[38]

Our thinking goes beyond simple counting and observation. People are able to evaluate things, in terms of whether they are GOOD or BAD, though significantly, apparently not universally in terms of 'right' and 'wrong'. As the primes in the field of time indicate, we can deal with abstract concepts. Whatever our cultural traditions about reasoning and argument, authority and tradition, there seems to be a basic understanding of causation; some things are the case BECAUSE of something else. We know that knowledge is not always complete, that sometimes a MAYBE is required. Whatever we call it, doubt and uncertainty appear to be universal concepts. We can apprehend similarity and dissimilarity, of something LIKE and NOT LIKE something else; we can imagine contingencies or future events, we have the concept of IF.

Wierzbicka has used the primes to compose a script that expresses what is good for people, providing a way of thinking about what a suitable environment for people would look like. The following lines set out much of what is already implicit in the primes.

At all times in all places people think that:

1. it is good for people to live
2. it is good for people to live with other people
3. it is good for people to know many things
4. it is good for people to be able to do some things because they want to do these things, not because they have to do these things.[39]

The first two lines state what could be considered facts. People live, thus for people to be people – to exist – they need at least to live. This takes for granted the notion that it is better for people to exist than not and as such is not problematic for human rights, as they presuppose the existence of humans. The second line can be read as a recognition that people depend on each other for their existence. For people to continue to exist, more than one person is required. The third and fourth spell out what seems to be implicit in the primes themselves. For a person to really be a person, it is good if she can do what a person does; that is, think, want and do.

38 HAVE is also a reasonably recent addition, appearing from 2002, see Durst (n 6) 160.

39 Wierzbicka, *What Did Jesus Mean?* (n 27) 169.

Wierzbicka regards these four things as being akin to the values posited by natural law though suggests that they may be different from 'absolute moral (or religious) values'.[40] Her proposals can also be connected to the human rights proposed so far. The fact that people live, and that we would probably rather have some people than no people, requires environmental protection and the protection of basic needs to food, water, shelter and sleep. This basic nature of human life has been considered through the frame of the body and the frame of the globe. The ability to be a person (in 3 and 4) to know, think and do something, obviously depends on having basic needs met. It also depends on having meaningful choices because a person is a being that can think, know and do.

To paraphrase the Proclaimers,[41] I don't want to complicate what the primes make simple. But what the primes tell us is in a sense so obvious that it may be missed. People are thinking, feeling, seeing, hearing and doing entities. People exist in relation with other people and with the world. People assess the world in temporal, spatial and evaluative terms. A person is a someone. What the primes point to in terms of human universals may well be more allusive than declarative, but this just means it provides us not so much with a map, but with a lens. Looking at people as someones rather than somethings matters. In terms of human rights it is really the only thing that matters. However, history tells us that this does not always happen. I return to this presently. First, having established that something like 'human' is universal, it is worth considering whether 'rights' are universal too.

'Rights'

There is nothing in the list of primes that is obviously connected with the usual understanding of 'rights'. This is not very surprising, as Wierzbicka has documented the lack of universality of this concept observing '... that *rights* and *obligations* are English words without exact semantic equivalents in most other languages, including other European languages like French or German'.[42] It is, however, understandable that an English speaker would see 'right' as a straightforward category. As Wierzbicka argues 'everyday English words like *right*, *wrong*, *fact*, *evidence*, *reasonable*, *fair*, and *unfair* are important instances of words that are "used automatically" and yet contain "a wealth of history"'.[43] This is not a universal history, however, but one that is specific to English culture.[44]

There have been arguments for a universal concept of 'right', but this does not include human rights, instead, it is concerned with

40 Wierzbicka, *What Did Jesus Mean?* (n 27) 169.

41 'Don't let me complicate what you made simple', The Proclaimers, 'Beautiful Truth', *This Is the Story* (Chrysalis, 1987).

42 Anna Wierzbicka, 'Theory and Empirical Findings: A Response to Jackendoff' (2007) 4(3), *Intercultural Pragmatics* 399, 402.

43 Wierzbicka, 'A Response to Jackendoff' (n 42) 406.

44 Wierzbicka, *English* (n 10).

> rather more mundane sorts of right such as those involved in possession (one has the right to use this object as one wishes, within parameters, and the right to give it away), agreements and contracts (one has the right to demand that the other person fulfil his/her side of the deal), authority (one has the right to impose demands on others), and marriage (one has the right to engage in sexual relations with this person).[45]

It may well be the case that all people engage in similar kinds of relations, but as the examples show, even this 'mundane' meaning of right involves power relations and what look very much like contractual relations. Even if these are universal, as Chapter 5 argued, construing human relationships like contracts is problematic.

As mentioned, Wierzbicka takes a different view and argues that in English the meaning of 'right' is connected to the development of English democracy and a particular mode of reasoning.[46] Moreover, tracing this development suggests a primitive that could be used in the place of 'rights' in the context of 'human rights'. Wierzbicka argues that 'right' was originally connected to the practice of 'thinking well', making judgements about what is 'good' in a scientific or rational way, that is, a 'good' way. This particular mode of thinking well then began to be discussed in terms of 'right' and 'wrong'.

> Thus, the ascendancy of *right* and *wrong* over *good* and *bad* seems to reflect a more 'rational', more 'procedural', more 'reason-based' approach to human life, and a retreat from a pure distinction between 'good' and 'bad' unsupported by any appeal to reason, procedures, methods, or intersubjectively available evidence. An ethics of 'right and wrong' is an ethics in which the choice between 'good' and 'bad' is seen as something that can be decided by reason, by good thinking, and something that can be interpersonally validated – like science. It is a 'rational ethics', an ethics which does not need to be grounded in metaphysics (in particular, in God) but can be grounded in reason.[47]

'Right' is thus ultimately connected to what is 'good' especially in terms of thinking, arguing and choosing a particular method for arriving at conclusions. Clearly this is a slightly different meaning from that of a legal or moral right. However, as Wierzbicka observes, they are related.[48] And as the shift from 'good' to 'right' that Wierzbicka described took place in the seventeenth and eighteenth

---

45 Ray Jackendoff, 'Conceptual Semantics and Natural Semantic Metalanguage Theory have Different Goals' (2007) 4(3), *Intercultural Pragmatics* 411, 413. See also Anna Wierzbicka, 'NSM Semantics versus Conceptual Semantics: Goals and standards (A response to Jackendoff)' (2007) 4(4), *Intercultural Pragmatics*, 521.

46 Anna Wierzbicka, 'Right and Wrong: From Philosophy to Everyday Discourse' (2002) 4(2), *Discourse Studies* 225, 236.

47 Wierzbicka, 'Right and Wrong' (n 46) 236.

48 Wierzbicka, *English* (n 10) 317, n 7.

centuries,[49] the same time as the development of what are now considered early human rights texts, it does not seem unreasonable to apply what has been said about the adjectival 'right' to the nominal form.

As mentioned, before this shift, 'right' was about speaking well 'an evaluation supported with a reference to truth'.[50] It then became associated with thinking well, reasoning in a way that would lead to the right conclusion. What is 'right' is that which is straight and well considered. If this is applied to the question of human rights, arriving at an appropriate set of rights requires thinking well about people. Human rights, then, become that which protects people as people. This is far from controversial (see Chapter 1). But focusing on the 'good', on thinking well about people, makes clear that the primary object of consideration in human rights is not the 'rights' part of the collocation but the 'human' portion. It also suggests that human rights are what people need to be human. Protection of the natural environment and protection of bare life are the first two human rights, as these protect the person as referent, ensuring her survival. The third human right protects what a person is over and above her corporeal state.

Dehumanisation

The primes set out what it is to be a person in the world. They show that people are thinking, feeling, sensing, corporeal beings. A someone is not a something. However, history demonstrates that people are very often treated as things. In fleshing out what it means to be a person, NSM helps make sense of the primary declarative of human rights: 'a person is a person'. Bearing the primes in mind, and taking into account the corporeality of people, it seems to me that the third human right needs to be a prohibition, that is, a prohibition against dehumanisation. After discussion of the definition of dehumanisation, I will explore some of the practical consequences of this, that is, what the prohibition would mean in practice before considering the ideological causes of dehumanisation.

Stollznow provides an NSM explication of dehumanisation.

a. everyone knows: people are all the same kind of thing
b. because of this, it is good if people don't do very bad things to other people
c. when X doesn't think like this about Y, X thinks like this:
d. 'Y is something very bad
e. Y is not like me in any way
f. it is like Y is not a person
g. because of this, I can do anything to Y
h. it is not bad if something happens to Y because of this
i. because of this, something very bad can happen to Y'

49 Wierzbicka, *English* (n 10) 95.
50 Wierzbicka, *English* (n 10) 95.

j. people think: it is very bad to do something like this.[51]

In a sense, this is a straightforward definition of dehumanisation. The thinking that underlies treating a person as a thing is captured in lines (d) to (h). Bad things can be done to a thing that is not considered a person. If a person is not recognised as a someone these bad things become more likely. The script captures these consequences in line (i). The definition does rely on two things, present in lines (a) and (b). First, it insists that everyone realises that a person is a person. Second, it asserts that treating people as people is a good thing. These are actually rather difficult to argue for in isolation. In terms of (a), I suggest that logic, and thinking 'well', leads to confirmation of the fact that a person is a person. Given a person is a person, it is logical, it is 'right thinking', to treat a person as a person. Moreover, treating people as something other than people is bad for these people; it would be to treat them as things rather than someones and would does not allow them to be what they are. Moreover, if we take the interconnectedness of people seriously, treating people as things is bad for everyone as all people are 'part of the same thing' in so far as we all inhabit the earth, rely on it and on each other.

It is also important to consider the preconditions necessary for seeing people as people. As Rorty suggests, a person who is safe, secure, with basic needs met is much more likely to see the other as a person.[52] Thus, a necessary consequence of the prohibition against dehumanisation is the creation of basic levels of security, both physical and psychological, for all people. I am not suggesting that we can completely rid the world of bad things, but it seems to me that it is possible to create an environment, physical and social, that is much more hospitable to and understanding of the human condition than that in which we currently live. Such an environment should pay attention to the needs of the body and the needs of people as thinking, feeling, beings.

There is another aspect of dehumanisation that needs to be considered. In the lines above, dehumanisation is very much caused by human agents; it is a person who does bad things to other people. While this clearly covers acts of commission, the prohibition against dehumanisation should also cover acts of omission as these are no less devastating in their effects. Here, I take the case of food security in order to explain the consequences of the right against dehumanisation and to argue that this right applies even in apparent absence of human cause.

We are perhaps used to thinking about lack of food security as an environmental issue, a kind of natural disaster, one that occurs in cases of catastrophic flooding or prolonged drought. At a basic level, food security depends on the functioning of the environment. But ensuring food security in the contemporary world requires

---

51 Karen Stollznow, 'Dehumanisation in Language and Thought' (2008) 7(2), *Journal of Language and Politics* 177, 184.

52 Richard Rorty, 'Human Rights, Rationality and Sentimentality' in Obrad Savić (ed.), *The Politics of Human Rights* (Verso 1999) 67. See also P.a.p.-Blog // Human Rights Etc. http://filipspagnoli.wordpress.com/. Accessed 12 May 2013.

more than protection of the environment. Food may be produced and yet still be unavailable to those who need it. The increasing reliance on food banks in the United Kingdom makes this plain.[53] For someone in the United Kingdom (or in similar political and economic context) to have real food security, they need to have secure employment at a living wage, be supported through welfare payments at a reasonable level or simply have enough money that they need neither work nor seek financial assistance. A living wage, and what amounts to a reasonable level of welfare payments, depends in turn on the price of food. This, along with availability of employment and financial sustainability of government support programmes, are not issues for the individual. They depend on complex, global, financial considerations.[54]

In order to protect something as 'basic' as food security, we need to examine the systems in which we live. That is, we need to think about the dehumanisation that can happen even in the apparent absence of a human agent.[55] For example, in the case of natural disasters like earthquakes and floods, it is clear that bad things have happened to people. In the wake of such events, the 'international community' is usually called upon to assist. It is good for other people to do something when these bad things happen. It is not necessary to specify a single responsible duty bearer for a right to exist, rather, the duty to do something attaches to those who

53 Of course, the issue is even more pronounced in the developing world. Charlie Cooper, 'UN official alarmed by rise of food banks in UK', *The Independent* 17 February 2013 http://www.independent.co.uk/news/uk/home-news/un-official-alarmed-by-rise-of-food-banks-in-uk-8498791.html#. Accessed 7 March 2013.

54 See Paul McMahon, *Feeding Frenzy: The New Politics of Food* (Profile 2013).

55 Stollznow makes this point through describing 'mechanisation', one of the three ways in which people are dehumanised. The other two are brutalisation and objectification/animalisation. Mechanisation is defined as follows: 'This is literal de-personalisation, to make a process "mechanical" or "impersonal" by removing an element of human involvement (typically resultant of the industrial age). This suggests an affected individual or group of people (e.g., employees lose their jobs due to the implementation of a computerised system, or, customers lose a personalised service)' (180). Brutalisation is the second form: 'In usage this is akin to "brain washing" or "cognitive programming" and is often institutionalised. This suggests that a passive experiencer is "numbed" to emotion and responsiveness (e.g., army training leads to the dehumanisation of soldiers). This sense refers to severe treatment or the conditioning of personality and emotions, so that an affected person appears compassionless, emotionally unresponsive and is therefore seemingly "less human". This implies the oppression, indoctrination or cognitive control of an individual or group (e.g., cult members suffer dehumanisation). Furthermore, this act of "programming" can desensitise a person, enabling them to perform violent acts without emotion, self-restraint or the human instinct for empathy' (181). Objectification/animalisation is the third form of dehumanisation: 'This is to disregard the equal human status of an individual or group as fellow members of the same species. This involves the perception of a target as somehow "unhuman", and often results in the mistreatment of the target. This sense conjures up a dichotomy of victimiser and victim …' (181). Stollznow (n 51).

are able to do something.[56] We understand this in cases of natural disaster. We are less willing to see this duty in other, less sudden, instances of human suffering.

It is also important to note that even the most agentless of actions – like natural disasters – may be disastrous for people because of underlying problems like poverty, lack of security and paucity of resources.[57] While not always obvious, these root causes can be connected to human action. I return to these root causes below. First, it helps to understand how systematic dehumanisation takes place.

What Makes Us Inhuman?

The dehumanisation of people happens not just at an individual level, but also more systematically. Here, I argue that the dehumanisation of people is linked to the personification of non-human entities. While my purpose here is not to examine the actual causes behind this dual shift, it is to suggest that dehumanisation seems to be driven by the dominance of capitalist ideologies. This results in corporations being personified, often so as to gain rights, while people are dehumanised. These two moves are linked to the same underlying ideology; that the market is the most important entity of all. The market is not only personified, it is also deified. I deal first with the personification of corporations before considering the dehumanisation of people by turning them into objects, specifically, products that can be sold. Finally, I consider the divine status of the market.

Humanisation and corporations

The dominance of the corporation has also been made with great cogency, precision and humanity by Anna Grear in the context of human rights. She warns against the claims corporations are making to human rights as while corporations are composed of people, there is no 'simple continuity between the corporation and its human sub-stratum for the purposes of attributing the individual human rights of human beings to the corporate form'.[58] Drawing attention to the distinction between real people and legal persons, Grear focuses on the body; 'Human beings are, fundamentally, body-persons – embodied personalities'.[59] The problem for embodied humans is that as shown in Chapter 3, law is not well suited to bodies and people.

---

56 Amartya Sen, 'Elements of a Theory of Human Rights' (2004) 32(4), *Philosophy and Public Affairs* 315; James Griffin, *On Human Rights* (OUP 2008).

57 Susan Marks, 'Human Rights and Root Causes' (2011) 74(1), *MLR* 57.

58 Anna Grear, 'Challenging Corporate "Humanity": Legal Disembodiment, Embodiment and Human rights' (2007) 7 *H. R. L. Rev*. 511, 517.

59 Grear 'Challenging Corporate "Humanity"' (n 58) 521.

> At the structural level, the artificiality of law better suits corporations than concrete human beings. At the ideological level, the construction of the archetypal liberal legal actor, law's privileged insider, the acquisitive, rational, narcissistic, will-driven, self-interested possessive, quasi-disembodied individual is an almost precise match for the corporation as the acquisitive *persona* of capital.[60]

Grear links this preference for legal entities over natural persons to broader patterns of economic globalisation. Further, this economic shift itself leads to human rights violations by corporations in a systematic way; and while corporations increasingly claim human rights, they are not held accountable to their violations. 'In this globalised age the power of economic actors requires, it is suggested, human rights to operate as critical concepts of resistance'.[61] The problem is that economic actors are now people, not just legally but also at the level of conceptual metaphor. Specifically, A CORPORATION IS A PERSON is a dominant metaphor, not only in law but also more generally. Here, I consider the use of this metaphor in a legal context. This is for two reasons. First, close attention to the language shows the instability of the conceptual metaphor when applied to actions that are essentially human. Second, the case examined here also makes clear what is driving this personification – the importance of the market. The metaphor A CORPORATION IS A PERSON works together with MONEY IS SPEECH.

Citizens and Corporations

The American case *Citizens United v. Federal Election Commission* (2010)[62] dealt with freedom of speech in relation to political campaigning and corporations. In particular, the case was concerned with the constitutionality of the specific rules that corporations had to follow in order to finance the promotion of a political party or candidate in an electoral period. The finer legal points at issue will not be covered here; suffice it to say that the real issue was whether there could be legislative restriction of the speech of non-human entities in the context of electoral politics. As mentioned, the decision ultimately depends on two conceptual metaphors; A CORPORATION IS A PERSON and MONEY IS SPEECH. For anyone not familiar with American Constitutional law, the treatment of money as speech is probably the most surprising aspect of the case. However, it appears that this is already well established in American jurisprudence and was not an issue.

60 Grear 'Challenging Corporate "Humanity"' (n 58) 524. Moreover, '... there is a remarkable degree of correspondence between law's person, particularly as exemplified by its dominant template – a template that forms the submerged but archetypal beneficiary of liberal law – and the corporation' Anna Grear, *Redirecting Human Rights: Facing the Challenge of Corporate Legal Humanity* (Palgrave 2010) 48.

61 Grear 'Challenging Corporate "Humanity"' (n 58) 521.

62 558 U.S. 310 (2010) < http://www.supremecourt.gov/opinions/09pdf/08-205.pdf>. Last accessed 17 May 2013.

In general terms, and certainly in the terms of arguments made in the judgments, the meaning of 'freedom of speech' was the central question. The judgments make clear the importance attached to freedom of speech generally in American constitutional law, most notably through recurrent reference to any restrictions on speech apparently having a 'chilling' effect.[63]

The metaphor SPEECH IS MONEY may not be seem to be as common as the more familiar TIME IS MONEY but it is far from new.[64] The classic instantiation is the phrase 'money talks' that is attested from the late nineteenth century (1880) if not before[65] and thus clearly well established in the English language. Of itself, this may not be problematic. However, close attention to the language used to argue for unrestricted speech – that in this case means unrestricted spending of money for political campaigning and advertising – makes plain the contradictions that arise when dealing with the 'speech' of corporations. The terms in which freedom of speech is endorsed in the judgments should present a problem for corporations. These difficulties, however, are largely glossed over.

> The rights of citizens to inquire, to hear, to speak, and to use information to reach consensus is a precondition to enlightened self-government and a necessary means to protect it.[66]

People speak, they hear, they think and they come to know things. To speak and hear, however, requires at least two interlocutors. A person hearing needs to hear something; a person saying is speaking to someone. Discussion and debate require, even according to the most basic models of communication, at least two parties. Fitting corporations into this model presents a challenge that the majority implicitly address. Justice Kennedy, for example, makes plain that corporations have 'views'[67] while accepting that these are not 'monolithic'.[68] But it is important to see these 'views' for what they are, that is, such views can only be a metaphor resulting from personification. Corporations can only have 'views' if one accepts that A CORPORATION IS A PERSON.

While a corporation is clearly a 'legal person', attributing it distinctly human features elaborates this metaphor in significant ways. It results in the proposition

---

63 Kennedy J, who gave the opinion of the court, at 9, 17, 19, 41; Thomas J at 5. There are many conceptual metaphors which inform these judgments. For example, the metaphor SILENCE IS COLD appears to be conventional, given its recurrence in the judgments.

64 For discussion of TIME IS MONEY, see George Lakoff and Mark Johnson, *Metaphors We Live By* (University of Chicago Press 1980). For discussion of SPEECH IS MONEY as used in American jurisprudence, see Linda L. Berger 'Of Metaphor, Metonymy, and Corporate Money: Rhetorical Choices in Supreme Court Decisions on Campaign Finance Regulation' (2007) 58 *Mercer L. Rev.* 949.

65 Oxford English Dictionary www.oed.com. There is an attested use from 1681.

66 (n 62) 23 (Kennedy J).

67 (n 62) 22.

68 (n 62) 48.

that a corporation can 'author' a message, one that a citizen will be able to 'hear'. In this case, the 'authoring' is closely connected to the MONEY IS SPEECH metaphor, as corporations can't literally speak thus their messages need to be 'authored' by purchasing a speaker. But even if one accepts that this makes the corporation an author, it does not make it an interlocutor. There is no way an individual can 'speak' to this entity in a meaningful way, that is, in a way that can be heard. Certainly one might argue that, citizens can 'speak' with their own purchasing power, or shareholders can speak with their votes (at Annual General Meetings). But this depends on a particular kind of relationship (many corporations don't deal with individual consumers as such and many shareholders are themselves corporations). Moreover, the effects of any consumer or shareholder communication may well take some time to come about. The citizen cannot 'inquire' and there can be no meaningful 'consensus'.

If corporations are people, their speech can be restricted in the same way that any person's speech may be limited. In the United States, however, the value placed on freedom of speech means that any such restriction is very carefully considered. The argument in this case was phrased in terms of identity. That is, limiting the free speech of corporations would be to limit speech on the basis of the identity of the speaker. As Justice Kennedy argues, 'Speech restrictions based on the identity of the speaker are all too often simply a means to control content.'[69] Hence, the restriction of corporate free speech is portrayed as being a form of censorship that is detrimental for 'the people'. What is lacking here is any consideration of the power of this corporate interlocutor. The only power that the majority seek to protect 'the people' from is the power of government to restrict speech.[70] Thus, when Justice Kennedy declares that 'The civic discourse belongs to the people',[71] he makes no distinction between corporate bodies and corporeal bodies. Indeed, the idea that one could do so is ridiculed, as '... the individual person's right to speak includes the right to speak in association with other individual persons'.[72] The corporation, then is construed simply as a group of people, as an 'association[] of citizens ... that have taken the corporate form'.[73]

The logic that informs the majority position is articulated and critiqued in legal and rhetorical terms by the dissenting opinion of Justice Stevens who describes 'the majority's incessant talk of a "ban" [on free speech as] aim[ing] at a straw man'.[74] Specifically, he points out the difference between legal persons and human persons: 'The fact that corporations are different from human beings might seem

69 (n 62) 24.
70 (n 62) 38 (Kennedy J).
71 (n 62) 57.
72 (n 62) 7 (Scalia J).
73 (n 62) 40 (Kennedy J).
74 (n 62) 28.

to need no elaboration, except that the majority opinion almost completely elides it.'[75] He then goes on to specify some of the differences between the two.

> It might also be added that corporations have no consciences, no beliefs, no feelings, no thoughts, no desires. Corporations help structure and facilitate the activities of human beings, to be sure, and their 'personhood' often serves as a useful legal fiction. But they are not themselves members of 'We the People' by whom and for whom our Constitution was established.[76]

Invoking models of communication discussed above, he asks who can be said to be 'speaking' when a corporation promotes a particular political candidate, thus making clear the difficulty in maintaining the entailments of THE CORPORATION IS A PERSON metaphor when it comes to speech.[77] In stark contrast to the majority, Justice Stevens' attention to 'real people' and the 'real world' takes account of the actual processes of communication, persuasion, deliberation and power.[78]

> In the real world, we have seen, corporate domination of the airwaves prior to an election may decrease the average listener's exposure to relevant viewpoints, and it may diminish citizens' willingness and capacity to participate in the democratic process.[79]

At the core of this case is the question: what is a person? The importance given to the 'speech' (money) of some 'people' (corporations) reveals the dominant modes of analysis at work here. Who matters most is made clear in Justice Scalia's closing lines.

> Indeed, to exclude or impede corporate speech is to muzzle the principal agents of the modern free economy. We should celebrate rather than condemn the addition of this speech to the public debate.[80]

Such celebration is even more of a triumph for some legal persons than others, as the fictional legal person has more rights and certainly more power than 'real'

75 (n 62) 75.

76 (n 62) 76.

77 (n 62) 77.

78 (n 62) 80.

79 (n 62) 83. Even without this passionate dissent, Justice Scalia's words are easily deconstructed. He argues 'The [first] Amendment is written in terms of "speech", not speakers' and yet then demonstrates how the former requires the latter when he continues 'Its texts offers no foothold for excluding any category of speaker...' (Scalia J at 8; see also Kennedy J at 26).

80 (n 62) 9; my emphasis.

people. What matters now is not democracy and people, but the 'modern economy' and its 'principle agents', corporations.

The humanisation of corporations has consequences for real people, not only in terms of cases like *Citizens United* but also in discursive and ideological terms. Specifically, the dominance of the 'modern economy' means that people must now identify themselves in terms that are compatible with this system. This is not to say that dehumanisation is only a result of political and economic changes as there have always been ways for dehumanising the other. Perhaps the most pervasive tactic, one that continues to be used, is the animalisation of people. And one of the most common groups to be turned into animals is immigrants. It is worth dealing with this process of animalisation and the related metaphors applied to immigrants as it shows two things. First, it recalls a metaphor that has already been discussed in Chapters 1 and 4, the nation as body. Second, it helps to understand the role of cognitive metaphors in dealing with fear and risk. As the modern world is one fraught with risk, it is important to understand the reflex of othering when people feel threatened.

Humans and Animals

The treatment of people as animals is a classic strategy for characterising an out-group. It is especially powerful in relation to human rights where being human is exactly what one needs to be in order to claim rights. Animals will always rank less highly than people in the hierarchical great chain of being.[81] This ranking is clear in Santa Ana's examination of metaphors used for immigrants in the US and demonstrates the power of a person is an animal metaphor as well as the way in which in-group borders can map directly onto national borders. The nation, construed as a body or a house, is defiled by immigrants who are construed as animals, parasites, criminals, carriers of illness or simply dirt.[82] Santa Ana also notes the presence of secondary metaphors, including seeing as immigrants as debased people, weeds and commodities.[83]

While seeing immigrants as animals is clearly racist and dehumanising, these metaphors are

> … manifestations of deeply-held concepts of what (not who) immigrants are. Such a world-view precludes any presumption that they are vested by birth with

81 Otto Santa Ana, '"Like an animal I was treated": Anti-immigrant Metaphor in US Public Discourse' (1999) 10(2), *Discourse and Society* 191, 202.

82 Santa Ana (n 81). See also Elisabeth El Refaie, 'Metaphors We Discriminate By: Naturalized Themes in Austrian Newspaper Articles about Asylum Seekers' (2001) 5(3), *Journal of Sociolinguistics* 352; Annabelle Mooney, 'Citizens, Immigrants, Anarchists and Other Animals', in Anne Wagner et al (eds), *Contemporary Issues in the Semiotics of Law* (Hart 2005) 35.

83 Santa Ana (n 81) 198.

> the same human rights as citizens, and that they should be shown due respect for the difficult and ill-paid work they provide for American society.[84]

Only citizens are people, as they are part of the national body.

Seeing other people as animals also makes empathy difficult. Indeed, the characterisation of people as animals can be understood as part of a broader set of processes that Lynne Cameron identifies as dypathy.[85] Dyspathy is defined in contrast to empathy; it is the inhibition of empathy that blocks recognition of the Other by exclusion, distance, resistance or hiding.[86] Cameron notes that this is an important consideration in trying to make sense of dialogue and cognition in conflict situations; it also seems to be relevant in responses to in-group and out-group members. It is linked to uncertainty. Describing social categorisation and social myths, Cameron explains that:

> Reducing uncertainty for one's own group operates as a factor that motivates self-categorization, i.e. alignment of the self with a group prototype, and the building of self-identity through negative attitudes to outgroups.[87]

In contemporary post-modernity, we are all living with uncertainty; few of us feel secure. We inhabit a risk society.[88] In the West, the economic crisis has only made this risk both more acute and more visible.[89] Dyspathy, the blocking of the Other, is sure to increase in times of crisis, apparent scarcity and threat. And whereas 'empathy individualizes and particularizes the Other, dehumanisation in violent/conflict situations works by stereotyping and generalising of entire social groups'.[90] Because of the radical uncertainty of the risk society we are always in a 'violent/conflict' situation, especially if this is understood in economic terms.[91]

---

84 Santa Ana (n 81) 218.

85 Lynne Cameron, 'Dyspathy: The Dynamic Complement of Empathy' (2012), *Living with Uncertainty* Working paper 5 www.open.ac.uk/researchprojects/livingwithuncertainty. Accessed 4 March 2013.

86 Cameron (n 85).

87 Cameron (n 85) 8.

88 Ulrich Beck, *Risk Society* (M. Ritter tr, Sage 1992).

89 And as Pogge points out, we can't ignore the 'risk' from global conditions such as poverty. Of course, the West poses a larger and more enduring risk to the rest of the world. Thomas Pogge, *World Poverty and Human Rights* (2nd ed. *Polity* 2008) 218.

90 Cameron (n 85) 9, drawing on J. Halpern and H.M. Weinstein 'Rehumanizing the Other: Empathy and Reconciliation' (2004) 26, *HRQ* 561.

91 This would help explain the criminalization of the poor that Helena Kennedy has described. Helena Kennedy, *Just Law: The Changing Face of Justice – and Why it Matters to us all* (Vintage 2005) Chapter 11.

In the UK at least, debates about migration are often framed in economic terms.[92] Migrants are portrayed as claiming financial assistance from the state to which they should not be entitled as well as 'taking' jobs from citizens. Certainly there are also strong elements of racism in here,[93] but the idea that migrants put pressure on the labour market is what I want to foreground here. While Santa Ana notes a secondary metaphor in immigration debates, one that sees migrants as commodities, this metaphor is now much more widespread. We are all commodities now, and it seems that part of the reason migration is seen as so threatening is that the marketplace is full.

Person as Commodity

In her account of the 'market society', that includes detailed discussion of the marketisation of education, public services and religion, Gerlinde Mautner examines the marketisation of the self.[94] People are no longer humans, they are products, commodities that need to be created, promoted and sold in the labour market.[95] Moreover, individuals are both agents and objects; they have to market themselves. We are all chattels now; but we also 'own' our selves. This explains how we can be held responsible when we don't perform well in the market. Unemployment, for example, is a personal failure rather than a necessary feature of the system.[96] Ownership of and responsibility for the self also means that we

92 See Greg Philo, Emma Briant and Pauline Donald, *Bad News for Refugees* (Pluto 2013).

93 Drawing on Žižek, Marks asks whether 'we exploit these [migrant] workers because we are racist' or whether '"we are racist in order to exploit" them'. Marks (n 57) 72–3, citing Slavoj Žižek, 'Human Rights and its Discontents' lecture at Bard College, 16 November 1999 < http://www.egs.edu/faculty/slavoj-zizek/articles/human-rights-and-its-discontents/>. Accessed 6 March 2013.

94 Gerlinde Mautner, *Language and the Market Society: Critical reflections on Discourse and Dominance* (Routledge 2010).

95 Mautner (n 94) 125ff.

96 Increasingly in the United Kingdom, unemployed people are represented as 'lazy scroungers' unwilling to work. However, the logic of the capitalist system is that there needs to be a ready labour pool, 'No economic system has ever kept people permanently in employment'. Kennedy (n 91) 233. The problem is not that there can't be full employment, the issue is that this fact is denied. Žižek remarks: 'I claim that – and this is my thesis that I developed in practically all of my last books — that isn't it that the power itself functions, the power itself has to disavow its own founding operation. For example, the classical example, which is for me the model of power: Let's take America in the '20s. You have the Ku Klux Klan. It was the necessary support of power, but it was disavowed, it was not publicly acknowledged. This is what interests me, this obscene underside of power, how power, in order to function, has to repress not the opponent, but has to split in itself. You have a whole set of measures which power uses, but disavows them; uses them, but they are operative but not publicly acknowledged. This is for me the obscenity of power.' Žižek (n 93).

are responsible for our own exploitation. This is biopolitics in its most advanced form; not in the interests of the state but in service of the market. What looks like the ultimate in freedom and autonomy is actually the playing out of late capitalism in all areas of lives, bodies and selves.[97]

While the 'commodified self' 'has complex political, cultural and socio-psychological underpinnings' it is also linked to 'celebrity culture and consumerism' as well as 'the role that consumption behaviour and mass-mediated, artificial lifestyles play in fashioning the project of the self'.[98] This project is connected to consumption in yet another way, as our identities can be understood as simply the sum total of our consumer preferences. And while consumption choices are choices in one sense, the way commodities are branded and sold along with the data that this generates means that our purchasing choices are used to encourage more consumption.[99] Our choices have consequences for our identity and for the consumer choices offered in future.

In relation to the self as brand, Mautner points out that people are both product and seller, encouraged, even compelled, to brand the self according to market demands.[100]

> In 'doing identity', the onus is placed firmly on the individual to manage his or her self, and it is the individual, too, that is made to bear full [134] responsibility for the success or failure of the project.[101]

The individual is not simply autonomous, she is completely responsible for both the construction of self and the reception of this identity project. The particular metaphor of marketing the self is that of a brand; 'based on an implied equivalence between self and product'.[102] Individuals are also encouraged to be like businesses, to have 'mission statements', to conduct 'image audits' and to see personal relationships as business assets and opportunities.[103] At the core of the commodification of self, then, is a tension between the object (A PERSON IS A

---

97 Mautner (n 94) 128. As well as being commodities on the labour market, people are also encouraged to style themselves in particular ways in order to be successful in the sexual market. Dating and relationship advice encourages us to approach personal relationships in the same way one might approach any other transaction. While in some ways this looks like older models of marriage, there is a level of personal responsibility for the success of the 'product', the possibility of reinvention and an altogether more thoroughgoing construction of the self along the lines of consumer goods.

98 Mautner (n 94) 131, 132.

99 Further, far from class becoming an obsolete social category, it is also implicated in this consumer landscape. Harry Wallop, *Consumed: How Shopping Fed the Class System* (Collins 2013).

100 Mautner (n 94) 127.

101 Mautner (n 94) 133–4.

102 Mautner (n 94) 136.

103 Mautner (n 94) 138–9.

BRAND) and the seller (A PERSON IS A BUSINESS). Neither of these selves are recognisably human; the brand is a product, a thing, and the seller is simply a functionary without deep personal investment in any interpersonal dealings that may occur ('it's only business'). There is also a tension between the construction of the brand and the authenticity it needs to sustain itself.[104] This can be understood as a fracture of the individual but it is also a consequence of the apparently necessary self-reflexive identity project of late modernity.[105]

Both metaphors necessarily erase the body. Instead, the self – as well as the body – are caught up in a complex, capitalist, construction of the person as signifier; including the commodification of the space on the surface of one's body as simply another surface for advertising. And while the idea of branding the self is described as a kind of necessary freedom, as Mautner notes, because of the discursive closure, it is difficult to challenge as it is not something that the individual can opt out of.[106] If one does not take an active role in this product development and placement of self, it will be done by others.

> If you opt out, you will not escape branding, but will simply be branded by your environment. The discursive closure thus achieved effectively precludes debate, so that the idea of branding the self is turned into an unassailable ideology.[107]

A parenthetical comment that Mautner makes, however, shows the absolute dehumanisation of this process. She notes that 'branding' referred originally to cattle, only later being applied to manufactured goods and finally as relevant to people.[108] This suggests that the individual is now often no more than an inanimate chattel. People may not even be attributed with the animacy of animals; we may be no more than 'manufactured goods'. Whatever form the metaphor insists upon, it is not the human form, as the market can only cope with products and brands.

> The commodified self is at once a product of the market society and one of its key drivers ... Human beings are no longer expected to merely sell their *labour*, as they were in the industrial age, but to market, brand and sell *themselves* in a much more comprehensive way. In doing so, responsibility for success and failure is made to rest squarely with the individual. Careers are desocialised and reconfigured as portable assets which the entrepreneurial self is called upon to continuously re-invent according to current market needs. In the process, personal relationships are also subjected to a market logic, either as networking

104 Mautner (n 94) 138, 140.

105 Anthony Giddens, *Modernity and Self Identity: Self and Society in the Late Modern Age* (Polity 1991).

106 Mautner (n 94) 142.

107 Mautner (n 94) 145.

108 Mautner (n 94) 136.

> opportunities helping to build one's personal brand, or as projects in their own right, designed as if they were marketable products and services.[109]

This inevitability is a consequence of the dominance of the market, not just as a global (human) entity, but also as the prime comparator for all value and decisions.

The Market is God

There are 'persons' in the world, but they are not human. While the principle agents of the modern economy may be corporations, the prime mover is another person: the market. Mautner writes

> There is ample linguistic evidence that, in general usage, 'the market' is reified (i.e., made into a 'thing') and at the same time anthropomorphised (i.e., treated as it if it were a human being).[110]

Thus, the market has a 'will of its own' it has moods that can be altered by some kind of external action; it can be encouraged, surprised and misled.[111] The survival of the market, and of corporations generally, has become more important than the survival of people. The primacy of the market should not be underestimated. It is the 'person' whose demands must be met, the entity whose moods must be responded to; 'far from being a neutral principle for organising economic affairs, the market has become "a totalising category"'.[112]

The market sits at the top of new, late modern, chain of being. The market has to be given what it wants; it is a deity that needs to be placated. People are simply objects to be offered, animals to be sacrificed and agents to placate the desires of the market. Humans are sacrificed to satisfy the demands of the market. The argument that capitalism is a religion is not new. But as Benjamin notes, it is a distinctive entity, 'a pure religious cult, perhaps the most extreme there ever was'.[113] He continues, 'Within it everything only has meaning in direct relation to the cult: it knows no special dogma, no theology.'[114] It is a cult of 'permanent duration', one that 'engenders blame'.[115] It is a religion with a clergy, corporations, and a god, the

109 Mautner (n 94) 144.

110 Mautner (n 94) 14.

111 Mautner (n 94) 14–15.

112 Mautner's point is not that markets as such a problematic, but that the 'market society' is; 'the mere existence of markets in a society does not in itself create a market society', that is, one where market values prevail over all else. Mautner (n 94) 15 citing P.R Trowler, 'Captured by the Discourse? The Socially Constitutive Power of New Higher Education Discourse in the UK' (2001) 8(2), *Organization* 183, 187.

113 Walter Benjamin, 'Capitalism as Religion.' In Michael W. Jennings (ed), *Walter Benjamin: Selected Writings* Vol. 1, 1913–1926 (Harvard University Press 2004) 259.

114 Benjamin (n 113) 259.

115 Benjamin (n 113) 259.

market. But everything else is more or less optional, contingent on the whims of an invisible god. This openness, the lack of theology, is clearest when capitalism appropriates that which opposes it. Žižek identifies

> … capitalism's drive towards its own ever-expanding reproduction: a capitalist who dedicates himself unconditionally to the capitalist drive is effectively ready to put everything, including the survival of humanity, at stake, not for any 'pathological' gain or goal, but simply for the sake of the reproduction of the system as an end-in-itself … .[116]

Moreover, at the end of history, there seems to be no other option.[117] This is the final victory of the cult. Nothing else seems possible.

This ideological victory is visible in discourse. Once these market discourses are widely enough used, they become naturalised and apparently irrefutable.[118] The result of this is that the 'person' category has been occupied by the market, displacing people and turning them into commodities. Because the market is a 'totalising category', people thus have to become both agent and object, they can only occupy the roles that this totalising category allows. The humanisation and deification of the market is central to the general dehumanisation of people.

Despite the naturalisation of this ideology, it is far from necessary. As the previous chapter showed, conceptual metaphors can (and sometimes should) be challenged. The difficulty of resisting the marketisation of society is exactly because it is a totalising ideology. We are all hailed and interpellated in it. Mautner observes

> From an anthropological perspective, the market is primarily a 'cultural model' and a 'cultural artefact' (Carrier, 1997, 14; 24) which is characteristically used to regulate behaviour. 'People invoke the laws of the marketplace', Carrier points out (1997, 16), 'in order to persuade people to think and act in certain ways.' In other words, monetarised exchange is no longer merely one type of social relationship among many. Instead, it is now presented as the optimal type,

116 Slavoj Žižek, *Living in the End Times* (Verso 2010) 335. See also Dorling who writes 'The signal that the market apparently wants to see is that officials are prepared to watch and stand aside as their citizens die, due, for instance, to lack of clean water as the supply is privatised by a Western contractor. Given this it is no wonder that popular books now describe how orthodox economists behave like members of a cult, as if in "… part of their training, their brains get … reprogrammed … everything they were taught when they were young as being right and true is removed and replaced by a new understanding of the laws of the universe".' Danny Dorling, *Injustice: Why Social Inequality Persists* (The Policy Press 2010) 228.

117 Francis Fukuyama, *The End of History and the Last Man* (Penguin 1992).

118 In discussing the real world consequences of metaphors like the market is a person, Mautner describes a 'dialectical loop' ((n 94) 28). As corporations, the media, religions and universities adopt a more marketised discourse, individuals also have to adopt this way of thinking, speaking and behaving.

> indeed the only viable one, at all times and in all social arenas – and hence that which must always be adopted. As Parker argues (2007, 222), the market is 'articulated as both a descriptive certainty and a prescriptive inevitability'.[119]

It is possible to challenge metaphors, but two things are required for this. First, another way of conceptualising people needs to be found. This is supplied by the body and the primes of NSM. Second, in terms of human rights, the connections between market metaphors and the pain that people suffer also needs to be made clear. That is, there has to be full recognition of the negative consequences of these metaphors for humans. Looking fully at these negative consequences leads us to the root causes of both the metaphors and human suffering.

Root Causes

The cult of capitalism and the associated deification of the market work to dehumanise people. Given that I have suggested that a prohibition against dehumanisation should constitute the third human right, it is worth connecting the cult to clear violations of human rights that have already occurred. Relating global capitalism and markets to human rights abuses is in one sense straightforward. The logic of the market makes it inevitable that human life will be treated as simply another cost to be accounted for (see Chapter 5). With the increasing marketisation of all spheres of life, the costing of people has become routine in everything from product development to health care. This costing is not explicated in terms of people, but rather in relation to more abstract concepts.[120] Moreover, as recent work argues, it is not the case that the analysis that takes place is defensible in terms of results. In *The Body Economic*, Stuckler and Basu examine the consequences of austerity for human lives. They show that not only do austerity policies not deliver in macro-economic terms, they also cause real human suffering: 'The price of austerity is calculated in human lives. And these lost lives won't return when the stock market bounces back.'[121] Here, I rely on Marks[122] who argues that even if root causes are documented when investigating human rights abuses (which is far

---

119 Mautner (n 94) 15 citing J.G. Carrier, 'Introduction' in *Meanings of the Market: The Free Market in Western Culture* (Oxford 1997).

120 For example, in deciding on the allocation of health care resources, Quality Adjusted Life Years (QALY) is a standard measure. See Annabelle Mooney, 'Quality of Life: Questionnaires and Questions' (2006) 11(3), *Journal of Health Communication* 327.

121 David Stuckler and Sanjay Basu, *The Body Economic: Why Austerity Kills* (Allen Lane 2013) xxi.

122 Marks (n 57). See also Paul Farmer, *Pathologies of Power: Health, Human Rights, and the New War on the Poor* (University of California Press 2005) and Pogge (n 89).

from consistent), they vanish when it comes to recommendations made for halting such violations.

As argued above, the prohibition against dehumanisation of all kinds means that action needs to be taken even in the absence of an obvious human cause. In order to do this, it is important to distinguish between causation and root causes.[123] Certainly the law of human rights has always been interested in causation, in finding an actor who 'can be held answerable for a legal wrong'.[124] Looking for *root* causes must go further as Marks demonstrates by paying attention to, among other things, the consequences of a natural disaster, the Haitian earthquake of 2010. She observes that in assessing the aftermath, the UN Human Rights Council noted the contribution made to fatalities by pre-existing poverty and inequality. When making recommendations, however, these factors were erased. Instead, poverty and discrimination 'are themselves depicted not as the outcome of determinate forces and relations, including forces and relations that stretch across the world, but as local dysfunctions and accidents of history'.[125] While 'natural disasters' don't always have human causes, how disastrous they are may well be related to pre-existing social and economic conditions that are amenable to human intervention if not ultimately caused by some kind of human action. Moreover, the negative consequences that can occur because of such conditions are predictable.

The importance of root causes is clear in the case of food security. While attention to food as a human right and to national policy and decision making matters, this is not enough as such a focus risks ignoring the 'organisation of the global economy that generated food crises, and does so not just contingently but necessarily, as part of its logic'.[126] Marks's argument is that famines aren't only (or even) natural disasters; people starve because of the way global food markets operate. Moreover, Marks argues that attention needs to be paid to those who benefit from these systems and abuses; 'the conditions which create vulnerability to hunger and malnutrition ... exist at least in part because they benefit some groups of people, even as they massively disadvantage others'.[127]

In short, because the problems that lead to death, dehumanisation and human rights violations are 'systemic, the solutions must be equally systemic'.[128] As Farmer observes:

> Human rights violations are not accidents; they are not random in distribution or effect. Rights violations are, rather, symptoms of deeper pathologies of power

---

123 Marks takes three examples; arbitrary detention, disaster relief and food crisis.

124 Marks (n 57) 60.

125 Marks (n 57) 67.

126 Marks (n 57) 69. See also Susan George, *How the Other Half Dies* (Penguin 1991).

127 Marks (n 57) 69.

128 Marks (n 57) 69. One of the blocks to identification of and attention to root causes is the position of the state, as it is seen as 'the primary agent of change'. Marks (n 57) 71.

> and are linked intimately to social conditions that so often determine who will suffer abuse and who will be shielded from harm.[129]

The current global system is essentially one of planned misery, 'the necessary suffering of those dispossessed, exploited and oppressed today'.[130] It is necessary only in the sense that it is required for the maintenance of the *status quo*. Moreover, while the oppression clearly has a global character, with whole countries being subject to vulnerabilities and abuse, it also has a local face in that some people benefit greatly from prevailing systems even though this relies on the exploitation of others. Finally, it is simply not the case that problems like poverty and famine are irresolvable. Pogge argues 'we could eradicate severe poverty worldwide if we chose to try – in fact, we could have eradicated it decades ago'.[131] Certainly this requires more than proposing new rights, it requires tackling root causes and keeping the human body clearly in sight.

Conclusion

In this chapter, I have argued that language provides the third frame for thinking about human rights. Paying attention to the Natural Semantic Metalanguage primes shows us what a person is over and above her embodiment. I suggested a third human right; a prohibition against dehumanisation. This is crucial, as attention to the way people are seen shows that a human is more likely to be represented as an animal or a brand. In the contemporary world, the only persons that matter are corporations. The god of contemporary life is the market. It is deity that rules over a world in which misery is planned, in the sense that human suffering is the inevitable consequence of the systems and ideologies that structure human life. While it is impossible to end all human suffering, as this is the human condition, it is possible to see it properly. It is therefore important to note that the divinity of the market is not 'just' ideological; it has profound effects in the world. Indeed, the most dominant cultural ideologies are the quotidian. I want to conclude this chapter by drawing attention to an absolutely banal aspect of human life in order to indicate how completely blinded we have become to the corporeality of people.

There is an endangered object in the United Kingdom – the public toilet. All over the country, it is becoming harder and harder to find a public convenience.[132] This may say something about the financial situation of local authorities and councils but it also tells us something about how the institutions previously

129 Farmer (n 122) 7.

130 Marks (n 57) 76.

131 Thomas Pogge, 'World Poverty and Human Rights' (2005) 19(1), *Ethics and International Affairs* 19(1) 1.

132 Rose George, *The Big Necessity: Adventures in the World of Human Waste* (Portobello Books 2008)

responsible for such facilities understand the human body. In short, there is no understanding of the human body. As was argued in Chapter 4, the embodied person brings with it particular existential presuppositions. All bodies, and hence all people, need air, water, food and sleep. These are the bare necessities for human life. A little mentioned but direct consequence of this is the fact that while the body must take in certain substances to live it must also expel them. Just as humans cannot live without taking in air, water and food, neither can they function without expelling them.

We all need some way of dealing with waste, but that does not mean there is only one way to do it. Different societies deal with human waste in various ways, but it is inescapable. The interconnectedness of all people, on a single planet, can also be connected to human waste. Taking a global perspective, seeing that we all inhabit the same place has an effect on how we should think about human waste. When dealing with waste we need to consider not just practical issues related to health, protection of water supply and so on, it is also desirable for there to be consideration of human aesthetic preferences.

While the lack of public facilities can be read as a consequence of lack of money, it can also be understood as a complete lack of vision; blindness. We have learnt not to see people as people in a multitude of systematic ways. The dominance of metaphors that construe non-human entities as persons has helped to blind us to the embodiment of people.

This chapter has suggested that the primes of NSM provide a way of fleshing out the concept of human and leads to a third human right: a prohibition against dehumanisation. This has far-reaching consequences, as it demands that attention be given to the root causes of dehumanisation of whatever kind. Human rights are what people need to be people. The body is at the base of this; it is our zero institution and it shows what we need at a physical level. Even these needs have consequences for social and cultural norms. People live, but they also feel, think and know. There is more to the human than bare physical life but it is with bare life that we need to start.

Conclusion
Three Rights and Three Frames

The human body is the fundamental frame for human rights. It needs to be acknowledged as our absolute zero institution, that without which nothing else has meaning. I have suggested that seeing the body as an index allows the human body its proper place. Once this is done, it becomes clear that the most important human rights are those that protect the environment on which we all depend and those that provide people with food, water, shelter, clean air and sleep. In the previous chapter, a third right was proposed, a prohibition against dehumanisation. This right can be seen as connecting back to environmental rights and the body as index (in so far as it acknowledges the person as our object of analysis) but also as suggesting other rights, structures and systems. Exactly what these will be depends on local social, political and economic contexts. The particular ways in which people are protected as people do not matter so long as they are protected as people. In Chapter 6 I argued that as well as seeing the body as the frame for human rights, the frame provided by looking at the earth from outside also needs to be considered. This was to stress the interrelationship between people and between people and the natural world. That is, to fully consider the frame of the body, it needs to be framed in terms of the globe. This kind of global framing, looking at the world from outside, is a direct challenge to the discourses and practices of economic globalisation which dehumanise people.

The primes of NSM provide the necessary complement to the human body and the globe as frames for human rights. And while these may be translated directly into rights that are already conventional, this would be to miss the point I made in relation to root causes and systems. For example, given that 'say' is a prime, it is tempting simply to argue that 'freedom of speech' is a human right. I am not suggesting that freedom of speech is not a good thing, but the point is rather to recognise that people are beings who 'say'. This would stop, for example, corporations claiming freedom of speech. Indeed, even if systems are proposed, rights suggested and structures put in place after paying attention to the body as frame supplemented by the frame that NSM provides, this must not result in these frames being put out of sight.

Thus, I propose three rights and three frames: environmental rights, rights to live (that is, to food, water, shelter and sleep) and the right against dehumanisation. The frame of the globe is required to provide a context for the frame of the body, which grounds the human condition, which in turn should be supplemented by the frame provided by language.

This is nothing less than a paradigm shift, a complete reinvention of human rights which focuses on the 'human'. It is difficult to say more about what this new world of human rights would look like. What matters is making the shift, acquiring a new way of looking at humans, their connection with each other and our connection with the world. Once this has happened, fully, once this new lens has been acquired, what is required in terms of specific practices and structures should be obvious; necessary changes would become immediately inescapable. Similar processes have, however, been described in fictional contexts.

In Haden-Elgin's *Native Tongue* trilogy, linguists hold a large measure of political power. With the importance of interplanetary trade, their linguistic skills are valued. Linguist women, however, are subordinate to their male counterparts. Their lived experiences are neither acknowledged nor captured in any language. Thus, the linguist women develop a new language, Láadan, which they must hide from their men. While they start to teach it to their own girl children, eventually they find a way to send it into the world. Like every language, it encodes a view of the world.[1] Once it spreads outside the linguist community, Láadan changes the world. One woman, Nazareth, had suspected this would happen.

> It had been Nazareth who had known – while the other women were wasting their energies in 'contingency plans' against a list of potential reactions from the men, should they discover the existence of Láadan – that there was in fact nothing to do except wait and be ready. It had been Nazareth, and only Nazareth, who had truly understood that it wasn't possible to make plans that obliged you to extrapolate from one reality to another. She had been the only one who understood that such planning had to be postponed until after the reality shift brought about by the language had taken hold, and who had stood firm and silent and watchful while they thrashed about, flatly refusing to be drawn into their fretful arguments.[2]

Once the new way of seeing the world becomes the norm, once Láadan is in the world and used by people, the world itself necessarily changes. If people are seen as people, rather than commodities or brands, they will not be bought, sold and traded. When the natural environment is understood not as an asset but as a human trust, exploitation for financial gain becomes illogical. When we realise that people depend on each other, everyone becomes a neighbour.

1 Benjamin Lee Whorf, 'The Relation of Habitual Thought and Behaviour to Language' in S.I. Hayakawa (ed.), *Language, Meaning and Maturity: Selections from Etc., A Review of General Semantics*, 1943–1953 (Harper 1954) 197–215.

2 Suzette Haden Elgin, *The Judas Rose* (The Feminist Press at the City University, New York 2002) 72.

***

Human rights has been so much discussed, so contested, that it is easy to lose sight of what they are. While texts (like this book) proliferate, suffering continues. In all the texts I have consumed, one in particular has haunted my thinking about human rights. Eleanor Roosevelt, Chair of the UN Human Rights Commission, tasked with drafting the UDHR, said:

> Where, after all, do universal human rights begin? In small places, close to home – so close and so small that they cannot be seen on any maps of the world. Yet they are the world of the individual person; the neighbourhood he lives in; the school or college he attends; the factory, farm or office where he works. Such are the places where every man, woman and child seeks equal justice, equal opportunity, equal dignity without discrimination. Unless these rights have meaning there, they have little meaning anywhere. Without concerned citizen action to uphold them close to home, we shall look in vain for progress in the larger world.[3]

The workplace, the home, the school, the street – this is where we find out whether we count as people or not. After all, in the end, where do we begin? In the small places, close to home, the places we do not map, but rather the places from which we start, from where we begin. We begin horizontally. We begin asleep.

> What does sleeping consist in? To sleep is to suspend physical and psychic activity. But an abstract being, hovering in the air, lacks an essential condition for this suspending: a place. The summoning of sleep occurs in the act of lying down. To lie down is precisely to limit existence to a place, to position.
> A place is not an indifferent 'somewhere,' but a base, a condition … Sleep re-establishes a relationship [70] with a place qua base.[4]

Awake or asleep we are placed in the world. Awake or asleep we begin and are limited by our bodies. We are bodies in our workplaces, our homes, in public and in private. We are all bare life. This is not all we are, or at least it is not all we can be, but this is where we begin.

Without a functioning environment, bodies cannot receive the food, water, shelter and sleep they need. Without understanding the interconnection of the natural world and our dependence on it, we will not survive. Without acknowledging that, for better or worse, we rely on other people, humanity has no future. There

---

3 Eleanor Roosevelt, 'In Our Hands' (1958) Speech delivered on the tenth anniversary of the Universal Declaration of Human Rights http://www.un.org/en/globalissues/briefingpapers/humanrights/quotes.shtml. Accessed 16 October 2013.

4 Emmanuel Levinas, *Existence and Existents*, A. Lingis (trans) (Matiinus Nijhoff 1978) 69–70.

is more to being human than bare life. We are all thinking, feeling, saying beings, engaged with the world and interacting with each other. While we want to know things, there are some things we can never know. We can never know the Other. We can never understand fully what it means to be another body; the limits of our understanding are the limits of our embodiment. We are embodied beings. But we can greet the Other, we can establish relationships with her, we can treat her as a person even without knowing exactly what kind of person she is. We are all unique, singular and unsubstitutable. We are all connected and we are all the same.

What does it mean to be human? It means to be in a body, in a place, to be thinking, feeling, wanting and saying beings. Being human begins in small places, in a body, a space. Human rights should protect these small places, because humans can live nowhere else. These small places are where we are; these small places are where we are human.

References

Adams M., 'Coke, Pepsi Used as Agricultural Pesticides by India Farmers' (2008) *Natural News* http://www.naturalnews.com/News_000590_Coke_Pepsi_pesticides.html. Accessed 31 July 2012.

Agamben G., *Homo Sacer Sovereign Power and Bare Life*, Daniel Heller-Roazen (trans) (Stanford University Press 1998).

Agamben G., *The Coming Community*, Michael Hardt (trans) (University of Minnesota Press 1993).

Agier M., *On the Margins of the World: The Refugee Experience Today*, David Fernbach (trans) (Polity, 2008).

Aiyer A., 'The Allure of the Transnational: Notes on Some Aspects of the Political Economy of Water in India' (2007) 22(4), *Cultural Anthropology* 640–58.

Amos O., 'Rights and Wrongs' (2008) 10 December, *The Northern Echo* 18.

An-Na'im A.A., 'Human Rights in the Muslim World: Socio-Political Conditions and Scriptural Imperatives – A Preliminary Inquiry' (1990) 3, *Harvard Human Rights Journal* 13–52.

Atkin A., 'Peirce on the Index and Indexical Reference' (2005) 41(1), *Transactions of the Charles S. Peirce Society: A Quarterly Journal in American Philosophy* 161–88.

Bakker K., 'The "Common's" versus the "Commodity": Alter-globalization, Anti-privatization and the Human Right to Water in the Global South' (2007) 39(3), *Antipode* 430–55.

Banerjee T., 'Right to Water: Some Theoretical Issues' (2010) 6(1), *Contemporary Issues and Ideas in Social Sciences.* http://journal.ciiss.net/index.php/ciiss/article/view/79/76. Accessed 31 July 2012.

Barker C., 'Paraphrase is not Enough' (2003) 29, *Theoretical Linguistics* 201–9.

Baxi U., 'Voices of Suffering and the Future of Human Rights' (1998) 8, *Transnat'l L. & Contemp. Probs.* 125–69.

BBC/Open University, *The Foods that Make Billions: Episode 1 – Liquid Gold*, first broadcast 23 November 2010.

Beck U., *Risk Society*, M Ritter (trans) (Sage 1992).

Beitz C.R., *The Idea of Human Rights* (Oxford University Press 2009).

Belsey C., 'Biology and Imagination: The Role of Culture', in Robin Headlam Wells and Johnjoe McFadden (eds), *Human Nature: Fact and Fiction* (Continuum 2006) 111–27.

Benjamin W., 'Capitalism as Religion' in Michael W. Jennings (ed.), *Walter Benjamin: Selected Writings* Vol. 1 1913–1926 (Harvard University Press 2004).

Bentham J. (nd), 'Auto-icon; or. Farther uses of the Dead to the Living'. A Fragment. From the Mss. of Jeremy Bentham (not published) 1832. http://www.preservedproject.co.uk/jeremy-bentham-auto-icon/. Accessed 16 January 2013.

Bentham J., *The Works of Jeremy Bentham*, vol. 2, The Online Library of Liberty 1843 http://files.libertyfund.org/files/1921/Bentham_0872-02_EBk_v6.0.pdf. Accessed 19 February 2013.

Berger J., *Ways of Seeing* (Penguin 2008).

Berger L.L., 'Of Metaphor, Metonymy, and Corporate Money: Rhetorical Choices in Supreme Court Decisions on Campaign Finance Regulation' (2007) 58, *Mercer L. Rev.* 949–90.

Blackburn R., 'Reclaiming Human Rights' (2011) 69, *New Left Review* 126–38.

Bland A., 'Should Government Be Allowed to Hold So Much Data on its Citizens: The Big Question' (2008) 5 December, *The Independent*, 46.

Bohnemeyer J., 'NSM without the Strong Lexicalization Hypothesis' (2003) 29, *Theoretical Linguistics* 211–22.

Bottomley A., 'The Many Appearances of the Body in Feminist Scholarship' in Andrew Bainham, Shelley Day Sclater and Martin Richards (eds), *Body Lore and Laws* (Hart 2002) 127–48.

Britain D., 'Exploring the Importance of the Outlier in Sociolinguistic Dialectology' in David Britain and Jenny Cheshire (eds), *Social Dialectology: in honour of Peter Trudgill* (John Benjamins 2001) 191–208.

Brown C., 'Universal Human Rights: A Critique' (1997) 1(1), *Intl J Hum Rts* 41–65.

Brown M.F., 'Cultural Relativism 2.0' (2008) 49(3), *Current Anthropology* 363–83.

Burks A.W., 'Icon, Index and Symbol' (1949) 9(4), *Philosophy and Phenomenological Research* 673–89.

Butler J., *Bodies that Matter: On the Discursive Limits of 'Sex'* (Routledge 1993).

Butler J., 'How Can I Deny That These Hands and This Body Are Mine?' in Tom Cohen, Barbara Cohen, J. Hillis Miller, Andrzej Warminski (eds), *Material Events: Paul de Man and the Afterlife of Theory* (University of Minnesota Press 2001) 254–73.

Butler J., *Giving an Account of Oneself* (Fordham University Press 2005).

Butler J., *Precarious Life: The Powers of Mourning and Violence* (Verso 2006).

Butler J., *Frames of War: When is Life Grievable* (Verso 2010).

Cahill A., '"The Human Right to Water – A Right of Unique Status": The Legal Status and Normative Content of the Right to Water' (2005) 9(3), *Intl J.Hum Rts* 389–410.

Cameron D., *Verbal Hygiene* (Routledge 1995).

Cameron, D., 'Language: Sociolinguistics and Sociobiology' (1997) 39(4) *Critical Quarterly* 81-4.

Cameron D., 'Sex/Gender, Language and the New Biologism' (2009) 31(2), *Applied Linguistics* 173–92.

Cameron J. and Abouchar J., 'The Precautionary Principle: A Fundamental Principle of Law and Policy for the Protection of the Global Environment' (1991) 14(1), *B.C. Int'l & Comp. L. Rev*, 1–27.

Cameron L., 'Dyspathy: The Dynamic Complement of Empathy' (2012), *Living with Uncertainty* working paper 5 www.open.ac.uk/researchprojects/livingwithuncertainty. [Accessed 4 March 2013]

Carter R., 'The Limits of Imagination' in Robin Headlam Wells and Johnjoe McFadden (eds), *Human Nature: Fact and Fiction* (Continuum 2006) 128–43.

Cavarero A., *Stately Bodies: Literature, Philosophy and the Question of Gender*, Robert de Lucca and Deanna Shemek (trans) (University of Michigan Press 2002).

Cavarero A., *For More Than One Voice: Toward a Philosophy of Vocal Expression*, Paul A. Kottman (trans) (Stanford University Press 2005).

Chakrabarty D., 'The Climate of History: Four Theses' (2009) 35(2), *Critical Enquiry* 197–222.

Chase A.T., 'Legitimizing Human Rights: Beyond Mythical Foundations and into Everyday Resonances' (2012) 11(4), *Journal of Human Rights* 505–25.

Cheah P. and Grosz E., 'The Body of the Law: Notes towards a Theory of Corporeal Justice' in Pheng Cheah, David Fraser and Judith Grbich (eds), *Thinking Through The Body Of The Law* (New York University Press 1996) 3–25.

Citizens United v Federal Election Commission 558 US 08-205, (2010) http://www.supremecourt.gov/opinions/09pdf/08-205.pdf. [Accessed 24 August 2011].

Clark R., 'So what about the Human Rights of the Law-abiding?' Leader (2009) 20 February, *The Express*, 10.

Coates J., 'Denominal Adjectives: A Study in Syntactic Relationships between Modifier and Head' (1971) 27, *Lingua* 160–69.

Cobain I., *Cruel Britannia: A Secret History of Torture* (Portobello Books 2010).

Collier P., *The Plundered Planet: How to Reconcile Prosperity with Nature* (Allen Lane 2010).

Collins-Chobanian S., 'Beyond Sax and Welfare Interests: A Case for Environmental Rights' (2000) 22(2), *Environmental Ethics* 133–48.

Conklin W.E., 'Human Rights, Language and Law: A Survey of Semiotics and Phenomenology' (1995) 27(1), *Ottawa Law Review* 129–73.

Commission on a Bill of Rights, (2012) http://www.justice.gov.uk/about/cbr. Accessed 8 January 2013.

Committee on Economic, Social and Cultural Rights, 'The Right to Water' General Comment no 15, (2002) http://www.unhchr.ch/tbs/doc.nsf/0/a5458d1d1bbd713fc1256cc400389e94/$FILE/G0340229.pdf. Accessed 4 June 2013.

Cooper C., 'UN Official Alarmed by Rise of Food Banks in UK' (2013) 17 February, *The Independent* (London) < http://www.independent.co.uk/news/uk/home-news/un-official-alarmed-by-rise-of-food-banks-in-uk-8498791.html#>. Accessed 7 March 2013.

Coupland J., Coupland N. and Robinson J.D., (1992), '"How Are You?": Negotiating Phatic Communion' (1992) 21(2), *Language in Society* 207–30.

Cripps E., 'Saving the Polar Bear, Saving the World: Can the Capabilities Approach do Justice to Humans, Animals and Ecosystems?' (2010) 16, *Res Publica* 1–22.

Cullet P., 'Water Sector Reforms and Courts in India: Lessons from the Evolving Case Law' (2011) 19(3), *R.E.C.I.E.L.* 328–38.

Daily Mail, 'Human Rights Scandal' Letter (2008), 16 October, 72.

Dallmayr F., '"Asian Values" and Global Human Rights' (2002) 52(2), *Philosophy East and West* 173–89.

Dawes J.R., 'Language, Violence and Human Rights Law' (1999) 11, *Yale Journal of Law & the Humanities* 215–50.

Deese R.S., 'The Artifact of Nature: "Spaceship Earth" and the Dawn of Global Environmentalism' (2009) 33(2), *Endeavour* 70–75.

Dembour M.-B., 'What are Human Rights? Four Schools of Thought' (2010) 32(1), *Hum. Rts. Q.* 1–20.

Derrida J. and Dufourmantelle A., *Of Hospitality*, Rachel Bowlby (trans) (Stanford University Press 2000).

Deva S., 'Human Rights Realization in an Era of Globalization: The Indian Experience' (2006) 12, *Buff. Hum.Rts. L. Rev.* 93–138.

Donnelly J., *Universal Human Rights: In Theory and Practice* 2nd ed. (Cornell University Press 2003).

Donnelly J., 'The Relative Universality of Human Rights' (2007) 29(2), *Hum. Rts. Q.* 281–306.

Donoghue (or McAlister) v Stevenson [1932] AC 562.

Dorling D., *Injustice: Why Social Inequality Persists* (The Policy Press 2010).

Doumas C, 'The Emergence of Central Authority in the Aegean' in Paul Sinclair (ed.), *The Development of Urbanism from a Global Perspective*, (Uppsala University 1996) http://www.arkeologi.uu.se/digitalAssets/9/9397_doumas.pdf. Accessed 5 October 2010.

Douzinas C., *The End of Human Rights* (Hart 2000a).

Douzinas C., 'Human Rights and Postmodern Utopia' (2000b) 11, *Law & Crit.* 219–40.

Douzinas C., 'The End(s) of Human Rights' (2002) 26, *MULR* 445–65.

Durst U., 'The Natural Semantic Metalanguage Approach to Linguistic Meaning' (2003) 29, *Theoretical Linguistics* 157–200.

Dwivedi G., *Revisiting Important Water Conflicts in Kerala* (Forum for Policy Dialogue on Water Conflicts in India (2011) http://www.conflicts.indiawaterportal.org/sites/conflicts.indiawaterportal.org/files/Kerala%20Water%20Conflicts%20Report%20Final.pdf. Accessed 2 July 2013.

Eagleton T., 'Local and Global in The Politics of Human Rights', in Obrad Savić (ed.) *The Politics of Human Rights* (Verso 1999) 258–67.

El Refaie E., 'Metaphors We Discriminate by: Naturalized Themes in Austrian Newspaper Articles about Asylum Seekers' (2001) 5(3), *Journal of Sociolinguistics* 352–71.

Evans N. and Levinson S. C., 'The Myth of Language Universals: Language Diversity and its Importance for Cognitive Science' (2009) 32(5), *Behavioral and Brain Sciences* 429-4.

Evans N. and Wilkins D. 'In the Mind's Ear: The Semantic Extensions of Perception Verbs in Australian Languages' (2000) 76(3), *Language* 546.

Evening Chronicle (Newcastle, UK), *Letters to the Editor* (2009) 12 June, 28–9.

Fairclough N., *New Labour New Language?* (Routledge 2000).

Farmer P., *Pathologies of Power: Health, Human Rights, and the New War on the Poor* (University of California Press, 2005).

Fielding H.A., 'Multiple Moving Perceptions of the Real: Arendt, Merleau-Ponty, and Truitt' (2011) 26(3), *Hypatia* 518–34.

Fineman M.A., 'The Vulnerable Subject: Anchoring Equality in the Human Condition' (2008) 20(1), *Yale J.L. & Feminism* 1–23.

Finnis F., *Natural Law and Natural Rights* (Clarendon 1980).

Freeman M., 'Universalism, Communitarianism and Human Rights: A Reply to Chris Brown' (1998) 2(1), *Intl J Hum Rts* 79–92.

Freeman M., *Human Rights: Key Concepts* (Polity 2002).

Freeman M., 'Putting Law in its Place: An Interdisciplinary Evaluation of National Amnesty Laws' in Meckled-García, S. and Çali, B., *The Legalization of Human Rights: Multidiscplinary Perspectives on Human Rights and Human Rights Law* (Routledge 2006) 49–64.

Freud S., 'The Uncanny' in James Strachey (trans), Albert Dickson (ed.), *Art and Literature*, vol. 14 (Penguin 1985) 335–76.

Fukuyama F., *The End of History and the Last Man* (Penguin 1992).

Garland-Thomson R., *Staring: How We Look* (Oxford University Press 2009).

Garrett P., Evans B. and Williams A., 'What does the word "globalisation" mean to you?: Comparative Perceptions and Evaluations in Australia, New Zealand, the USA and the UK' (2006) 27(5), *Journal of Multilingual and Multicultural Development* 392–412.

Gearty C., 'Is the Idea of Human Rights Now Doing More Harm than Good?' (2004) 12 October Human Rights Public Lecture, LSE, London. http://www2.lse.ac.uk/publicEvents/events/2004/20040907t1535z001.aspx, Last accessed 27 January 2013.

Gearty C., *Can Human Rights Survive?* The Hamlyn Lectures (Cambridge University Press 2006).

Gearty C., 'Do Human Rights Help or Hinder Environmental Protection?' (2010) 1(1), *JHRE* 7–22.

Geeraerts D. and Marín-Arrese J.I., 'Dirk Geeraerts: Cognitive Sociolinguistics and the Sociology of Cognitive Linguistics' Interview (2007) 5, *Annual Review of Cognitive Linguistics* 289–305.

George R., *The Big Necessity: Adventures in the World of Human Waste* (Portobello Books 2008).

George S., *How the Other Half Dies* (Penguin 1991).

Geurts B., 'Semantics as Lexicography' (2003) 29, *Theoretical Linguistics* 223–6.

Gewirth A., 'Why there are Human Rights' (1985) 11(2), *Social Theory and Practice* 235–48.
Gibbs R.W. Jr., 'Embodied Experience and Linguistic Meaning' (2003) 84, *Brain and Language* 1–15.
Giddens A., *Modernity and Self Identity: Self and Society in the Late Modern Age* (Polity Press 1991).
Goddard C., 'Natural Semantic Metalanguage: The State of the Art', in Goddard, Cliff (ed.), *Cross-Linguistic Semantics* (John Benjamins 2008a) 1–34.
Goddard C., 'Towards a Systematic Table of Semantic Elements', in Goddard, Cliff (ed.), *Cross-Linguistic Semantics* (John Benjamins 2008b) 59–81.
Goddard C., 'Semantic Primes, Semantic Molecules, Semantic Templates: Key Concepts in the NSM Approach to Lexical Typology' (2012) 50(3), *Linguistics* 711–43.
Goddard C. and Wierzbicka A., 'Semantic Primes and Cultural Scripts in Language Learning and Intercultural Communication' in Gary Palmer and Farzad Sharifian (eds), *Applied Cultural Linguistics: Implications for Second Language Learning and Intercultural Communication* (John Benjamins 2007), 105–24.
Goddard C. and Wierzbicka A. (eds), *Meaning and Universal Grammar: Theory and Empirical Findings* (John Benjamins 2002).
Goodhart M., 'Origins and Universality in the Human Rights Debate: Cultural Essentialism and the Challenge of Globalisation' (2003) 25(4), *Human Rights Quarterly* 935–64.
Goudge T.A., 'Peirce's Index' (1965) 1(2), *Transactions of the Charles S. Peirce Society* 52–70.
Gould C., 'The Theory of Universal Human Rights: A Comment on Talbott' (2008) 9(2), *Human Rights Rev* 157–65.
Granath S. and Wherrity M., 'Thinking in Space: The Lexis of Thinking from a Cognitive Perspective' (2008) 24(1), *English Today* 41–8.
Grear A., 'Challenging Corporate "Humanity": Legal Disembodiment and Human Rights' (2007) 7. *H.R.L. Rev.* 511–43.
Grear A., *Redirecting Human Rights: Facing the Challenge of Corporate Legal Humanity* (Palgrave 2010).
Gregory R.L., *The Intelligent Eye* (Oxford University Press 1971).
Griffin J., *On Human Rights* (Oxford University Press 2008).
Grosz E., *Volatile Bodies: Toward a Corporeal Feminism* (Indiana University Press 1994).
Guager A., Rabatel-Fernal M.P., Kulbicki L., Short D. and Higgins P., 'Ecocide is the Missing 5th Crime against the Peace' (2012) http://www.sas.ac.uk/sites/default/files/files/hrc/Events%20Documents/Ecocide%20is%20the%20missing%205th%20Crime%20Against%20Peace.pdf. Accessed 21 January 2013.
Haden Elgin S., *The Judas Rose* (The Feminist Press at the City University New York 2002).

Hanafin P. Patrick, 'Refusing Disembodiment. Abortion and the Paradox of Reproductive Rights in Contemporary Italy' (2009) 10(2), *Feminist Theory* 227–44.

Hardin G., 'The Tragedy of the Commons' (1968) 162, *Science*, 1243–8. http://dieoff.org/page95.htm. Accessed 2 August 2012.

Hauser M.D., *Moral Minds: The Nature of Right and Wrong* (Harper Collins 2006).

Higgins P., *Eradicating Ecocide: Laws and Governance to Stop the Destruction of the Planet* (Shepheard-Walwyn 2010).

Higgins P., *Earth is our Business: Changing the Rules of the Game* (Shepheard-Walwyn 2012).

Higgins R., *Problems and Process: International Law and how we use it* (Clarendon Press 1994)

Hindustan Coca-Cola Beverages v Perumatty Grama Panchayat, 2005 (2) KLT 554 http://www.ielrc.org/content/e0515.pdf. Accessed 24 May 2011.

Hiskes R.P., 'Environmental Human Rights and Intergenerational Justice' (2006) 7(3), *Human Rights Rev* 81–95.

Hoffman Lord, 'The Universality of Human Rights' (2009), Judicial Studies Board Annual Lecture 19 March, [Online]. Available: http://www.judiciary.gov.uk/training-support/judicial-college/Annual+Lectures. Accessed 16 May 2011.

Homer, *The Odyssey*, Samuel Butler (trans) (Plain Label Books 2009).

Howard R.E., 'Cultural Absolutism and the Nostalgia for Community' (1993) 15, *Hum,.Rts.,Q.* 315–38.

Huang L.-Y., 'Not Just another Drop in the Human Rights Bucket: The Legal Significance of a Codified Human Right to Water' (2008) 20, *Fla.J.Int'l L.* 353–70.

Hughes R.A., 'Pro-Justice Ethics, Water Scarcity, Human Rights' (2009–10) 25, *J. L. & Religion* 521–40.

Hume D., *A Treatise of Human Nature* (John Noon 1739).

Hunt L., *Inventing Human Rights: A History* (Norton 2007).

Hunter G., 'Hume on Is and Ought' (1962) 37(140), *Philosophy* 148–52.

Ibarretxe-Antuñano I., 'Mind-as-body as a Cross-linguistic Conceptual Metaphor' (2002) 25, *Miscelánea. A Journal of English and American Studies* 93–119.

Ibarretxe-Antuñano I., 'Vision Metaphors for the Intellect: Are they really Cross-linguistic?' (2008) 30(1), *Atlantis: Journal of the Spanish Association for Anglo-American Studies* 15–33.

Ignatieff M., *Human Rights as Politics and Idolatry* (Princeton University Press 2001).

Ishay M., 'What are Human Rights? Six Historical Controversies' (2004) 3(3), *Journal of Human Rights* 359–71.

Ishay M.R., *The History of Human Rights: From Ancient Times to the Globalization Era* (University of California Press 2004).

Jackendoff R., 'Conceptual Semantics and Natural Semantic Metalanguage Theory have Different Goals' (2007) 4(3), *Intercultural Pragmatics* 411–18.

Jackendoff R., 'The Natural Logic of Morals and of Laws' (2009) 75(2), *Brook. L. Rev.* 379–403.
Jakobson R., 'Closing Statements: Linguistics and Poetics' in Thomas A. Sebeok (ed.), *Style in Language* (MIT Press 1960) 350–77.
Janis M.W., 'Individuals as Subjects of International Law' (1984) 17, *Cornell International Law Journal* 67–78.
Jitha S.R., 'Bureaucracy and Sustainable Development' (2011) Oct–Dec, *PRAGATI Quarterly Research Journal* 23–31.
Johnson M., *The Meaning of the Body: Aesthetics of Human Understanding* (Chicago University Press 2007).
Johnson M. and Lakoff G., 'Why Cognitive Linguistics Requires Embodied Realism' (2002) 13(3), *Cognitive Linguistics* 245–63.
Jones M., 'Landscape, Law and Justice: Concepts and Issues – a Preliminary Overview' in Z. Roca, T. Spek, T. Terkenli, T. Plieninger and F. Höchtl (eds), *European Landscapes and Lifestyles: The Mediterranean and Beyond* (Edições Universitárias Lusófonas 2007) 438–59.
Jones P., 'Human Rights, Group Rights, and Peoples' Rights' (1999) 21(1), *Hum. Rts. Q.* 80–107.
Jünger E., *On Pain*, David C. Durst (trans) (Telos Press 2008).
Kay P., 'NSM and the Meaning of Color Words' (2003) 29, *Theoretical Linguistics* 237–45.
Kayman M.A., 'Bodies of Law and Sculptural Bodies: Writing, Art and the Real' (2010) 24(5), *Textual Practice* 791–817.
Kennedy H., *Just Law: The Changing Face of Justice – and Why it Matters to us all* (Vintage 2005).
Kjær A.L. and Palsbro L., 'National Identity and Law in the Context of European Integration: The Case of Denmark' (2008) 19(5), *Discourse and Society* 599–627.
Klug F., 'The Human Rights Act: Origins and Intentions' (2010), Tenth Anniversary of the Human Rights Act Symposium 24 September, St John's College, Durham University.
Kohen A., 'The Problem of Secular Sacredness: Ronald Dworkin, Michael Perry and Human Rights Foundationalism' (2006) 5(2) *Journal of Human Rights* 235–56.
Kohen A., *In Defense of Human Rights: A Non-religious Grounding in a Pluralistic World* (Routledge 2008).
Koonan S., 'Legal Implications of Plachimada: A Case Study' (2007), IELRC Working Paper 2007-05 www.ielrc.org/content/w0705.pdf. Accessed 31 July 2012.
Koptjevskaja-Tamm M. and Ahlgren I., 'NSM: Theoretical, Methodological and Applicational Problems' (2003) 29, *Theoretical Linguistics* 247–61.
Kövecses K., *Metaphor in Culture. Universality and Variation* (Cambridge University Press, 2005).

Kövecses Z., 'Conceptual Metaphor Theory: Some Criticisms and Alternative Proposals' (2008a) 6, *Annual Review of Cognitive Linguistics* 168–84.
Kövecses Z., 'Universality and Variation in the Use of Metaphor' in N.-L. Johannesson and D.C. Minugh (eds), *Selected Papers from the 2006 and 2007 Stockholm Metaphor Festivals* (Department of English, Stockholm University 2008b) 51–74.
Kysar D.A., 'Sustainable Development and Private Global Governance' (2005) 83, *Tex. L. Rev.* 2109–66.
Lacey N., 'Unspeakable Subjects, Impossible Rights: Sexuality, Integrity and Criminal Law' in *Unspeakable Subjects: Feminist Essays in Legal and Social Theory* (Hart 1998) 98–124.
Lakoff G., 'The Metaphor System for Morality', in Adele D. Goldberg (ed.), *Conceptual Structure, Discourse and Language* (CSLI Publications, Centre for the Study of Language and Information 1996) 249–66.
Lakoff G. and Johnson M., *Metaphors We Live By* (University of Chicago Press 1980).
Lakoff G. and Johnson M., *Philosophy in the Flesh* (Basic Books 1999).
Lambooy T., 'Corporate Social Responsibility: Sustainable Water Use' (2011) 19, *Journal of Cleaner Production* 852–66.
Lametti D., 'The Objects of Virtue' in Gregory S. Alexander and Eduardo M. Peñalver (eds), *Property and Community* (Oxford University Press 2010) 1–38.
Laurance J., 'Hospital patients "left so thirsty doctors had to prescribe water"', *The Independent* 26 May 2011 www.independent.co.uk. Accessed 5 June 2013.
Lazier B., 'Earthrise; or, The Globalization of the World Picture' (2011) 116(3), *The American Historical Review* 602–30.
Leung K. and Tong K.-K., 'Justice Across Cultures: A Three-stage Model for Intercultural Negotiation' in Michele J. Gelfand and Jeanne M. Brett (eds), *The Handbook of Negotiation and Culture* (Stanford Business Books, 2004) 313–33.
Levinas E., *Existence and Existents*, A. Lingis (trans) (Matiinus Nijhoff 1978).
Levinas E., *Éthique et infini: Dialogues, avec Philippe Nemo* (Livre de Poche, 1982)
Levinas E., *Otherwise than Being or Being Beyond Essence* (Kluwer1991).
Levinas E., *Collected Philosophical Papers*, Alphonso Lingis (trans), (Duquesne University Press 1998).
Levinas E., 'Signification and Sense' in *Humanism of the Other*, Nidra Poller (trans) (University of Illinois Press, 2003) 9–44.
Levinas E., 'The/ and The Totality' in *Entre Nous*, Michael B. Smith and Barbara Harshaw (trans) (Continuum 2006) 11–33.
Levinson S.C., 'Vision, Shape, and Linguistic Description: Tzeltal Body-part Terminology and Object Description' (1994) 32, *Linguistics* 791–855.
Lévi-Strauss C., 'Do Dual Organizations Exist?' in *Structural Anthropology*, Claire Jacobsen and Brooke Grundfest Schoepf (trans) (Basic Books 1963) 132–63.
Loux Jarman A., 'Urban Commons: From Customary Use to Community Right on Scotland's Bleaching Greens', in A. Lewis et al (eds), *Law in the City* (Four Courts Press 2007a) 319–45.

Loux Jarman A., 'Customary Rights in Scots Law: Test Cases on Access to Land in the Nineteenth Century' (2007b) 28(2), *The Journal of Legal History* 207–32.
Love N., 'Cognition and the Language Myth' (2004) 26, *Language Sciences* 525–44.
MacIntyre A.C., '"Is" and "Ought"' (1959) 68(4), *The Philosophical Review* 451–68.
MacKinnon C.A., *Are Women Human? And Other International Dialogues* (The Belknap Press of Harvard University Press 2006).
MacNeil W., 'Law's Corpus Delicti: The Fantasmatic Body of Rights Discourse' (1998) 9(1), Law & Crit. 37–57.
MacNeil W., 'Taking Rights Symptomatically – Jouissance, Coupure, Objet Petit a.' (1999) 8, *GLR* 134–51.
Madhu P., 'Business Ethics: Should it Remain an Oxymoron?' (2010) 1(1), *MES Journal of Technology and Management* 83–98.
Malabou C., 'An Eye at the Edge of Discourse' (2007) 17, *Communication Theory* 16–25.
Malik K., 'What Science Can and Cannot Tell us about Human Nature' in Robin Headlam Wells and Johnjoe McFadden (eds), *Human Nature: Fact and Fiction* (Continuum 2006) 164–83.
Manderson D., *Proximity, Levinas, and the Soul of Law* (McGill-Queen's University Press 2006a).
Manderson D., 'Levinas and the Philosophy of Negligence' (2006) 14 *Tort L Rev* 1–18.
Margalit A., 'Commons and Legality' in Gregory S. Alexander and Eduardo M. Peñalver (eds), *Property and Community* (Oxford University Press 2010) 141–64.
Marks S., 'Human Rights and Root Causes' (2011) 74(1), *MLR* 57–78.
Matthewson L., 'Is the Meta-language Really Natural?' (2003) 29, *Theoretical Linguistics* 263–74.
Mautner G., 'Time to Get Wired: Using Web-based Corpora in Critical Discourse Analysis' (2005) 16, *Discourse and Society* 809–28.
Mautner G., 'Mining Large Corpora for Social Information: The Case of *elderly*' (2007) 36, *Language in Society* 51–72.
Mautner G., *Language and the Market Society: Critical Reflections on Discourse and Dominance* (Routledge 2010).
Mautner G., 'The Entrepreneurial University: A Discursive Profile of a Higher Education Buzzword' (2005) 2(2), *Critical Discourse Studies* 95–120.
McFarland S., and Matthews M., 'Who Cares About Human Rights?' (2005) 26(3), *Political Psychology* 365–85.
McIntosh A., *Hell and High Water: Climate Change, Hope and the Human Condition* (Birlinn 2008).
McNamara L., *Human Rights Controversies: The Impact of Legal Form* (Routledge Cavendish 2007).
McMahon P., *Feeding Frenzy: The New Politics of Food* (Profile 2013).

McWilliams J., 'Coca-Cola Will Face Claims in India' (2011), *The Atlanta Journal – Construction* 26 Feb p 12A http://www.lexisnexis.com/uk/nexis/.

Meckled-García S. and Çali B. (eds) *The Legalization of Human Rights: Multidisciplinary Perspectives on Human Rights and Human Rights Law* (Routledge 2006).

Merleau-Ponty M., *The Primacy of Perception: And Other Essays on Phenomenological Psychology, the Philosophy of Art, History, and Politics* (Northwestern University Press, 1964).

Merleau-Ponty M., *Maurice Merleau-Ponty: Basic Writings, Thomas Baldwin* (ed.) (Routledge 2004).

Midgley M., 'Towards an Ethic of Global Responsibility' in Timothy Dunne and Nicholas J Wheeler (eds), *Human Rights in Global Politics* (Cambridge University Press 1999) 160–74.

Mikhail J., 'Moral Grammar and Human Rights: Some Reflections on Cognitive Science and Enlightenment Rationalism' in Ryan Goodman, Derek Jinks and Andrew Woods (eds), *Understanding Social Action, Promoting Human Rights* (Oxford University Press 2012) 160–98.

Mills S., *Language and Sexism* (Cambridge University Press 2008).

Mooney A., 'Citizens, Immigrants, Anarchists and Other Animals', in Anne Wagner, Tracy Summerfield and Farid, Samir, Benavides, Vanegas (eds), *Contemporary Issues in the Semiotics of Law* (Hart 2005) 35–56.

Mooney A., 'Quality of Life: Questionnaires and Questions' (2006) 11(3), *Journal of Health Communication* 327–41.

Mooney A., 'Human Rights: Law, Language and the Bare Human Being' (2012) 32, *Language and Communication* 169–81.

Moyn S., *The Last Utopia: Human Rights in History* (The Bellknap Press of Harvard University Press 2010).

Murphy A.V., 'Corporeal Vulnerability and the New Humanism' (2011) 26(3), *Hypatia* 575–90.

Murphy J., *Street on Torts* 12th ed. (Oxford University Press 2007a).

Murphy J., 'Rethinking Injunctions in Tort Law' (2007b) 27(3), *OJLS* 509–35.

Naffine N., 'Who are Law's Persons – From Cheshire Cats to Responsible Subjects' (2003) 66, *MLR* 346–67.

Nancy J.-L., *Corpus*, Richard A. Rand (trans) (Fordham University Press 2008).

Nedelsky J., 'Law, Boundaries, and the Bounded Self' (1990) 30, *Representations* 162–89.

Nedelsky J., 'Embodied Diversity and the Challenges to Law' (1997) 42, *McGill L. J* 91–117.

New Indian Express, 'Chidambaram urged to forward Plachimada Bill' (2011) 24 September from http://www.lexisnexis.com/uk/nexis/.

Núñez R.E. and Sweetser E., 'With the Future Behind Them: Convergent Evidence from Aymara Language and Gesture in the Crosslinguistic Comparison of Spatial Construals of Time' (2006) 30, *Cognitive Science* 401–50.

O'Neill O., 'The Dark Side of Human Rights' (2005) 81(2), *Int'l Aff. (UK)* 427–39.

Obokata T. and O'Connell R., 'Ambition, Achievement and Potential: the UK and the Universal Declaration of Human Rights at Sixty' (2010) 14(3), *Intl J Hum Rts* 394–406.

Ochoa C., 'Advancing the Language of Human Rights in a Global Economic Order: An Analysis of a Discourse' (2003) 23, *B. C. Third World L. J.* 57–114.

O'Hare U.A., 'Realizing Human Rights for Women' (1999) 21(2), *Hum. Rts. Q.* 364–402.

Okazaki S., 'Happiness in the Eye and the Heart: Somatic Referencing in West African Emotion Lexica' (2006) 32(2), *The Journal of Black Psychology* 117–40.

Pagden A., 'Human Rights, Natural Rights and Europe's Imperial Legacy' (2003) 31(2), *Political Theory* 171–99.

Parekh B., 'Non-ethnocentric Universalism', in Timothy Dunne and Nicholas J. Wheeler (eds), *Human Rights in Global Politics* (Cambridge University Press) 128–59.

Parekh S., 'Resisting "Dull and Torpid" Assent: Returning to the Debate over the Foundations of Human Rights' (2007) 29, *Hum. Rts. Q.* 754–78.

Parsons A.S., 'The Conventions of the Senses: The Linguistics and Phenomenological Contributions to a Theory of Culture' (1988) 11(1), *Human Studies* 3–41.

Pauwels A., 'Linguistic sexism and feminist linguistic activism' in Janet Holmes and Miriam Meyerhoff (eds), *The Handbook of Language and Gender* (Blackwell 2003) 487–508.

Peirce C.S., *The Commens Dictionary of Peirce's Terms*, Mats Bergman and Sami Paavola (eds), (2003) http://www.helsinki.fi/science/commens/dictionary.html.

Perrin C., 'Breath from Nowhere: The Silent "Foundation" of Human Rights' (2004) 13(1), *Social and Legal Studies* 133–51.

Perry M.J., 'The Morality of Human Rights: A Nonreligious Ground?' (2005) 54, *Emory Law Journal* 97–150.

Perumatty Grama Panchayat vs State of Kerala, 2004 (1) KLT 731 http://www.ielrc.org/content/e0328.pdf. Accessed 30 July 2012.

Pinker S., 'The Biology of Fiction' in Robin Headlam Wells and Johnjoe McFadden (eds), *Human Nature: Fact and Fiction* (Continuum 2006) 27–39.

Pires de Olivera R., 'Language and Ideology: An interview with George Lakoff', in René Dirven, Bruce Hawkins and Esra Sandikcioglu (eds), *Language and Ideology: Volume I: Theoretical Cognitive Approaches* (John Benjamins 2000) 23–47.

Philo G., Briant E. and Donald P., *Bad News for Refugees* (Pluto 2013).

PLoS Medicine Editors, 'Clean Water Should be Recognised as a Human Right' (2009) 6(6), *PLoS Medicine* 1 www.plosmedicine.org.

Poe E.A., 'The Purloined Letter' in Andrew Barger (ed.), *Edgar Allan Poe's Annotated Short Stories* (Bottletree Books LLC 2008) 462–73.

Pogge T., 'World Poverty and Human Rights' (2005) 19(1), *Ethics and International Affairs* 1–7.

Pogge T., *World Poverty and Human Rights*, 2nd ed. (Polity 2008).

Poole R., *Earthrise: How Man First Saw the Earth* (Yale University Press 2008).
The Proclaimers, 'Beautiful Truth', *This Is the Story* (Chrysalis, 1987).
Putnam H., 'Are Values Made or Discovered' in *The Collapse of the Fact/Value Dichotomy: and other essays including the Rosenthal lectures* (Harvard University Press 2002) 96–110.
Putnam H., *Ethics Without Ontology* (Harvard University Press 2004).
Radin M.R., 'Market Inalienability' (1987) 100(8), *Harv. L. Rev.* 1849–1937.
Rakova M., 'The Philosophy of Embodied Realism: a High Price to Pay?' (2002) 13(3), *Cognitive Linguistics* 13(3) 215–44.
Raman K.R., 'Transverse Solidarity: Water, Power, and Resistance' (2010) 42(2), *Review of Radical Political Economics* 251–68.
Rampton B., 'Speech Community and Beyond', in Nikolas Coupland and Adam Jaworski (eds), *The New Sociolinguistics Reader* (Macmillan 2009) 694–713.
Reidy D.A., 'William Talbott's Which Rights Should be Universal?' (2008) 9(2), *Human Rights Rev* 181–91.
Renteln A.D., 'The Unanswered Challenge of Relativism and the Consequences for Human Rights' (1985) 7(4), *Hum. Rts. Q.* 514–40.
Renteln A.D., 'Relativism and the Search for Human Rights' (1988) 90(1), *American Anthropologist* 56–72.
Ricoveri G., *Nature for Sale: The Commons versus Commodities* (Pluto 2013).
Robbennolt J.K. and Studebaker C.A., 'News Media Reporting on Civil Litigation and Its Influence on Civil Justice Decision Making' (2003) 27(1), *Law & Hum. Behav.* 5–27.
Rohrer T., 'Pragmatism, Ideology and Embodiment: William James and the Philosophical Foundations of Cognitive Linguistics' in René Dirven, Bruce Hawkins and Esra Sandikcioglu (eds), *Language and Ideology: Volume I: Theoretical Cognitive Approaches* (John Benjamins 2000) 49–81.
Roosevelt E., 'In Our Hands' (1958), Speech delivered on the tenth anniversary of the Universal Declaration of Human Rights http://www.un.org/en/globalissues/briefingpapers/humanrights/quotes.shtml. Accessed 16 October 2013.
Rorty R., 'Human Rights, Rationality, and Sentimentality' in *Truth and Progress: Philosophical Papers*, Vol. 3 (Cambridge University Press 1998) 167–85.
Rose C.M., 'The Several Futures of Property: Of Cyberspace and Folk Tales, Emission Trades and Ecosystems' (1998), Faculty Scholarship Series paper 1804 http://digitalcommons.law.yale.edu/fss_papers/1804. Accessed 17 May 2011; (1998-1999) 83 *Minn. L. Rev.* 129–82.
Rose C.M., 'Expanding the Choices for the Global Commons: Comparing Newfangled Tradable Allowance Schemes to Old-Fashioned Common Property Regimes' (1999), Faculty of Scholarship Series paper 1803 http://digitalcommons.law.yale.edu/fss_papers/1803. Accessed 17 May 2011; (1999) 10 (1) *DELPF* 45–72
Rose C.M., 'Common Property, Regulatory Property and Environmental Protection' in Elinor Ostrom et al (eds), *The Drama of the Commons* (National Academies Press 2002) 233–58.

Rose C.M., 'Romans, Roads and Romantic Creators: Traditions of Public Property in the Information Age' (2003) 66(1/2), *LCP* 89–110.

Rose H. and Rose S., 'Darwin and After' (2010) 63, *New Left Review* 91–113.

Sachedina A., 'The Clash of Universalisms: Religious and Secular in Human Rights' (2007) 9(3), *The Hedgehog Review* 49–62.

Santa Ana O., '"Like an animal I was treated": Anti-immigrant Metaphor in US Public Discourse' (1999) 10(2), *Discourse and Society* 191–224.

Sax J.L., 'The Public Trust Doctrine in Natural Resource Law: Effective Judicial Intervention' (1970) 68(3), *Mich. L. Rev.* 471–566.

Sax J.L., 'The Search for Environmental Rights' (1990) 6, *J. Land Use & Envtl. L.* 95–105.

Scarry E., *The Body in Pain: The Making and Unmaking of the World* (Oxford University Press 1985).

Schaefer B., 'Human Rights: Problems with the Foundationless Approach' (2005) 31(1), *Social Theory and Practice* 27–50.

Schapiro R.A., 'The Consequences of Human Rights Foundationalism' (2005) 54, *Emory Law Journal* 171–86.

Schmidt P.F., 'Some Criticisms of Cultural Relativism' (1955) 70, *Journal of Philosophy* 780.

Sen A., 'Elements of a Theory of Human Rights' (2004) 32(4), *Philosophy and Public Affairs* 315–56.

Shapiro I. and Kymlica W. (eds), *Ethnicity and group rights* (New York University Press 1997).

Sharma P., 'Bills fall Victim to rocky Centre-state relationship' (2013) 12 May, *Sunday Standard* newsindiaexpress.com. Accessed 5 June 2013.

Sharma R., 'Green Courts in India: Strengthening Environmental Governance?' (2008) 4(1), *Law, Environment and Development Journal* 52–71.

Shaw D., 'The Specter of Water Piracy: The World Trade Organization Threatening Water Security in Developing Nations' (2008) 19, *Colo. J. Int'l Envtl. L. & Pol'y* 129–53.

Shestack J.J., 'The Philosophical Foundations of Human Rights' (1998) 20, *Hum. Rts. Q.* 201–34.

Shue H., *Basic Rights: Subsistence, Affluence, and U.S. Foreign Policy* (Princeton University Press 1980).

Silverstein M., 'Shifters, Linguistic Categories, and Cultural Description' in K. Basso and H. Selby (eds), *Meaning in Anthropology* (Albuquerque University of New Mexico Press 1976) 11–55.

Silverstein M., 'Indexical Order and the Dialectics of Sociolinguistic Life' (2003) 23, *Language and Communication* 193–229.

Singh Chauhan K. and Sing Chauhan S., 'Ecological Destruction vis-à-vis Environmental Jurisprudence in India: A Survey' (2009) 27(3), *Journal of Human Ecology* 207–16.

Sinha C. and Jensen de Lopez K., 'Language, Culture and the Embodiment of Spatial Cognition' (2000) 11(1/2), *Cognitive Linguistics* 17–41.

Skutnabb-Kangas T., *Linguistic Genocide in Education – Or Worldwide Diversity and Human Rights?* (Orient Longman 2008).
Skutnabb-Kangas T., 'Language Ecology' in Jan-Ola Östman and Jef Verschueren (eds), *Pragmatics in Practice* (John Benjamins 2011) 177–98.
Skutnabb-Kangas T. and Phillipson R., 'Human Rights Perspective on Ecology' in Angela Creese, Peter Martin and Nancy Hornberger (eds), *Ecology of Language, Volume 9, Encyclopedia of Language and Education*, 2nd edition (Springer 2008) 3–14.
Slapper G. and Kelly D., *The English Legal System*, 7th ed (Cavendish 2004).
Spini D. and Doise W., 'Organizing principles of involvement in human rights and their social anchoring in value priorities' (1998) 28, *European Journal of Social Psychology* 603–22.
Stenner P., 'Subjective Dimensions of Human Rights: What do Ordinary People Understand by "human right"?' (2011) 15(8), *Intl J Hum Rts* 1215–33.
Stollznow K., 'Dehumanisation in Language and Thought' (2008) 7(2), *Journal of Language and Politics* 177–200.
Stone C.D., *Should Trees Have Standing? Law, Morality and the Environment*, 3rd ed. (Oxford University Press 2010).
Stuckler D. and Basu ., *The Body Economic: Why Austerity Kills* (Allen Lane 2013).
Stychin C.F., 'Same-Sex Sexualities and the Globalization of Human Rights Discourse' (2004) 49, *McGill L. J* 951–68.
The Sun, Letters (2009) 15 April , 41.
The Sun, 'Rights Wrong', Editorial (2009) 20 February, 8.
Sweetser E., 'Regular Metaphoricity in Gesture: Bodily Based Models of Speech Interaction', in Actes du 16e Congrès International des Linguistes (CD-ROM) (Elsevier 1998) http://linguistics.berkeley.edu/~sweetser/sweetser.cil.98.pdf accessed 10th August 2011.
Sweetser E., *From Etymology to Pragmatics. Metaphoric and Cultural Aspects of Semantic Structure* (Cambridge University Press 1990).
Takacs D., 'The Public Trust Doctrine, Environmental Human Rights and the Future of Private Property' (2008) 16, *N. Y. U. Envtl. L. J.* 711–65.
Talbott, W.J., 'Reply to Critics: In Defense of One Kind of Epistemically Modest But Metaphysically Immodest Liberalism' (2008) 9 (2) *Human Rights Rev* 193–212.
Talbott W.J., *Which Rights Should be Universal?* (Oxford University Press 2005).
Talbott W.J., *Human Rights and Human Well-Being* (Oxford University Press 2010).
The Hindu, 'Calls for presidential asset to Plachimada Bill' (2012) 5 June www.thehindu.com. Accessed 25 July 2012.
The Plachimada Coca-Cola Victims Relief and Compensation Claims Special Tribunal Bill 2011 http://www.niyamasabha.org/bills/12kla/plachimada%20victims.pdf. Accessed 27 July 2012.
Thomas M., *Belching Out the Devil: Global Adventures with Coca-Cola* (Ebury Press 2008).

Thompson M.R., 'Whatever Happened to "Asian Values"?' (2001) 12(4), *Journal of Democracy* 154–65.

Turner B.S., *Vulnerability and Human Rights* (Penn State Press 2006).

Upadhyay V., 'Water Rights and the "New" Water Laws in India: Emerging Issues and Concerns in a Rights Based Perspective' in *India Infrastructure Report 2011: Water: Policy and Performance for Sustainable Development Infrastructure* (Oxford University Press 2011) 56–66. http://www.idfc.com/pdf/report/IIR-2011.pdf. Accessed 1 August 2012.

United Nations, 'The Human Right to Water and Sanitation', General Assembly Resolution 64/292 (2010) 28 July http://www.un.org/ga/search/view_doc.asp?symbol=A/RES/64/292. Accessed 16 October 2013.

Waldmann M.R., Nagel J. and Wiegmann A., 'Moral Judgment' in K.J. Holyoak and R.G. Morrison (eds), *The Oxford Handbook of Thinking and Reasoning* (Oxford University Press 2012) 364–89.

Wall I.R., 'On Pain and the Sense of Human Rights' (2008) 29, *A Fem L J* 53–76.

Wallop H., *Consumed: How Shopping Fed the Class System* (Collins 2013).

Weizman E., *The Least of All Possible Evils: Humanitarian Violence from Arendt to Gaza* (Verso 2011).

West S., *First Names* (Puncher and Wattmann 2006).

Westcoat J.L. Jnr, 'Submerged Landscapes: The Public Trust in Urban Environmental Design, from Chicago to Karachi and Back Again' (2009) 10, *Vermont Journal of Environmental Law* 435–75.

Western Morning News, 'Abusing our Right to our own Legal System", *Western Morning News*. 9 April 2009 10.

White F., *The Overview Effect: Space Exploration and Human Evolution* (Houghton Mifflin 1987).

Whitney S.Y., 'Dependency Relations: Corporeal Vulnerability and the Norms of Personhood in Hobbes and Kittay' (2011) 26(3), *Hypatia* 554–74.

Whorf B.L., 'The Relation of Habitual Thought and Behaviour to Language' in S.I. Hayakawa (ed.), *Language, Meaning and Maturity: Selections from Etc., a Review of General Semantics, 1943–1953* (Harper 1954) 197–215.

Wierzbicka A., *Semantics, Culture, and Cognition: Universal Human Concepts in Culture-Specific Configurations* (Oxford University Press 1992).

Wierzbicka A., *Semantics, Primes and Universals* (Oxford University Press 1996).

Wierzbicka A., *What Did Jesus Mean?* (Oxford University Press 2001).

Wierzbicka A., 'Right and Wrong: From Philosophy to Everyday Discourse' (2002) 4(2), *Discourse Studies* 225–52.

Wierzbicka A., *English: Meaning and Culture* (Oxford University Press 2006).

Wierzbicka A., 'Bodies and their Parts: An NSM Approach to Semantic Typology' (2007a) 29, *Language Sciences* 14–65.

Wierzbicka A., 'Theory and Empirical Findings: A Response to Jackendoff' (2007b) 4(3), *Intercultural Pragmatics* 399–409.

Wierzbicka A., 'NSM Semantics versus Conceptual Semantics: Goals and Standards (A response to Jackendoff)' (2007c) 4(4), *Intercultural Pragmatics* 521–9.

Wierzbicka A., 'Is "remember" a Universal Human Concept? "Memory" and Culture', in Mngistue Amberber (ed.), *The Language of Memory in a Crosslinguistic Perspective, Human Cognitive Processing* 21 (John Benjamins 2007d) 13–39.
Wierzbicka A., 'Mental Lexicon', in Tilman Berger, Kalr Gutschmidt, Sebastian Kempgen and Peter Kosta (eds), *The Slavic Languages: An International Handbook of their History, their Structure and their Investigation* (Mouton de Gruyter 2009) http://www.une.edu.au/bcss/linguistics/nsm/nsm-downloads.php.
Wierzbicka A., 'Is Pain a Human Universal?' (2012) 4(3), *Emotion Review* 4(3) 307–17.
Wolcher L.E., 'The Third Mountain: A Meditation on Chaos and Order' (2002) 15, *International Journal for the Semiotics of Law* 25–52.
Wolcher L.E., 'Senseless Kindness: the Politics of Cost-Benefit Analysis' (2007) 25, *Law and Inequality: A Journal of Theory and Practice* 147–202.
Wolcher L., 'The Tragic Foundations of Human Rights' (2006) 24, *Wis. Int'l L. J.* 523–56.
Wolcher L., *Law's Task: the Tragic Circle of Law, Justice and Human Suffering* (Ashgate 2008).
Wolterstorff N., 'Response: the Irony of it all' (2007) 9(3), *The Hedgehog Review* 63–9.
Woodiwiss A., *Human Rights* (Routledge 2005).
Yu N., 'Metaphor, Body and Culture: The Chinese Understanding of Gallbladder and Courage' (2003) 18(1) *Metaphor and Symbol* 13–31.
Zaylia J L, 'Questioning the Coke Side of Life: Groundwater Appropriation, Absolute Property Rights, the Public Trust Doctrine and Gender Inequality in India' (2009) 6(2), *Manchester Journal of International Economic Law* 159–90.
Žižek S., 'Human Rights and its Discontents', lecture at Bard College, 16 November 1999 at http://www.egs.edu/faculty/slavoj-zizek/articles/human-rights-and-its-discontents. Accessed 6 March 2013.
Žižek S., *Enjoy your Symptom! Jacques Lacan in Hollywood and Out*, 2nd ed. (Routledge 2001).
Žižek S., 'Against Human Rights' (2005) 34, *New Left Review* 115–31.
Žižek S., *Living in the End Times* (Verso 2010).

Index